Study Guide and Workbook
to Accompany
Economics of Development
Fifth Edition

Study Guide and Workbook
to Accompany
Economics of Development
Fifth Edition

Dwight H. Perkins
Steven Radelet
Donald R. Snodgrass
Malcolm Gillis
Michael Roemer

by
Bruce R. Bolnick
and
Berhanu Abegaz
College of William and Mary

W·W·Norton & Company
New York   London

ISBN 0-393-97649-1 (pbk.)

W. W. Norton & Company, Inc., 500 Fifth Avenue, New York, N.Y. 10110
    www.wwnorton.com
W. W. Norton & Company, Ltd., Castle House,75/76 Wells Street, London W1T 3 QT

1 2 3 4 5 6 7 8 9 0

Contents

Preface

To the Student

Do you find that you absorb more from your reading if you first have a preview of the material? After reading through a chapter of one of your school books, do you ever wonder, "What exactly am I supposed to *know* from all this?" Do you find that it is useful to have practice tests to provide feedback on your understanding and recall of course material and to help you spot material that requires more careful study? Do you like to see additional applications of the concepts, formulas, and tools covered in class? Is your comprehension enhanced by exercises that lead you systematically through the analytical and technical material, in detail?

If your answer to even one of these questions is yes, then you will find this *Study Guide and Workbook* to be a valuable aid in learning the economics of development. First, an introductory chapter reviews some basic principles of economics that you will encounter repeatedly in the textbook. Then, for each chapter of the textbook, the *Study Guide* provides:

1. An overview of the contents

2. A summary of the main learning objectives

3. A list of economic tools and techniques developed or applied in the chapter

4. A list of key terms and concepts that you should understand and be able to explain

5. A self-test, which generally contains 30 questions that are split between completion, true-false, and multiple-choice formats

6. A Worked Example analyzing in detail an application of one of the main technical tools or economic concepts from the chapter

7. Exercises that walk you step by step through applications of each major analytical topic and tool in the chapter

8. Answers for all the self-test questions (Answers to the Exercises are contained in the *Instructor's Manual* for the textbook; ask your instructor about how access to these answers are to be handled in your class.)

This *Study Guide* is designed to make your study time more productive and to *help you learn* the technical and analytical material. The best way to master such material is by doing exercises. Think of it this way: you can't learn to play the oboe by reading an oboe book and listening to oboe lectures, no matter how clear the book and the lectures may be.

We hope you will find the *Study Guide* material to be challenging and rewarding—even enjoyable.

While studying the economics of development, you will be exploring problems faced by more than 100 countries around the world. You will certainly encounter the names of countries with which you aren't entirely familiar. When this happens, grab an atlas or encyclopedia and look up the country. This will help you to fill gaps in your knowledge of world geography.

To the Instructor

One of the outstanding strengths of the Perkins, Radelet, and Snodgrass textbook is that it integrates solid applications of economic analysis into the discussion of the economics of development. This *Study Guide and Workbook* provides the pedagogical support that most students need in order to learn the material more easily and more thoroughly. It contains summaries that point out what they should know, question sets that provide feedback on major concepts, facts, terms, and tools, examples illustrating basic analytical material, and problem sets that provide hands-on experience with the economics of development.

In using the *Study Guide* for your course, three points should be called to your attention. First, you may not want to hold your students responsible for 100 percent of the material in some chapters. The format of the *Study Guide* allows you to identify specific learning objectives, key terms, economic tools, and/or exercises that you want them to master.

Second, consider motivating your students to use the *Study Guide* by adopting an explicit policy of using questions from this book—either as is or with minor variations—on course exams. If students have mastered what is in the *Study Guide*, then they have mastered a lot.

Third, the answers to all the exercises are contained in the *Instructor's Manual*, not in the *Study Guide* itself. This arrangement gives you the option of assigning exercises as homework problems. In return for this flexibility, you will have to make an arrangement to let students have access to the answers. Perhaps the easiest way to do this is to place a copy of the answers on reserve at your library.

We welcome your comments on the *Study Guide*. You can contact Berhanu Abegaz at the Department of Economics, College of William and Mary, Williamsburg, VA 23187.

Principles of Economics: A Refresher

The economics of development is a field that applies the basic principles of economics. In some cases, these principles are extended or adapted to reflect the special features of low-income economies. The basic microeconomic tools of supply and demand and such fundamental concepts as markets, equilibrium, elasticity, opportunity cost, information, and competition are used repeatedly. The macroeconomic tools of aggregate demand and supply also are deployed along with such concepts as income, expenditure, saving, investment, exchange rates, and money supply to study issues of stabilization and growth.

A major objective of the *Study Guide* is to help you master the basic economic tools and concepts needed to understand the economic challenges facing developing economies. This introductory chapter reviews the most basic principles of economics, which you will frequently encounter in the textbook. If you feel a little rusty or your previous classes did not cover some of the basic concepts, this brief review will help you prepare for the more in-depth analyses that come later in the course.

PRINCIPLES OF MACROECONOMICS: A SELECTIVE REVIEW

Macroeconomics of Development

Development economics generally focuses on long-term issues of growth and structural change. However, the events following the OPEC oil shocks of the 1970s have drawn much attention to the short-run issues of macroeconomic stability in developing economies. The most notable examples are the Latin American debt crises of the 1980s, and the **financial crises** in Mexico, in the transition economies, and in the emerging economies of East Asia in the 1990s. Issues involving open-economy macroeconomics are central to the material in a number of chapters (especially Chapters 2, 11–14, and 19).

A brief look at the national income and balance of payments accounting systems will give you a good idea of the major channels of interaction among the primary actors in the economy (households, firms, foreigners, or government). Since there are so many conceptual balls to juggle, we sketch out a highly simplified but useful framework for thinking about the complex relationships of trade flows and capital flows between the domestic economy and the rest of the world.

Gross Domestic Product (GDP) and Gross National Product (GNP)

By the magic of double-entry bookkeeping, we can think of the **gross *domestic* product (GDP)** from many alternative and illuminating perspectives. This gives us several identities that will reappear in different guises.

One perspective defines GDP (the value of **final goods and services** produced annually inside a country) as the **value added** that shows up as payments to labor and capital. The idea behind it is that sales revenue shows up as income to someone. **Intermediate goods** are income to the firm that makes them, wages are income to workers, and profits are income to the people who own the firm. As a result, GDP for some purposes can be usefully thought of as measuring either income or output.

A second look at GDP comes from the perspective of purchases of final goods; that is, who buys them (consumers, firms, governments, or foreigners). The most common decomposition of this sort is given by the accounting **identity**:

$$GDP = C + I + G + NX \qquad [1]$$

Net exports (NX; trade balance) refers to exports (E) minus imports (M), or $NX = E - M$. Consumption (C) is expenditures on consumer goods by households. Investment (I) here refers to the accumulation of physical capital: purchases of new buildings and machines, plant, equipment, and accumulation of inventories. Government consumption (G) here consists of purchases of goods and services. Note that, although they are used interchangeably here, an identity is true by definition while an equilibrium is not.

Given the definition of net exports, the national income accounting identity [1] can be rewritten as

$$GDP + M = C + I + G + E \qquad [2]$$

The left-hand side of the expression represents the total supply of goods available in the country; such a supply is the sum of domestic supply (GDP) and foreign supply of goods (M). The right-hand side ($= A + E$) says that the total supply of goods is purchased either by private consumers (C), firms for investment purposes (I), the government for its own public consumption (G), or foreign agents in the form of exports (E). **Absorption** (A), total spending by residents on domestically produced as well as imported goods, is the sum of consumption ($C + G$) and investment (I).

The Current Account and Foreign Debt

The **gross *national* product (GNP)** measures the income received by residents from activities at home *and* abroad. The **current account** (CA) provides the broadest measure of a country's trade surplus by adding to net exports such income flows as net factor receipts (and net transfer receipts, assumed in this discussion to equal zero).

Given the definition of GNP, CA can be derived as follows:

$$GNP = GDP + NFR = C + I + G + CA \qquad [3]$$

where

CA = current account ($= NX + NFR$);

NFR = **net factor receipts** (factor receipts from foreigners net of factor payments to foreigners).

Most developing countries have large current account deficits, even when they report trade surpluses. That is because they tend to be net recipients of foreign investment or net borrowers of capital from abroad or both. Foreign interest payments, repayment of principal on foreign debt, and profit repatriations can exceed any trade surplus (plus any net transfers such as foreign aid and worker remittances).

To better understand why a country may be running a current account deficit or surplus, it would be helpful to note that the current account is the difference between what a country produces (GNP) and what that country spends or absorbs. That means

$$CA = GNP - A \qquad [4]$$

where $A = C + G + I$.

If a country produces more than it spends (i.e., $GNP > A$), the excess of goods produced over those bought at home for consumption and investment must be exported to the rest of the world. This means that the external balance is positive or, equivalently, the current account is in surplus. The reverse is the case for $GNP < A$.

Note also that the current account can be recast as the difference between **national savings** (S) and **national investment** (I). To see this, we define national savings as the difference between national income and national consumption (private plus government):

$$S = GNP - C - G \qquad [5]$$

Using [4] and [5], CA can be reformulated interestingly as the balance between what a nation saves and what it invests:

$$CA = S - I \qquad [6]$$

If a country invests more than it saves, the excess of investment over savings implies that the country is running a current account deficit. It is very important to understand that if a country runs a current account deficit ($CA < 0$), as often is the case in most developing countries, this means that the country is borrowing from the rest of the world and its stock of **foreign debt** will increase over time. Thus, **flows** (saving, investment, or trade deficits/surpluses) translate into changes in **stocks** (the stock of capital, government **domestic debt**, or net foreign debt).

A current account deficit may be caused by an increase in national investment or a fall in national savings (i.e., privates savings or increases in budget deficits). The important point to note here is that a country may be borrowing funds from the rest of the world for good or bad reasons. So, a current account deficit and the ensuing accumulation of foreign debt may be good, sustainable, and lead to higher long-run growth. As you will see in Chapter 14, it also may turn out to be unsustainable and lead to a currency and debt crisis, depending on what drives the current account deficit.

The Balance of Payments and the Domestic Money Supply

Global financial integration also means a close relationship between international financial flows and a developing country's domestic **money supply**. We know for sure that a country can do two things to finance the excess of investment over savings: run down its foreign financial assets (if there are enough foreign assets to be run down) or borrow from the rest of the world to finance the new investment.

These points jump at you from the very definition of the **balance of payments**:

$$CA + F_n = \Delta IR \qquad [7]$$

where

F_n = **net capital inflows** (into deficit country);
ΔIR = changes in the stock of **international reserves**;
$CA + F_n$ = balance of payments.

Equation [7] makes it clear that a current account deficit ($CA < 0$) has to be financed by private net capital inflows ($F_n > 0$); that is, net imports of **foreign savings**. If private inflows are inadequate to cover the deficit (i.e., the sum on the left-hand side still is negative), the difference has to be made up by the monetary authorities, say, by drawing down previously accumulated international reserves ($\Delta IR < 0$).

Unfortunately, changes in international reserves also have potentially undesirable consequences for the domestic money supply. To appreciate this linkage, remember from your principles course that the consolidated T-accounts for the domestic banking system can be written as

$$M = DC + IR \qquad [8]$$

where

M = domestic **money supply**;
DC = **domestic credit** (private and public);
IR = international reserves (gold, forex).

Expressing [8] in terms of changes and using [7], you can see that

$$\Delta IR = \Delta M - \Delta DC \qquad [9]$$

To make things even more intuitive, rearrange terms to obtain

$$\Delta M = CA + F_n + \Delta DC \qquad [10]$$

For a given level of domestic credit, a country with a balance of payments surplus ($CA + F_n = \Delta IR > 0$) will automatically see its domestic money supply increase as **foreign exchange** receipts are converted into domestic currency. By the same token, a deficit country experiences a contraction of its money supply as it depletes its international reserves. In other words, the central bank sells its foreign assets and buys back the domestic currency, thereby reducing the domestic money supply.

Since the supply of international reserves (including emergency loans from international financial institutions) is not unlimited, the country eventually will be forced to deal with the underlying causes of persistent CA deficits. You will see later in the course that these adjustments may take the forms of changes in the level of domestic spending (reduction of budget deficits) or the composition of spending in favor of domestically produced goods (via changes in exchange rates, or trade measures). The bottom line is that, in an **open economy**, intimate linkages lie between domestic activity and international activity in both the goods markets and the asset markets.

PRINCIPLES OF MICROECONOMICS: A SELECTIVE REVIEW

Production Possibilities Frontier

The **production possibilities frontier** (PPF) illustrates the fundamental problem of **scarcity** facing every economy. It does so by using the very simple case of an economy that produces only two goods, X and Y. Figure 1 shows an economy with the capacity to produce Y_{max} of good Y if it devotes all its resources to Y. Or it can produce X_{max} if it devotes all its resources to X. More likely, the economy will allocate its resources to achieve a point such as A, involving production of both goods. The PPF shows all feasible combinations of X and Y production, given the available resources and technology.

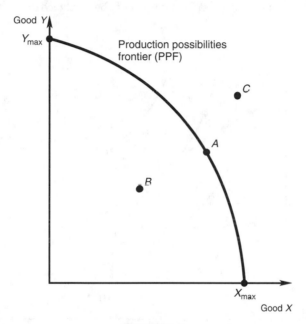

FIGURE 1

At any point such as A, the economy can produce more of Y only by reallocating resources away from producing X. The loss of X production is called the **opportunity cost** of the additional Y. Similarly, extra production of X entails an opportunity cost in the form of the Y goods that are forgone. The slope of the PPF at each point embodies the terms of this trade-off.

An economy that is underutilizing its resources or one that is producing inefficiently would operate at a point inside the PPF, such as point B. In this case the economy has the capacity to produce more of both goods. Many LDCs could increase production significantly by adopting policies that encourage available resources to be used more fully and more productively. However, any combination of outputs lying outside the PPF, such as point C, cannot be produced unless the economy's productive capacity expands.

Economic efficiency for an economy involves operating on the PPF and also selecting the "best" attainable combination of X and Y. The "best" attainable point is illustrated using **indifference curves** to represent society's preferences. Consider point H in Figure 2. This point represents certain amounts of goods X and Y, and hence a particular level of welfare. Exactly the same level of welfare could be achieved with less X if this loss is compensated by a sufficient amount of extra Y, as at point H'. Likewise, the same level of welfare could be achieved with less Y, if enough extra X were available, as at point H''. The curve I_1 connects all such points of equal welfare; this is an indifference curve. Another indifference curve, such as I_2, lying further from the origin, connects points yielding a higher level of welfare. A curve closer to the origin, such as I_3, contains combinations of X and Y yielding a lower level of welfare.

Given the PPF in Figure 2, point H is the best production outcome since it lies on the highest indifference curve the economy can attain from its limited resources. In Chapter 18 you will see how trade can expand the possibilities and permit the economy to *consume* combinations that lie outside the PPF, such as point C, even though such combinations cannot be produced domestically.

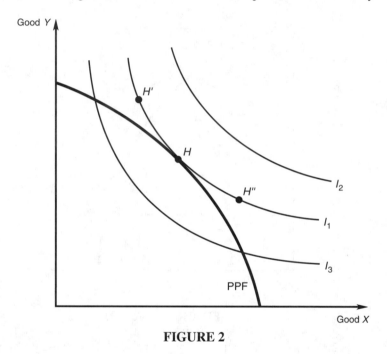

FIGURE 2

Markets

Except in a highly planned command economy, markets play a vital role in determining how resources are allocated, how much of each good will be produced, what prices will be paid for products or inputs, and who will receive what income. Quite generally, a market consists of interacting buyers and sellers engaged in transactions for a particular set of products or services. **Factor markets** are markets for factors of production such as labor, capital, and land. **Product markets** are markets for goods and services. **Financial markets** are markets in which funds are borrowed and lent.

A **competitive market** is one in which the number of buyers and sellers is large enough that no single participant is able to manipulate the market price significantly. In a competitive market, buyers and sellers respond to market-determined prices. Where markets are reasonably competitive, they serve as an efficient social mechanism for decentralized coordination of individual decisions about production and expenditures.

Supply and Demand

The principles of supply and demand provide the basis for understanding the market mechanism, as well as many development policy issues that involve market operations. The key to supply and demand is to analyze separately the behavior of the buyers and sellers: How would buyers react *if* faced with various possible market prices? How would sellers react? The **equilibrium price** is that which coordinates the supply and demand decisions.

The law of demand states that as the price of any good rises, the quantity that buyers are willing and able to buy will fall. Conversely, as the price falls the quantity demanded will rise. This behavior is summarized in the negatively sloped market **demand curve** for good X, as shown in Figure 3. The amount of X demanded at a given price depends, of course, on other factors such as consumer incomes, tastes, and prices of related goods. The demand curve shows how buyers react to various prices, assuming that these other factors are held constant. A change in any of these other variables will shift the position of the demand curve. For example, an increase in real incomes would generate more demand for X at any given price. The demand curve then shifts to the right.

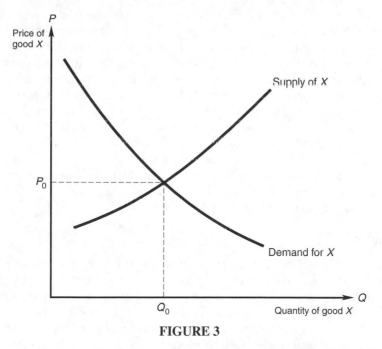

FIGURE 3

In similar fashion the **supply curve** shows the alternative quantities that sellers would be able and willing to put up for sale at various possible prices. In general, a higher price will induce production that is not profitable at a lower price, along with the possible entry of new suppliers into the market. Thus the market supply curve typically slopes upward: The higher is the price, the greater the quantity supplied.

The quantity of X that suppliers choose to supply depends on more than just the price of X. The decision depends also on the available capacity and on production costs. The supply curve is drawn assuming these other conditions are held constant. The curve will shift position when these variables change. For example, given a market price for X, an increase in costs would render some marginal units of output unprofitable. So supply would fall. On the graph, the supply curve then shifts to the left.

With the supply and demand curves shown in Figure 3, P_0 is the equilibrium price. At that price, the quantity Q_0 that suppliers decide to supply coincides with the quantity that buyers choose to demand. Furthermore, the price P_0 is the natural outcome of **market forces** in a competitive market. At any price above P_0, there is an excess of supply over demand, which will cause the price to fall; and at any price below P_0, the consequent excess demand creates a powerful tendency for the price to rise.

The market equilibrium has very important economic properties. Suppose $P_0 = \$10$ and buyers and sellers choose to transact 500 units of X at this price. The fact that the buyers are willing and able to buy 500 units of X, but no more, implies that each of these units is worth forgoing $10 of other things. It also implies that additional units are not worth $10.

Similarly, the suppliers' choice to sell 500 units of X, but no more, implies that $10 covers the cost of producing each of these units (including an adequate profit margin to compensate for the use of capital). It also implies that extra units entail a cost exceeding $10.

Put these insights together. For every unit of output up to the market equilibrium of 500, the value to consumers compensates for the cost of production; for every unit in excess of 500, the cost of production exceeds the value to consumers! In this sense, the market picks out the *best* level of production, and hence the best point on the economy's PPF. The market price serves a dual role here; it provides the incentive for production, while rationing the supply to the buyers for whom the product is worth at least the cost of production.

This conclusion applies only to *competitive* markets. The claim that the market output is best also must be questioned when there are serious inequities in the underlying distribution of income and purchasing power. These qualifying remarks are often pertinent to the analysis of economic problems in developing countries, where monopoly power and extreme income inequalities are frequent features of the economic landscape.

Elasticity

Elasticity means responsiveness. How responsive is the quantity demanded to a change in the price? The answer is the "price elasticity of demand." How does the capital-labor ratio in an industry respond to a change in the relative price of the two factors of production? The answer is the "elasticity of substitution." Elasticity is a convenient tool for summarizing the magnitude of response effects.

Specifically, elasticity is a calculation of *proportional* responsiveness. If a price increase of 15 percent produces a 10 percent decline in the quantity demanded, the elasticity is $10/15 = 0.667$ (in absolute value). The denominator represents the percentage change in the independent variable, and the numerator is the percentage change in the dependent variable.[1] The response is called **inelastic**

---

1. The percentage change in any variable X usually is calculated as

$$100 \times [X(1) - X(0)]/X(0) = 100 \times [X(1)/X(0)] - 100.$$

For example, if $X(0) = 50$ and $X(1) = 63$, the percentage change is $100 \times (63 - 50)/50 = 26$ percent.

if the value of the elasticity is less than 1 (in absolute value); it is **elastic** if the value is greater than 1; a value equal to 1 is referred to as **unit elastic**.

Production Functions and Isoquants

A production function identifies how much output can be produced using a given set of factors of production. Let Q be the quantity of output for a firm or an industry, and suppose that capital (K) and labor (L) are the only factors of production. The production function can be expressed as $Q = F (K, L)$.

The **marginal product** of labor is the amount of *extra* Q that could be produced by adding one extra unit of the labor, holding capital unchanged. The marginal product of capital is defined in similar fashion. As more and more of one factor is added to a fixed amount of the other, the marginal product of the variable factor typically declines. This means that increments to output grow smaller and smaller. Economists call this the **law of diminishing returns** to a factor of production.

A factor's **marginal revenue product** is the extra *value* of output that could be produced by adding one extra unit of the factor. In competitive markets, the marginal revenue product is simply the marginal product times the price of the good being produced.

Production functions are often diagrammed as **isoquants**. An isoquant is a line showing the alternative factor combinations that can be used to produce a given level of output. In Figure 4, an output of $Q = 100$ tons of steel can be produced using 50 units of capital along with 30 units of labor (point A). The same output can be produced using a more labor-intensive process involving just 20 units of capital and 60 units of labor (point B). Or it can be produced using any other factor combination lying on the curve $Q = 100$. The curve labeled $Q = 200$ shows the various combinations of capital and labor sufficient to produce an output of 200 tons of steel. Similar curves can be drawn for any possible values of Q. These curves are isoquants.

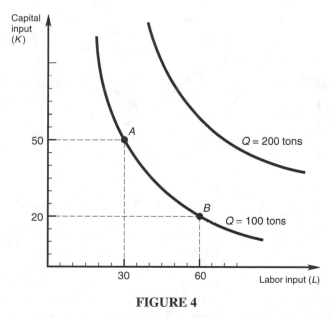

FIGURE 4

Among the options indicated by any given isoquant, which production technique will be used? This depends on the relative prices of the **factors of produc-**

tion. Producers generally try to use the production technique that minimizes the cost of producing any given output. If capital is expensive relative to labor, then a point to the southeast would be used, whereas a point to the northwest would be preferred by producers who face labor costs that are high relative to capital costs.

The **elasticity of substitution** measures how responsive the capital-labor ratio is to a change in the relative **factor prices**. Isoquants that are relatively un-bowed reflect a high elasticity of substitution; this indicates that the capital-labor mix would respond strongly to changes in relative factor prices. Isoquants that are tightly bowed reflect a very low elasticity of substitution; in this case there is little room for changing the capital-labor mix. The important case of L-shaped isoquants is introduced in Chapter 3.

Monopoly

A firm has **monopoly** power when it is large enough to influence significantly the market price of its product. In perfect competition, prices are determined by market interactions and each firm responds with an output decision. In contrast, a monopolist can choose what price to charge. A **pure monopoly** exists when there is a sole producer who can select the product price without fear of losing customers to competitors.

The law of demand still imposes a constraint on the monopolist. The higher is the price selected, the smaller the volume of output that the monopolist can sell. This can be graphed as a demand curve facing the monopolist, as shown in Figure 5.

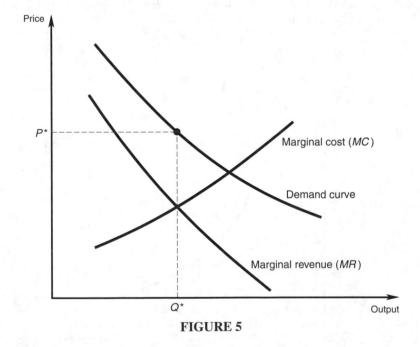

FIGURE 5

Suppose, quite generally, that the monopolist chooses to charge a price P and sell Q units of output, with Q's being determined by the demand curve. The firm's total revenue is $P \times Q$. How much will revenue increase if another unit of output is to be sold? The demand curve shows that $Q + 1$ units of output can be sold only if the monopolist lowers the price. The gain from selling one more unit is offset to some extent by lower revenues on the first Q units. Hence the **marginal revenue**—defined as the extra revenue produced by a unit increase in output—is less than the price P. The line labeled MR in Figure 5 shows the marginal revenue associated with each increment of output.

Given the demand curve, which price will the monopolist choose? The key is this: As long as the marginal revenue generated by an additional unit of output exceeds the **marginal cost** (MC) of producing that unit, the extra output increases profits, despite the need to lower the price. The monopolist, therefore, chooses to produce up to the point where $MR = MC$ and to charge the price that the demand curve allows for that level of sales. In Figure 5, the curve MC shows the marginal cost of each successive unit of output. The profit-maximizing output is then Q^*, and the monopoly price is P^*.

Compared with a competitive market, a monopolist finds it profitable to restrict output and charge a higher price. As a result, the market efficiency conditions presented are violated in monopoly markets.

Key Terms and Concepts

absorption (A)

balance of payments

competitive markets

current account (CA)

demand curve

domestic credit

domestic (national) debt

economic efficiency

elastic

elasticity of substitution

equilibrium price

factor markets

factor prices

factors of production

final goods and services

financial crisis

financial markets

flows

foreign (external) debt

foreign exchange

foreign savings

gross domestic product (GDP)

gross national product (GNP)

identity

indifference curves

inelastic

intermediate goods and services

international reserves (IR)

isoquants

law of diminishing returns

marginal cost

marginal revenue

marginal revenue product

marginal product

market forces

money supply

monopoly

national investment

national savings

net capital inflows

net exports

net factor receipts (NFR)

open economy

opportunity cost

product markets

production possibilities frontier (PPF)

pure monopoly

scarcity

stocks

supply curve

unit elastic

value added

Part I   Theory and Patterns

CHAPTER 1 | Introduction

OVERVIEW

The textbook opens with the story of Rachmina Abdullah, a young Malay woman who left her family to work in a modern electronic factory in the city. Rachmina's story personifies many of the changes that confront 4 billion inhabitants of developing countries in their quest for economic well being.

Modern economic growth started with England's Industrial Revolution in the late eighteenth century and spread to other areas of European settlement and Japan in the century that followed. Most countries started the process in earnest only after World War II. Even then, the process is more advanced in East Asia and Latin America than in Africa and Central America.

The textbook defines economic development as growth cum structural change. Economic development also implies popular participation in the production and distribution of economic prosperity. The uneven gains in real per capita income that one observes across world regions generally are characterized by industrialization, urbanization, and rising literacy rates and life expectancy. Around these broad patterns, however, one finds considerable variation from country to country.

An important historical lesson that stands out from the great diversity of historical experience, institutions, and policies is that successful development is a complex process. No simple formula assures success in initiating and sustaining development in some countries; no simple set of barriers can account for the persistence of underdevelopment in others. Through a combination of economic theory and evidence, the textbook identifies many of the conditions that facilitate the congruence of initial conditions, institutions, and policies that trigger a virtuous cycle of sustainable development.

MAIN LEARNING OBJECTIVES

After studying this chapter, you ought to understand and be able to explain

1. The profound nature of the economic and social changes that accompany economic development, as exemplified in the story of Rachmina Abdullah.

2. The fundamental distinction between economic growth and economic development.

3. The uneven process of growth and development across countries.

4. How differences in historical background and resource base have influenced the prospects for modern economic growth.

5. The fundamental point that no simple formula explains the complex question of why some countries are so rich while others remain so poor.

ECONOMIC TOOLS AND TECHNIQUES

From what you have learned in this chapter, you should be able to

1. Analyze patterns of structural change accompanying economic development, using international data such as those presented in Tables 1–1, 1–2, and 1–3 in the text.

2. Use the purchasing power parity (PPP) method of conversion to improve the accuracy of intercountry comparisons of income.

3. See how various competing explanations of the development record reflect differences in theoretical perspective and in emphasis on the various correlates of economic development.

KEY TERMS AND CONCEPTS

colonialism	institutional context
demographic transition	modern economic growth
developed countries	new industrializing countries (NICs)
developing countries	North vs. South
economic development	political obstacles
economic growth	purchasing power parity (PPP)
environmental degradation	substitutes (for prerequisites)
export processing zone (EPZ)	sustainable growth
HIV/AIDS	third world
Industrial Revolution	transitional economies

SELF-TEST

Completion

1. The key element in the epoch of modern economic growth has been the application of _____ to problems of economic production.

2. In 1992 Madagascar had a population of 12.4 million people and GNP estimated at the equivalent of U.S.$8,929 million dollars (using the PPP conversion method). Madagascar's per capita income was U.S.$_____.

3. In the World Bank's classification system, countries like Malaysia, Brazil, Korea, and Colombia fall in the category of _____-income countries.

4. International data comparisons reveal that energy consumption per capita generally _____ as an economy becomes more developed.

5. The process of economic development involves both _____ and structural change.

6. The electronics plant where Rachmina Abdullah worked was located in an _____ processing zone in Penang, Malaysia.

7. All the international data presented in the textbook tables of Chapter 1 can be found in the *World Development Report*, which is published annually by the _____ _____.

8. In developing countries, taken as a group, manufacturing output has been growing _____ rapidly than GDP.

9. In countries where per capita income is growing by 2 percent per year, average incomes will double in about _____ years.

10. Most countries that have suffered declines in per capita income since 1965 are on the continent of _____.

True-False

If false, you should be able to explain why.

_____ 1. The terms *economic growth* and *economic development* are interchangeable, each referring to a rise in national income per capita.

_____ 2. While working in the electronics factory, Rachmina Abdullah was able to earn an average of $80 per month.

_____ 3. The textbook classifies countries as low-income economies if income in 1992 was below U.S.$2,000 per capita (using the PPP measure).

_____ 4. The electronics factory where Rachmina Abdullah worked was owned and operated by a Japanese company that was attracted to Malaysia by generous tax exemptions and low wages.

_____ 5. By 1992 the adult literacy rate exceeded 75 percent in virtually all LDCs.

_____ 6. The study of economic development relies heavily on theory because not much data is available to provide an empirical record of the characteristics of most LDCs.

_____ 7. The World Bank is a large international bank with branches that take in deposits and extend commercial loans in over 130 countries.

_____ 8. Two major structural changes accompanying economic development are a rising share of industry and a falling share of agriculture in total output.

_____ 9. Statistical indicators of health and education, across countries, bear no significant correlation to differences in per capita income.

_____ 10. The label *PPP* stands for "purchasing power parity."

Multiple Choice

1. Which term does not belong with the others?
   a. LDCs
   b. Low-income countries
   c. North
   d. Third world

2. Which of the following changes is *not* typical of the structural changes that accompany development?
   a. Increasing poverty in rural areas.
   b. An increase in manufacturing output as a share of GDP.
   c. An increase in urbanization of the population.
   d. A decrease in the infant mortality rate.

3. Which statement reflects the attitude of Rachmina Abdullah and her friends toward overtime work?
   a. The women felt compelled to work long hours of overtime.
   b. The women had no interest in working overtime since their standard workday was so long to begin with.
   c. The women felt no need to earn additional money by working overtime.
   d. The women welcomed opportunities to work overtime, to supplement their pay.

4. Which country falls in the category of a transitional economy?
   a. Poland
   b. Korea
   c. Mexico
   d. Ghana

5. On the basis of data tables in the textbook, which generalization is broadly valid for low-income countries?
   a. The average life expectancy remained under 40 years in 1992.
   b. Around 90 percent of the labor force worked in agriculture in 1992.
   c. Per capita income did not improve from 1965 to 1992.
   d. Infant mortality rates declined significantly from 1965 to 1992.

6. Typically, how do economic theories of development treat the *institutional context*?
   a. It is ignored as irrelevant to the economic analysis.
   b. It is taken as given.
   c. It enters explicitly into much of the analysis.
   d. Institutions are assumed to adjust in conformity to the economic theory.

7. Members of the Organization for Economic Cooperation and Development (OECD) are
   a. high-income industrial countries.
   b. high-income oil-exporting countries.
   c. newly industrializing countries like Korea and Singapore.
   d. Eastern European countries in decline.

8. According to the textbook, what remarkable characteristic was shared by poor countries like China, India, Kenya, and Sri Lanka in 1992?
   a. Primary education was virtually universal.
   b. Foreign companies dominated the industrial sector.
   c. Infant mortality rates were as low as in the United States.
   d. For two decades, GNP per capita had grown by more than 5 percent per year.

9. In 1992, the average life expectancy at birth ranged from as high as 79 years in a rich country like Japan to as little as _____ in a poor African country like Mali.
   a. 27 years   c. 48 years
   b. 35 years   d. 66 years

10. The textbook authors view economic development as being first and foremost a process involving
   a. technology,   c. degradation of the environment.
   b. international trade. d. people.

APPLICATIONS

Worked Example: Examining Cross-Country Development Patterns

Cross-country data are frequently used for the inductive analysis of development patterns and also for testing theoretical hypotheses about development. Let's see what the data reveal about patterns of change in infant mortality rates.

In Figure 1–1 the horizontal axis measures GNP per capita (call this Y) in 1992 U.S. dollars, based on the PPP method of comparison. The vertical axis measures the infant mortality rate (call this IM) per 1,000 live births in 1992. The data for each country can be considered as one snapshot observation of an underlying dynamic relationship between Y and IM. For present purposes we use only the data reported in textbook Table 1–3 for low- and lower-middle-income countries. The result is the scatter plot of points shown in Figure 1–1.

There is a visible pattern to the scatter plot of points. To quantify this pattern, economists use statistical techniques such as regression analysis; you can think of it as a calculation of the best-fit line through the data points. The line PP in Figure 1–1 is the best-fit regression line for the plotted data. The exact equation for the line, calculated using a standard spreadsheet program, is $IM = 113.7 - 0.022Y$.

The various points obviously don't stick very closely to line PP. Deviations from the line could be explained by considering other explanatory variables. In addition to GNP per capita, one might expect the level of education to be an important determinant of IM. Indeed, in countries such as China, Sri Lanka, and the Philippines, which all have IM values well below the "pattern" line, adult illiteracy is also low (see text Table 1–1). In contrast, Mali, Pakistan, and Egypt have *IM* values well above the line *PP*; in each case adult illiteracy rates are quite high. As always, there are exceptions: have a careful look at the data for Bolivia and Indonesia.

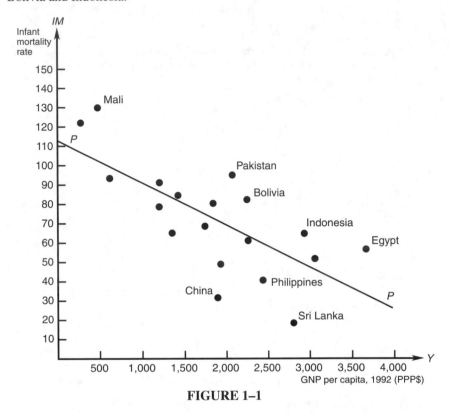

FIGURE 1–1

Two Notes to Students

1. When you encounter references to countries that you don't know much about, it is a good idea to look them up. Any handy encyclopedia will do. You can also form a mental picture of economic conditions in each country by scanning the data tables in the back of the latest *World Development Report*, which should be available in your library.

2. Examine the horizontal axis in the textbook graphs. Equal distances along the axis do not represent equal increments in GNP per capita. The *X* axis is drawn using a *natural logarithmic scale*, so equal distances along the axis represent equal *proportional* changes. The points 10,000 and 20,000 are separated by the same horizontal distance as the points 500 and 1,000. Given wide differences in GNP per capita, with lots of countries clustered at low values, the logarithmic scale tends to spread out the data plot and provide a clearer picture of patterns. Scanning these graphs, you should interpret each jump to the right as a proportional increase in per capita income.

Exercises

1. Now it is your turn to examine a development pattern. Consider differences in the child mortality rate (call this *CMR*) across the continuum of

development, as measured by GNP per capita (call this Y). The database for this exercise is given in Table 1–1. (The topic of nutrition is covered in detail in Chapter 10.)

a. To simplify your work, the graph will be drawn using only three group-wise average values of CMR and Y. From the data in Table 1–1, calculate the average values of CMR and Y for

Low-income countries: $CMR =$ _____; $Y =$ _____ .

Lower-middle-income countries: $CMR =$ _____ ; $Y =$ _____ .

Upper-middle-income countries: $CMR =$ _____; $Y =$ _____ .

Table 1–1

Child Mortality Rates and Per Capita Income for 24 Selected LDCs

	GNP per capita (PPP$)	Under-5 mortality rate per 1,000 live births
*Low-income economies**		
Ethiopia	340	216
Tanzania	630	158
India	1,210	104
Bangladesh	1,230	127
Kenya	1,360	110
Senegal	1,750	113
China	1,910	43
Honduras	1,930	70
*Lower-middle-income economies**		
Pakistan	2,130	142
Bolivia	2,270	115
Cameroon	2,300	124
The Philippines	2,480	56
Sri Lanka	2,810	24
Indonesia	2,970	98
Peru	3,080	75
Egypt	3,670	93
*Upper-middle-income economies**		
Tunisia	5,130	63
Brazil	5,250	76
Hungary	5,740	21
Colombia	5,760	29
Argentina	6,080	38
Mexico	7,490	49
Malaysia	8,050	20
Korea, Republic of	8,950	18

*The classifications used here adhere to PPP$ ranges used in the textbook.

Source: World Bank, *World Development Report 1994* (New York: Oxford University Press, 1994), pp. 214–15, 220–21.

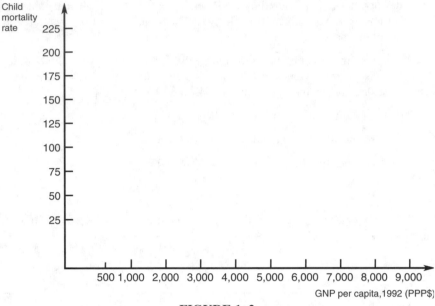

FIGURE 1–2

b. (i) In Figure 1–2 plot the three points corresponding to the averages you calculated in part a. Then draw line segments connecting the three data points.

  (ii) What do you observe about the general relationship between Y and CMR?

c. Now examine several individual countries in relation to the pattern that you derived from the group averages.

  (i) From Table 1–1, what are the values of CMR and Y for each of the following eight countries?

	CMR	Y
Ethiopia	_____	$_____
China	_____	$_____
Honduras	_____	$_____
Pakistan	_____	$_____
Cameroon	_____	$_____
Sri Lanka	_____	$_____
Brazil	_____	$_____
Malaysia	_____	$_____

  (ii) Plot these eight data points on Figure 1–2.

  (iii) What factors other than Y might account for the deviations between CMR values and the average pattern established in part b? Give two plausible answers.

d. Do the country-specific statistics invalidate the presumption that there is a pattern to the changes in child mortality rates that occur in the course of economic development?

2. Chapter 1 points out that international comparisons of income per capita require converting each country's statistics to a common currency, typically U.S. dollars. The standard approach has been to convert using exchange rates. In recent years, international data have been compiled using purchasing power parity (PPP) as the basis for converting to a common currency unit. This exercise presents a simple example to show how exchange-rate conversions can produce misleading results and how the PPP methodology works.

a. In 1990, Zambia's GDP was K113 billion (where K stands for kwacha, the national currency). The population was 8.1 million people. To get GDP per capita in local currency units, divide GDP by the number of people. Be sure to take into account that GDP is in billions and population is in millions.

GDP per capita = K_____ in 1990.

To convert this figure from kwacha units to U.S. dollar units using the exchange-rate method, divide by the exchange rate (kwacha per dollar). In 1991, the exchange rate averaged K29 per U.S.$, so in dollar units

GDP per capita = U.S.$_____ in 1990.

b. A year later, Zambia had a population of 8.4 million people and GDP of K218 billion. The large rise in GDP was due entirely to inflation; real GDP was virtually unchanged. The exchange rate averaged K65 per U.S.$ in 1991. From these numbers, you can calculate that:

In kwacha units, GDP per capita = K_____ in 1991.

In dollar units, GDP per capita = $_____ in 1991.

c. Compare the results of converting Zambia's per capita GDP into U.S. dollars using the exchange-rate method. In 1990, Zambia's GDP per capita in dollars was $_____; the following year, GDP per capita was $_____. The 1991 figure is lower than the 1990 figure by _____ percent.

Yet real GDP did not change: Even taking population growth into account, GDP per capita fell less than 4 percent, measured in kwacha units at constant prices. The conversion to dollars gives a very different result because the change in the exchange rate did not accurately reflect the change in purchasing power of the kwacha. Using the exchange rate to convert from kwacha to dollars introduced a large distortion into the dollar value of GDP per capita.

d. The PPP method avoids this by valuing each country's output in dollar terms product by product. Take a simple example using the following data for a hypothetical economy. Calculate nominal GDP for each year by multiplying output *times* price for each product and then totaling the output values:

	1990		1991	
	Output	Price (K)	Output	Price (K)
Copper (tons)	50,000	29,000	50,000	58,000
Maize (bags)	8,000,000	200	8,000,000	400
Furniture (units)	1,000,000	100	1,000,000	200
Nominal GDP	K_____ million		K_____ million	

Note that output remains constant but prices double between 1990 and 1991. To convert to dollar values, the PPP methodology bypasses the exchange rate altogether. Instead, *each product* is valued at a consistent set of dollar prices, such as

Copper $1,000 per ton
Maize $100 per bag
Furniture $50 per unit

Multiply the outputs for 1990, item by item, by the respective dollar prices to obtain GDP in dollar units. Do the same for 1991 outputs. The result, in dollar units, is

GDP = $_____ million in 1990.

GDP = $_____ million in 1991.

Suppose that the population of this economy is 2.0 million in 1990 and 2.1 million in 1991. What is GDP *per capita* in dollar units, on the basis of the PPP conversion methodology?

GDP per capita = $_____ million in 1990.

GDP per capita = $_____ million in 1991.

Compared to the exchange rate method, this calculation gives a more accurate picture of the situation and a more consistent set of output valuations for use in making international comparisons.

3. This exercise uses stylized graphs to capture some basic patterns of development.

   a. Figure 1–3 shows a cross-country development pattern, but the labels are missing. Think about the relationship expressed by the two lines in this figure. Then pair each item in the left-hand column of the following table to the appropriate *letter* label from the graph.

Item	Letter label
Percentage of age group enrolled in primary school	_____
GNP per capita	_____
1965	_____
1995	_____

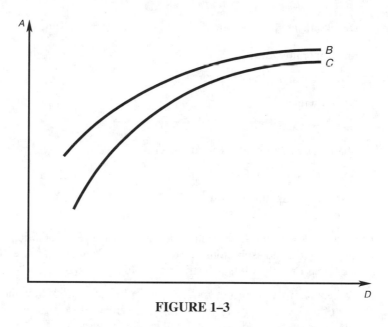

FIGURE 1–3

b. In Figure 1–4, line *A* shows a negative correlation between per capita income and variable *X*, while line *B* shows a positive correlation.

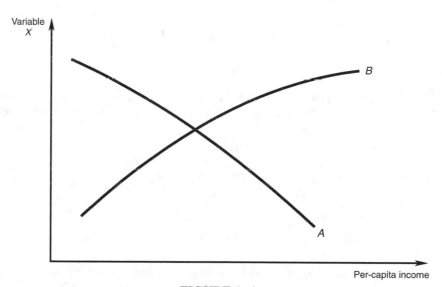

FIGURE 1–4

Consider the variables in the following list as alternative definitions of *X*, one by one. For each variable, indicate whether line *A* or line *B* best captures its relationship with per capita income, as countries move through the development continuum. The first blank is filled in as an example.

Development characteristic	Line
Infant morality rates	__A__
Energy consumption per capita	_____
Adult literacy	_____
Life expectancy	_____
Share of population living in rural areas	_____
Share of industry in GNP	_____
Percentage of population with access to clean water	_____

4. The story of Rachmina Abdullah portrays a set of working conditions, living standards, and aspirations that differ greatly from the lifestyle of most citizens of the world's industrial countries.

   a. Write a brief word portrait conveying your impressions of how the life of a 17-year-old girl from a Malaysian village differs from that of a 17-year-old girl in a small town in Massachusetts.

   b. Write a brief word portrait conveying your impressions of how the life of a lathe operator in Maputo, Mozambique, differs from that of a lathe operator in Tokyo.

   c. Write a brief word portrait conveying your impressions of how life on a small family farm in Malawi differs from life on a small family farm in Wisconsin.

5. The text mentions that when income per capita grows by 4 percent per year, average incomes "double in less than a generation." A convenient way to grasp the significance of different growth rates is to calculate "doubling times." How long does it take for a variable to *double* in value if it grows continuously at the rate R percent per year? One way to answer this question is to use the equation for compound growth:

$$\text{(Value at year } T)/\text{(initial value)} = e^{rT}$$

where T is the time, in years, and $r = R/100$ is the growth rate expressed in decimal form. For this particular problem, we want the ratio on the left-hand side to equal exactly 2, representing a doubling of the value. Taking the logarithm of both sides, the equation can be expressed as $\ln 2 = rT$, or $100 \times \ln 2 = RT$ when the growth rate is expressed in percentage units rather than decimal units. Since $\ln 2 = 0.7$, approximately, the formula reduces to $70 = RT$, or $T = 70/R$. If income per capita grows at $R = 4$ percent per year, then doubling takes approximately $T = 70/4 = 17.5$ years.

a. Using the growth rates of GNP per capita from textbook Table 1–2, calculate the number of years required for GNP per capita to double in each of the following countries:

	Growth rate	Doubling time
India	_____%	_____ years
Sri Lanka	_____%	_____ years
Honduras	_____%	_____ years
Ghana	_____%	_____ years
Korea, Republic of	_____%	_____ years

b. Even moderate differences in growth rates can cause astonishing differences in the doubling time. This is most apparent when we look at longer periods of time. Notice that when income doubles once, twice, and then three times, the overall value is multiplied eightfold ($2 \times 2 \times 2$). Thus, three doubling periods generate an eightfold increase. Suppose that the growth rate experienced by each country listed can be sustained indefinitely. How many years are needed for each country's GNP per capita to grow eightfold? Also, what level of GNP per capita (in 1992 PPP dollars) would each country attain after an eightfold increase? (Table 1–1 in the textbook gives initial values needed to answer the second part of the question.)

	Time required to grow eightfold	GNP per capita after growing eightfold
India	_____ years	$_____
Sri Lanka	_____ years	$_____
Honduras	_____ years	$_____
Ghana	_____ years	$_____
Korea, Republic of	_____ years	$_____

(Note: The last figure, for Korea, is an extrapolation based on a period of extremely rapid growth, which almost certainly cannot be sustained.)

ANSWERS TO SELF-TEST

Completion

1. science
2. 720
3. upper-middle
4. rises
5. growth
6. export
7. World Bank
8. more
9. 35
10. Africa

True-False

1.	F	6.	F
2.	T	7.	F
3.	T	8.	T
4.	T	9.	F
5.	F	10.	T

Multiple Choice

1.	c	6.	c
2.	a	7.	a
3.	d	8.	a
4.	a	9.	c
5.	d	10.	d

CHAPTER 2	Economic Growth: Theory and Empirical Patterns

OVERVIEW

Chapter 2 (on growth) and Chapter 3 (on development) provide the theoretical foundations for much of the rest of the book. This chapter examines the factors that account for the pace and sustainability of aggregate economic growth within a country over time or across countries and over time. It introduces the various models development economists use to explain the process of growth and the empirical tools they employ to test or illustrate the predictions of those theories. Some of the material is difficult, so the chapter requires careful study.

The analysis starts with a definition of *gross national product* (GNP) and an explanation of the conceptual and statistical problems inherent in measuring such aggregate indicators of overall living standards. The historical patterns of levels of income per capita across world regions and countries then are used as a backdrop for an examination of the evolution of theories of growth that purport to explain the often puzzling record on growth.

The text provides a detailed presentation of the two workhorses of growth economics: the Harrod-Domar model, which focuses on saving and investment, and the Solow model, which highlights the role of saving and factor substitution. The empirical evidence on the key assumptions (e.g., fixity of capital-out ratios) and implications (e.g., convergence of per capita incomes) are examined in some detail. In light of this, more recent attempts to account for the sources of technological progress also briefly are reviewed in the section on endogenous growth models. The uses and misuses of both models for identifying constraints on growth are discussed, too. The appendix provides a nice antidote for those with a phobia for the high-school algebra used here for teasing out the implications of the models.

MAIN LEARNING OBJECTIVES

After studying this chapter, you ought to understand and be able to explain

1. The problems that arise in measuring aggregate output and making comparisons across countries and over time.

2. The major trends in per capita income across major world regions in the past century.

3. The role of technology (production function), saving, investment, and labor force growth as the basic building blocks of growth theory.

4. The implications for developing countries of the basic Harrod-Domar model of growth.

5. The implications for developing countries of the basic Solow model of growth and its extension to accommodate exogenous technological progress.

6. The empirical evidence for conditional and unconditional convergence in real per capita income across countries or regions.

7. The decomposition of aggregate growth into sources related to factor accumulation and total factor productivity growth.

8. Endogenous growth models that account for self-generated technological progress, and its implications including the possibility of a permanent increase in the rate of economic growth.

9. The importance of compounding, which shows how small gains in efficiency can have substantial cumulative effects on real per capita income over time.

ECONOMIC TOOLS AND TECHNIQUES

From what you have learned in this chapter, you should be able to

1. Convert a country's GNP or GDP into a common currency such as the U.S. dollar, using the official exchange rate method or the purchasing-power parity exchange rate method.

2. Convert nominal GNP or GDP into real terms using a price index.

3. Apply the Harrod-Domar and Solow growth models to analyze economic growth.

4. Calculate and interpret such parameters as the capital-labor ratio and the incremental capital-output ratio.

5. Explain how technological progress in the form of innovation and imitation affects long-run growth.

6. Explain the limitations of existing models in explaining the growth record, which reflects a multitude of conditioning factors related to endowments, policies, and institutions.

7. Apply the "rule of 70" to relate annual growth rates of developing economies to the number of years it would take their incomes to double at those rates.

KEY TERMS AND CONCEPTS

capital deepening versus capital
  widening
capital-intensive methods
capital-labor ratio
conditional convergence
diminishing returns to capital
effective units of labor
fixed-coefficients (Leontief)
  production function
Harrod-Domar model
human capital
increasing returns to scale
incremental capital-output ratio (ICOR)
index-number problem

knife-edge problem
labor-intensive methods
marketed versus nonmarketed output
neoclassical (variable-coefficients)
  production function
nontraded versus traded goods
positive externality
PPP versus official exchange rates
production function
Solow model
steady state
technological change
total factor productivity
unconditional convergence

SELF-TEST

Completion

1. In 1992 Korea's exchange rate averaged 781 won per dollar; Korea's GNP per capita was 5.3 million won. Converting to dollars using the exchange rate, Korea's per capita GNP was U.S.$_____.

2. As a measure of aggregate economic activity, gross _____ product excludes earnings outside the country by citizens, while it includes earnings inside the country by persons from other countries.

3. ICOR stands for the _____ _____ _____ _____.

4. The Harrod-Domar growth model is based on the premise that growth is determined mainly by the accumulation of _____.

5. A curve showing the various input combinations that produce a given amount of output is called an _____.

6. During the 1980s, Indonesia's ICOR was 4.8 while Nigeria's ICOR was 11.2. Capital investment was more efficient in _____.

7. If Senegal's savings rate averages 15 percent of GDP and the ICOR equals 4.6, then real GDP will grow by _____ percent per annum.

8. A one-time increase in the saving rate will increase _____ permanently and _____ temporarily.

9. Convergence in per capita income between India and Germany implies that India should grow _____ than Germany.

10. If China has an annual population growth rate of 2 percent and a GDP growth rate of 9 percent, it can expect to double its per-capita income every _____ years.

True-False

If false, you should be able to explain why.

_____ 1. GNP is the sum of the value of all final and intermediate goods and services produced in an economy.

_____ 2. Value added in the textile industry is equal to the sum of the earnings of the factors of production employed in the industry.

_____ 3. Using the traditional exchange-rate method to convert GNP statistics into dollars, one greatly overstates the level of GNP per capita for low-income countries like India.

_____ 4. With a neoclassical aggregate production function, the capital-output ratio for the economy is influenced by policies that alter the relative costs of capital and labor.

Multiple Choice

1. To say that a production function has constant returns to scale means that
   a. output is constant regardless of the scale of operation.
   b. output doubles when labor input doubles.
   c. output doubles when both the labor and capital inputs double.
   d. various levels of output can be produced with a constant stock of capital.

2. What special problem is associated with nontraded goods in measuring GNP?
   a. Nontraded goods are excluded because they are intermediate goods.
   b. Nontraded goods are excluded because they are not sold in the market.
   c. There is no value added in the production of nontraded goods.
   d. Nontraded goods are improperly valued by the exchange-rate conversion method for international comparisons.

3. From 1980 to 1990, real GDP in India grew by 5.8 percent per annum, while investment averaged 23.1 percent of GDP. The ICOR for India was
   a. 3.98.   c. 17.3.
   b. 0.25.   d. 28.9.

4. A production function with L-shaped isoquants is a
   a. two-sector model.
   b. neoclassical production function.
   c. fixed-coefficient production function.
   d. Marxian production function.

5. Because of population growth, Ghana's GNP must grow by 3 percent per year just to avoid a decline in average standards of living. With an ICOR of 6.0, achieving this minimum-growth target requires a saving rate of
   a. 18 percent.   c. 50 percent.
   b. 3 percent.   d. 9 percent.

APPLICATIONS

Worked Example: Multiple Growth Equilibria in a Developing Economy

Recent thinking in development economics suggests that underdevelopment may have as much to do with equilibrium traps precipitated by inertia or history as with missing institutions. Several metaphors invoked by the older generation of development economists (such as low-level equilibrium trap, takeoff, and vicious circle of poverty) now can be recast in a more illuminating light.

This worked example and the exercises that follow build on the insights of the Harrod-Domar and the Solow growth models to illustrate how the fictitious economy of Paradise Lost gets stuck in inferior equilibria. It brings out the crucial importance of good institutions or policies for rescuing economies out of stable, self-sustainable equilibria (growth traps).

The two growth models suggest that the steady-state growth rate of the capital stock (K) needed to maintain a constant capital-labor ratio (k) at equilibrium is equal to

$$\text{Harrod-Domar:} \quad s/v = n - d \quad \text{(from [2–11] of the text)} \qquad [2–1]$$

$$\text{Solow:} \quad sy/k = n - d \quad \text{(from [2–14] of the text)} \qquad [2–2]$$

Assuming that the depreciation rate (d) is equal to 0, the preceding equations give us the growth rate of income (g) that would ensure a constant per-capita income (y) in the face of population growth (n). Furthermore, equation [2–1] or [2–2] can be rewritten as (remember, $v = K/Y = k/y$):

$$s = nv \qquad [2–3]$$

Let us do some "what-if" exercises by modifying some of the key assumptions of the two models. This would generate some interesting conclusions about the dynamics of growth in an underdeveloped economy that faces several obstacles. Consider the following three changes of assumption:

1. The equilibrium implied by the equations may be an underemployment equilibrium ($g = n'$) rather than a full-employment equilibrium ($g = n^*$). Since we are dealing with a low-income economy, lets call the $n' < n^*$ equilibrium a *low-level equilibrium trap*. Policy makers, therefore, should have a strong incentive (but not necessarily the wisdom or the capability) to nudge the economy toward a superior equilibrium.

2. The saving rate, s, no longer is fixed or exogenously given. It is endogenous. That is, it depends on the distribution of income, the level of financial development, and the level of income itself.

3. The rate of population (labor force) growth, n, no longer is fixed either. it depends, in a neo-Malthusian fashion, on the level of per-capita income.

Using these three new assumptions, we rewrite [2–3] as

$$s(k) = n(k)v \qquad\qquad [2\text{–}4]$$

Furthermore, the "takeoff" from a low-income steady state to a high-income steady state means that the capital-labor ratio (k) needs to be pushed above the threshold. That is,

$$s(k) > n(k)v \qquad\qquad [2\text{–}5]$$

These possibilities are depicted in the reformulated Solow diagram (Figure 2–1) with nonlinear $s(k)$ and $n(k)$. Three equilibrium positions have been identified, two of which are unstable. Table 2–1 provides some illustrative data for a group of developing economies.

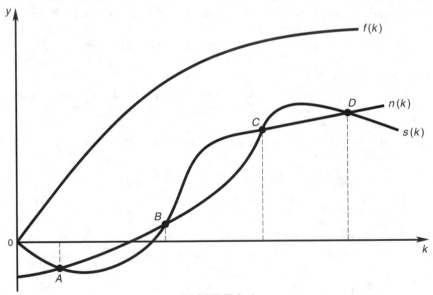

FIGURE 2–1

Exercises

1. We now apply our knowledge of the two growth models to the particular context just provided. Consider Figure 2–1.

    a. Identify the two unstable equilibria:
       (i) The "destitution" steady state is _____.
       (ii) The "pretakeoff" steady state is _____.

Table 2–1

The Timing of Takeoff for the Four Asian Tigers

Country/year	v	n	nv	s	$\Delta k/k$	g	Memo: F/I (%)
Taiwan							
1953	5.5	3.8	—	5.0	−15.9	5.7	40.7
1962	3.4	3.3	—	7.6	−3.6	5.5	40.0
1963	3.2	3.2	—	13.4	3.2	8.2	40.0
1977	2.1	1.8	—	32.3	28.5	6.8	−6.0
South Korea							
1960	2.4	2.9	—	−4.8	−11.8	−4.7	48.3
1965	2.0	2.6	—	1.9	−3.3	2.6	77.8
1966	1.9	2.5	—	7.0	2.2	0.3	77.8
1973	1.8	1.8	—	18.3	15.1	12.4	5.9
Hong Kong							
1961	1.4	3.0	—	−5.2	−9.4	5.5	60.1
1964	1.4	3.5	—	2.9	−0.6	5.2	−13.6
1965	1.4	2.7	—	7.2	3.4	15.2	−13.6
1974	1.3	3.8	—	15.0	10.1	−0.7	−13.8
Singapore							
1960	1.7	3.2	—	−14.0	−19.4	4.8	80.5
1965	1.4	2.7	—	−0.1	−3.9	4.9	80.5
1966	1.3	2.1	—	4.1	1.4	8.4	38.3
1974	1.5	1.4	—	19.6	17.5	4.6	37.9

Note: F/I = foreign capital inflows as percentage of gross domestic investment.

Source: Adapted from S. C. Tsiang and Rong-I Wu, "Foreign Trade and Investment as Boosters for Take-off: The Experiences of the Four Asian Newly Industrializing Countries." In: Walter Galenson, ed., *Foreign Trade and Investment: Economic Development in the Newly Industrializing Asian Countries* (Madison: University of Wisconsin Press, 1985), pp. 301–32.

  b. Identify the two stable equilibria:
    (i) The "low-level-trap" steady state is _____.
    (ii) The "takeoff" steady state is _____.

  c. Assuming a trap refers to a very low level of per capita income, this under-developed economy can escape the trap only if it can mobilize additional savings or if it experiences a cataclysmic drop in labor force growth.
    (i) At what point on the graph is the equilibrium position reached with the help of foreign transfers (aid)? _____
    (ii) At what point on the graph is the equilibrium position reached with the help of depopulation or massive emigration? _____
    (iii) What other possibilities might this economy use to escape the undesirable equilibrium?

d. Consider Table 2–1.

 (i) Calculate *nv* using the data from the first two columns.

 (ii) Determine the implied year of takeoff for each of the four countries:

> Taiwan _____
>
> South Korea _____
>
> Hong Kong _____
>
> Singapore _____

 (iii) Why is the takeoff accompanied by rapid growth in capital intensity (*k*)?

 (iv) What do the high growth rates coinciding with the takeoff year tell us about convergence in per capita income implied by the Solow model?

 (v) Look at the data in the last column. What might they tell us about closing financing gaps in natural-resource-poor developing economies?

2. *Measuring gross national product (GNP).* Begin this exercise by looking back over Table 2–1 in the textbook. A similar table with new data is reproduced here as Table 2–2.

 a. Calculate the following:

 (i) The market value of steel output for the United States is $_____ million.

 (ii) The market value of retail services for the United States is $_____ million.

 (iii) The total value of goods and services produced in the United States is $_____ million. This is GNP for the United States.

 (iv) Place this information in the column of blank spaces for the United States in Table 2–2.

 (v) In the same manner, calculate the value of India's steel output, retail services, and total GNP (in millions of rupees). Then fill in the column of blank spaces for India.

Table 2-2

GNP for the United States and India

	United States			India		
	Quantity	Price ($)	Value of output (million $)	Quantity	Price (Rs)	Value of output (million Rs)
Steel (millions of tons)	105	210 per ton	——	12	6,100 per ton	——
Retail services (millions of person-years)	2.1	5,100 per person-year	——	5	3,200 per person-year	——
Total GNP (in local currency)			——			——

b. You now have GNP figures for both countries in local currency units: millions of dollars and rupees, respectively. To compare GNP for the two countries, the GNP figures must be expressed in common currency units. Let's convert India's GNP to U.S. dollars using the exchange rate. Suppose that the Indian government maintains the exchange rate at Rs30 = $1.

   (i) You have calculated that India's GNP is Rs_____ million (in rupee units). At the prevailing exchange rate this is equivalent to $_____ million (in dollar units).

   (ii) With both values expressed in dollars, the ratio of GNP for the United States to GNP for India is

$$\text{(GNP U.S.)/(GNP India)} = \underline{\hspace{2cm}}.$$

c. Rather than using the exchange rate to convert from rupee values into dollars, one can apply pertinent dollar values directly to each of India's goods and services. This is the purchasing power parity (PPP) method.

   (i)   Using the U.S. price of $210 per ton, India's steel output has a total dollar value of $_____ million.

   (ii) Using the U.S. price of $5,100 per person-year, India's retail services have a total dollar value of $_____ billion.

   (iii) Adding these together gives India's total GNP, converted to dollars using the purchasing power parity method, as $_____ billion.

   (iv) Based on the PPP method for converting from rupee to dollars, the ratio of GNP for the United States to GNP for India is

$$\text{(GNP U.S.)/(GNP India)} = \underline{\hspace{2cm}}.$$

   (The economic differential is larger in *per-capita* terms since India's GNP serves $3\frac{1}{2}$ times as many people.)

   (v)   Briefly explain why switching from the exchange-rate method to the PPP method causes such a large change in India's GNP as measured in dollars.

d. To look at GNP measurements over time, suppose that the table used here represents data for 2000, while Table 2–1 in the textbook represents the corresponding data *for 1990.*

   (i) You have calculated that India's GNP is Rs _____ million in 2000 (in part b). In Table 2–1 in the textbook, the corresponding figure was Rs312,000 million in 1990. (Note: The textbook table gives GNP in billions; we are using millions here, to conform with the units given for quantity measurements.)

       These are *nominal* GNP figures. To get *real* GNP figures for comparing the change in output levels, one must value the outputs each year using a constant set of prices. Let's choose 1990 as the base year. The outputs for each year will now be valued at constant 1990 prices. For 1990, real and nominal GNP are identical; this must be true since the prices used to compute nominal GNP for 1990 happen to be the base-year prices. Thus real GDP for 1990 is Rs312,000 million. For 1996 things are different.

(ii) Using the *base-year* price of steel (Rs9,000 per ton) India's steel output for 1996 has a value of Rs _____ million.

(iii) Using the constant *base-year* price of retail services (Rs60,000 per person-year), India's retail services in 1996 have a value of Rs_____ billion.

(iv) India's GNP for 1996 (at constant 1990 prices) is Rs_____ million. This is *real* GNP for 2000.

(v)   Compare India's real GNP for 2000 with real GNP for 1990. Between 1990 and 2000 total output grew by _____ percent. If you rework this calculation using 2000 as the base year, rather than 1990, the answer is altered slightly. This occurs because the base-period prices serve as valuation *weights* for averaging the change in output levels for various goods and services.

The exercise provides a very simple illustration of the real-world problem of comparing national-account statistics across countries and over time. Inevitably, the results depend on the methodology. This is the index-number problem.

3. *Harrod-Domar growth model.*

   a. In Indonesia during the 1970s the incremental capital-output ratio (ICOR) averaged 2.50.

      (i)   Using the Harrod-Domar growth equation, what saving rate would have been required for Indonesia to achieve an aggregate growth rate of 8 percent per annum?

      $$s = _____\%.$$

      (ii) With the same ICOR, what growth target could be achieved with a saving rate of 27 percent?

      $$g = _____\%.$$

      (iii) If there is a large increase in the saving rate, and therefore a large increase in the amount of new capital formation, is the ICOR likely to rise, fall, or remain the same? Explain.

   b. The government of a poor developing country fears that a political upheaval will occur unless the growth rate is at least 4 percent per annum. The ICOR and the saving rate are projected to be $k = 5.0$ and $s = 14$ percent, respectively.

(i) Show that 4 percent growth cannot be achieved under these circumstances.

(ii) With the saving rate as given, what ICOR would be required to achieve the 4 percent growth target?

(iii) No doubt, the government faces a serious threat due to poor economic performance. What types of changes in economic conditions would alter the ICOR as needed to achieve 4 percent growth? Give a few examples.

c. *More difficult.* Over the period 1980 to 1992, the GNP in Peru grew by $g = -0.6$ percent per year, even though total savings (s) averaged 23 percent of GDP. How can you reconcile these figures with the Harrod-Domar growth model? What does the model suggest is the cause of Peru's poor growth performance?

4. *Isoquants and production functions.* Brrravia is a very cold country with a highly specialized economy. The only product is hot chicken soup. The aggregate production function shows how much chicken soup can be produced for any given quantity of labor (L) and capital (K). The relationship can be expressed graphically using isoquants, which show the various combinations of L and K needed to produce a given quantity of chicken soup.

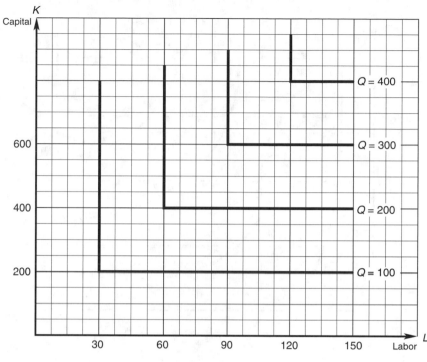

FIGURE 2–2

a. Figure 2–2 shows a set of fixed-coefficient isoquants for producing chicken soup. The label for each isoquant relates to a particular quantity (Q) of output. The farther the isoquant is from the origin, the higher the output level.

(i) With 400 units of K and 60 units of L, Brrravia could produce _____ barrels of chicken soup. The capital-output ratio would be $K/Q =$ _____.

(ii) With 600 units of K and 90 units of L, Brrravia could produce _____ barrels of soup. Hence the incremental capital-output ratio for Brrravia is ICOR = _____. (Hint: The ICOR is defined as $\Delta K/\Delta Y$.)

(iii) If Brrravia had $K = 600$ and $L = 120$, then _____ barrels of soup could be produced. The capital-output ratio would be $K/Q =$ _____.

(iv) In the last case, is there a labor surplus in Brrravia? Explain.

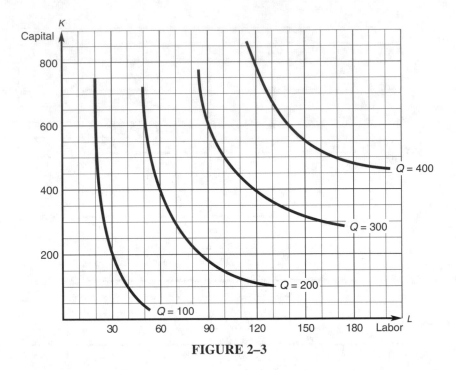

FIGURE 2–3

b. The isoquants in Figure 2–3 represent a neoclassical production function.
   (i) With 400 units of K and 60 units of L, Brrravia could produce
       _____ barrels of chicken soup. The capital-output ratio would
       (again) be $K/Q =$ _____.
   (ii) With 600 units of K and 90 units of L, Brrravia could produce
        _____ barrels of soup. Hence, the incremental capital-output ratio
        for Brrravia is ICOR = _____.
   (iii) If Brrravia had $K = 600$ and $L = 120$, then approximately _____
         barrels of soup could be produced. The capital-output ratio would
         be $K/Q =$ _____.
   (iv) In the last case, is there a labor surplus in Brrravia? Explain.

   (v) If Brrravia grew from $K = 400$ and $L = 60$ as in part (i) to $K = 600$
       and $L = 120$ as in part (iii), the incremental capital-output ratio
       would be ICOR = _____. This ICOR differs from the one you
       calculated in part (ii). Why?

c. In Figure 2–4, the vertical axis shows the level of chicken-soup
production, while the horizontal axis shows the amount of labor
input. Working from the information embodied in the isoquants
shown in Figure 2–3, plot in Figure 2–4 the various combinations
of L and Q consistent with a fixed capital stock of $K = 600$.

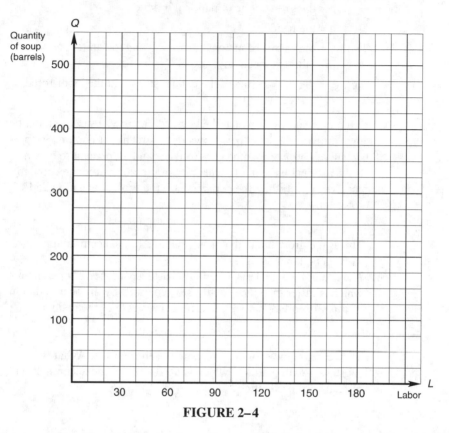

FIGURE 2–4

How does this neoclassical production function reflect diminishing
returns to labor?

d. *Optional.* Still assuming $K = 600$, plot in Figure 2–4 the relationship
between L and Q from Figure 2–2, where we assumed a fixed-
coefficient production function. In this case, how does the marginal
product of labor behave when the quantity of labor is increased?
Viewed broadly, this exercise has shown how production functions are
linked to the ICOR, the capital-output ratio, the marginal product of
labor, and the concept of surplus labor.

5. This exercise applies the sources-of-growth model. We will neglect land and natural resources for simplicity. With this modification, the sources-of-growth equation from the textbook is

$$g = a + W_K g_K + W_L g_L,$$

where g = the growth rate of national product,

   a = the residual,

   $W_K,\ W_L$ = the shares of national income going to capital and to labor, respectively,

   $g_K,\ g_L$ = the growth rate of the capital stock and the labor force, respectively.

a. Consider an economy in which the labor force grows by 2.7 percent per annum, while the capital stock grows by 4 percent per annum. Suppose 55 percent of national income goes to labor and 45 percent to capital.
   (i) If the residual were $a = 0$, what rate of growth would the economy achieve? (Hint: Plug the numbers into the growth equation and solve for g.)

   $g = $ _____% per annum.

   This is the growth rate that is attributable to the accumulation of capital and labor stocks.
   (ii) The country's actual rate of growth has been 4.5 percent per annum, which is faster than the growth rate generated by the accumulation of capital and labor stocks. Calculate the value of the residual.

   $a = $ _____% per annum.

   (iii) Then explain the economic meaning of the residual: What is causing growth over that which is derived from the accumulation of factors of production?

b. Consider a second economy in which labor's share of national income is 0.6; the remainder is capital's share. The capital stock is growing by 5 percent per annum and the labor force is growing by 3 percent per annum, while real GDP is growing by just 1 percent per annum.
   (i) Calculate the residual for this economy.

   $a = $ _____% per annum.

   (ii) You should find that the value of the residual is disturbingly low this time! What economic conditions might be responsible for such a low residual?

c. From 1970 to 1989 Singapore's growth rate averaged 8.4 percent per year. A recent growth-accounting study showed that the residual accounted for only 1.2 percent per year of Singapore's outstanding growth performance. This growth-accounting analysis used weights of 0.33 for labor and 0.67 for capital, *including* human capital.

   (i) Singapore's labor force grew by 2.6 percent per year during this period. What can you conclude about the annual growth rate of Singapore's capital stock? (Bear in mind that this includes both physical and human capital.)

   (ii) What fraction of the overall 8.4 percent growth rate is attributable to capital investment? (Hint: Calculate $W_K g_K / g$.)

   (iii) Briefly assess the sources of GDP growth in Singapore. Was the growth performance due primarily to capital accumulation? To population growth? To improvements in total factor productivity, as measured by the residual?

ANSWERS TO SELF-TEST

Completion

1. 6,786
2. domestic
3. incremental capital-output ratio
4. capital
5. *isoquant*
6. Indonesia
7. 3.26
8. per capita income; growth rate
9. faster
10. ten years

True-False

1. F
2. T
3. F
4. T

Multiple Choice

1. c
2. d
3. a
4. c
5. a

CHAPTER 3 | Structural Change

OVERVIEW

A defining characteristic of economic development is a transformation in the structures of production, employment, and consumption. On the supply side, these changes initially are triggered by reallocation of resources across industry sectors (industry, agriculture, services) and across economic actors (households, firms). In the long run, this process can be sustained only by gains in productivity resulting from continual improvements in technology broadly construed. On the demand side, changes in household income and taste alter the composition of consumer demand (Engel's law), to which producers respond.

The result is an increase in the share of industrial output and employment at the expense of agriculture. This compositional shift favors services in later stages of development, primarily at the expense of industry. Although this pattern of industrialization and postindustrial change is universal, the timing of the structural changes and even the sequencing at more disaggregated levels by no means are identical across countries.

To provide a deeper understanding of the links between industry and agriculture, the textbook presents multisector production, input-output, social accounting, and computable general equilibrium models to analyze the multitude of linkages and feedback mechanisms. The input-output model is a tool for analyzing the industry-by-industry output (input) requirements implied by a set of final output targets. The social accounting matrix (SAM) broadens the input-output framework to include data on household expenditures, government budgets, balance of payments, and financial flows. Both tools are "consistency" models used to test the feasibility of alternative growth targets set by policymakers.

In contrast, "optimality" models are used to identify the best plan or project that maximizes a constrained economic objective. In addition to the brief reference to linear programming models, the text introduces computable general equilibrium (CGE) models, which can be used to simulate a market economy's responses to changes in policy. All these models help us understand how the evolution of a country's industrial structure is influenced by strategies for balanced (unbalanced) growth, by policies of import substitution or export promotion, and by complex production or consumption linkage effects.

MAIN LEARNING OBJECTIVES

After studying this chapter, you ought to understand and be able to explain

1. Why industrialization and urbanization systematically accompany development and how these structural patterns are estimated empirically.

2. How industrialization is tied to conditions in agriculture in the context of two-sector growth models.

3. How population growth affects the process of structural change in the two-sector growth models.

4. The underlying theme that regularities characterize the development process, but each country must identify the path and patterns of development suitable to its own conditions.

5. The difference between a consistency model and an optimality model.

6. The structure of an input-output model.

7. The characteristics and advantages of a social accounting matrix.

8. The broad features and advantages of computable general equilibrium models.

ECONOMIC TOOLS AND TECHNIQUES

From what you have learned in this chapter, you should be able to

1. Explain the methodology developed by Hollis B. Chenery and his coauthors to analyze the average patterns of development for various categories of developing countries.

2. Explain the process by which surplus labor is mobilized to finance industrialization in the labor-surplus two-sector model of Lewis, Ranis, and Fei.

3. Contrast the assumptions and conclusions of the neoclassical two-sector model with the labor-surplus model.

4. Explain backward and forward linkage effects and how such links enter Albert O. Hirschman's theory of unbalanced growth.

5. Convert an input-output table into a matrix of input-output coefficients (the A-matrix) and explain how to compute sectoral gross output levels consistent with a set of final output targets.

6. Interpret the row and column entries of a social accounting matrix.

KEY TERMS AND CONCEPTS

average patterns of development
balanced vs. unbalanced growth
big push
computable general equilibrium
   (CGE) model
consistency model
Engel's law
economies of scale
final goods (demanded)
import substitution
input-output model

institutionally fixed wage
interindustry linkages
labor surplus
Leontief production function
linear programming model
linkages
marginal product
optimality model
social accounting matrix (SAM)
terms of trade (internal)
turning point

SELF-TEST

Completion

1. A model that computes the best feasible use of resources is called an

   _____ model.

2. Let sector 1 = agriculture and sector 3 = manufacturing. Manufacturing

   uses $200 million of agricultural inputs to produce $500 million of

   output. The input-output coefficient a_{13} (agricultural input per unit of

   manufacturing output) equals _____.

3. The acronym SAM stands for _____ _____

   _____.

4. An economic model is overdetermined when it has more equations than

   _____; in this case, some of the equations are _____.

5. A linear programming model determines the outcome that maximizes the

   value of an _____ function, subject to constraints such as

   resource availability.

6. The Lewis and Ranis-Fei two-sector models describe the dynamics of

   structural change in countries with surplus _____ in rural areas.

7. The Fei-Ranis model assumes that rural workers earn an institutionally

   fixed wage that is determined by the _____ product of labor in

   agriculture.

8. An industry that uses simple technologies to produce goods that are

   essential to poor households is called _____.

9. Economists use _____ _____ _____
   models to simulate how policies will influence market outcomes, as
   individuals respond to price signals.

10. The use of _____ coefficient production functions in input-
    output models rules out substitution effects that may be important elements
    of any economic adjustment.

True-False

If false, you should be able to explain why.

_____ 1. For a plan to be *consistent*, it must be feasible and it must be the
         best use of available resources.

_____ 2. Each column of an input-output coefficient matrix defines a fixed-
         coefficient production function for one sector of the economy.

_____ 3. Coefficient a_{ij} shows the ratio of output i to input j in sector i.

_____ 4. The basic equations of an input-output model show that for each
         production sector that total output equals the sum of intermediate
         uses and final uses.

_____ 5. Using a SAM, economists can study the income distribution effects
         of various policies.

_____ 6. A major advantage of CGE models is that they incorporate
         neoclassical production functions to allow for factor substitution.

_____ 7. An input-using industry is said to have a forward linkage.

_____ 8. A major conclusion from growth-accounting research is that capital
         accumulation is far more important than productivity gains as a
         source of growth for LDCs.

_____ 9. Chenery and his associates have shown that large countries, small
         industry-oriented countries, and small primary-product exporters
         all follow the same "normal" patterns of development.

_____ 10. Empirical evidence shows that countries with higher levels of per
          capita income tend to have a higher share of GNP produced in
          agriculture.

_____ 11. The turning point in the Fei-Ranis model is the point in the
          development process where labor demand has increased enough to
          generate rising real wages in both agriculture and industry.

_____ 12. The neoclassical two-sector growth model assumes that wages in agriculture equal the marginal product of labor.

_____ 13. The new approach to growth theory emphasizes increasing returns to scale and externalities that affect productivity.

_____ 14. If the supply curve of labor to industry is perfectly elastic, then an increase in the demand for labor in industry leaves the real wage unchanged.

_____ 15. According to proponents of balanced growth, industrialization requires an initial big push in order to balance demand expansion with supply expansion.

Multiple Choice

1. In Figure 3–1, which point represents a *consistent* target for a development plan?

   a. *A*　　　　　　　　　　c. *C*
   b. *B*　　　　　　　　　　d. all the above

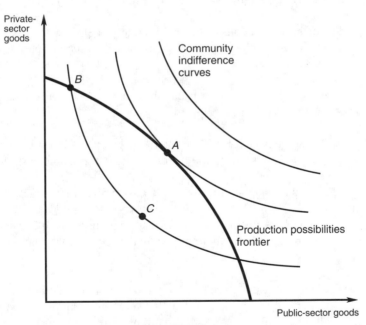

FIGURE 3–1

2. In the equation $\Delta Y_t = (1/k) (I_{t-1} - \delta K_{t-1})$, the parameter δ stands for the

   a. ICOR.
   b. rate of depreciation of the capital stock.
   c. savings rate.
   d. rate of growth of the capital stock.

3. A major problem with input-output models is that they
   a. can distinguish only four production sectors.
   b. capture intermediate-goods linkages but ignore final demands.
   c. cannot readily handle changes in input-output coefficients due to technological innovation, scale economies, or input substitutions.
   d. are subject to all the criticisms listed above.

4. Given the estimated bill of final uses for the output of each sector, input-output analysis can be used
   a. to compute the total required output for each sector.
   b. to identify sectors requiring more capital investment to increase production capacity.
   c. to compute the implied requirement for imports and foreign exchange.
   d. all the above.

5. If sector 3 is steel and sector 5 is coal, then $a_{35} = .09$ means that
   a. each unit of steel production requires an input of 0.09 units of coal.
   b. each unit of coal production requires an input of 0.09 units of steel.
   c. one unit of coal input is required per 0.09 units of steel production.
   d. one unit of steel input is required per 0.09 units of coal production

6. In applying the standard input-output model, the bill of final uses (F_i) for each sector's product is usually
   a. estimated separately on the basis of a predetermined target growth rate for the economy.
   b. calculated as part of the solution to the input-output model.
   c. measured directly from available national accounts data.
   d. identified by computing the point on the production possibilities frontier that is tangent to a community indifference curve.

7. The central idea of Engel's law is that rising family incomes cause
   a. a decline in the amount of money spent on food.
   b. a decline in the proportion of the budget spent on food.
   c. people to migrate to urban areas.
   d. an increase in the saving rate.

8. Chenery and his research associates estimated average patterns of development using
   a. fixed-coefficient production functions.
   b. cross-section data.
   c. purchasing power parity comparisons.
   d. a two-sector neoclassical growth model.

9. If the marginal product of labor in agriculture is positive, then drawing more workers into industry will cause the terms of trade between industry and agriculture to turn against
   a. labor.   c. agriculture.
   b. industry.   d. exports.

10. China's efforts to cope with labor surplus have included all the following policies *except*
    a. control of population growth.
    b. use of less-mechanized farming methods.
    c. reduced imports of food.
    d. encouraging growth of labor-intensive urban industries.

11. Which is a backward-linkage effect from establishing a steel factory?
    a. Stimulating construction activities using steel beams.
    b. Stimulating coal mining to provide fuel to the steel factory.
    c. Stimulating employment through job creation.
    d. All the above.

12. Industry in Pakistan has grown faster than agriculture. Due to index-number problems, Pakistan's growth rate will seem higher if real GNP is calculated using
    a. a base year when agriculture prices were unusually low.
    b. dollars rather than rupees.
    c. growth accounting rather than the Harrod-Domar growth model.
    d. data on the value added in each sector.

13. Which of the following is *not* true of SAMs?
    a. An input-output table often is embedded within a SAM.
    b. SAMs can integrate data from household surveys together with data from national income accounts.
    c. SAMs focus on domestic economic activity and exclude data on international trade and financial flows.
    d. In the process of compiling a SAM, economists may uncover inconsistencies across various data sources.

14. A major advantage of CGE models over linear programming models is that the CGE models
    a. incorporate welfare weights.
    b. allow for price adjustments, factor substitutions, and substitutability among consumer goods.
    c. include intersectoral linkages and international trade.
    d. take into account resource constraints.

APPLICATIONS

Worked Example: The Fei-Ranis Model

How does the lack of progress in agriculture hinder the development of *industry*?

Consider the case of Machismo, a small country that neglected agriculture in its drive to industrialize. Initially, the entire labor force of 1,000 people worked on farms producing bananas, worth 10 pesos per kilogram. Figure 3–2 shows the agricultural production function. You can see that the last 100 workers added nothing to farm output. Their marginal product was zero. With 1,000 workers producing 1.8 million kilograms of bananas per year, each worker consumed 1,800 kilograms (worth 18,000 pesos) per year.

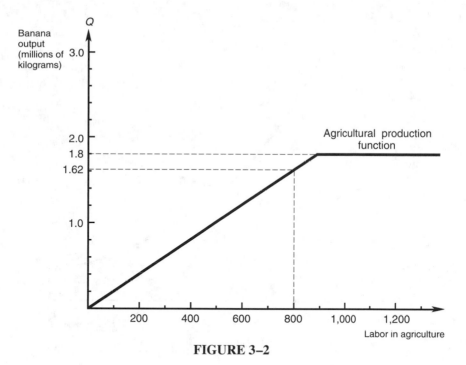

FIGURE 3–2

Workers were willing to migrate to urban industrial jobs as long a they could earn enough to eat as well as kinfolk back on the farm. Initially, industry could attract labor supply with a wage of 18,000 pesos per year.

After 100 workers had moved to industry, the situation looked like this: 900 workers remained in agriculture and produced 1.8 million kilograms of bananas (still), enough for each rural worker and each urban worker to maintain the traditional consumption of 1,800 kilograms per year per person. When 100 more workers migrated to industry, conditions changed markedly. With only 800 workers left on the farm, banana production dropped to 1.62 million kilograms per year; those who left for the city no longer had a zero marginal product on the farm. Workers still demanded 1.8 million kilograms but only 1.62 million kilograms were produced. The excess demand caused banana prices to rise to 12 pesos per kilogram. This price increase caused rural and urban workers to reduce their banana consumption to 1,620 kilograms per year. The quantity demanded matched the quantity supplied (1.62 million kilograms), but the terms of trade between agriculture and industry had shifted against industry.

Although urban workers consumed fewer bananas, the higher banana price raised their food bill to 24,300 pesos per year. Without higher wages to meet the higher food costs, workers would have moved back to the farm. In Figure 3–3, the supply curve of labor to industry (S_0S_0) reflects this circumstance. Industry could hire as many as 100 workers at a wage of 18,000 pesos. But to hire another 100 workers, the industrial wage had to rise to 24,300 pesos (point B). Despite the higher wage, workers are no better off; their real wage in terms of banana consumption has declined. But the real cost of labor to employers has risen.

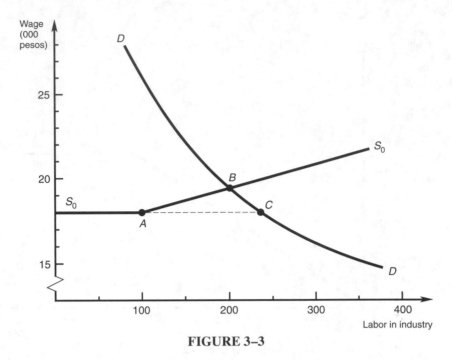

FIGURE 3–3

Suppose that agricultural productivity had risen to maintain production of 1.8 million kilograms of bananas with fewer rural workers, via a shift in the production function in agriculture. Then banana prices would not have risen. Rural and urban workers would not have faced a decline in banana consumption. The supply curve of labor to industry would not have turned up at point A. Given the demand curve (DD) for labor in industry, employment would have risen to point C rather than point B. In short, by neglecting agricultural productivity, Machismo ended up with fewer jobs, lower real incomes, less output, and lower profits for reinvestment and growth.

The example leads to three observations. First, it shows an increase in the nominal price of bananas; it is more accurate to say that the shortage caused the price of bananas to rise *relative to* the price of industrial goods. Second, if bananas could be imported, then industrial labor costs might not have to rise, but the need to import food would use valuable foreign exchange and the neglect of agriculture still would cramp industrialization and growth. Finally, a neoclassical version of the story there would have no horizontal portion to curve S_0S_0 in Figure 3–3. In this case, neglecting agricultural productivity pinches into banana output even before industrial employment expands to point A.

Exercises

1. *Analysis of two-sector labor-surplus model.* This exercise uses Figures 3–2 and 3–3. Be sure that you have read the Worked Example carefully.

   a. Let's see how the situation changes if the labor force in Machismo grows to 1,200 people. Start with all 1,200 workers placed in the agricultural sector.

(i) From Figure 3–2 you can see that total farm output would be
_____ million kilograms of bananas per year.

(ii) Assuming that everyone eats an equal amount, this level of output
permits each worker to consume _____ kilograms of
bananas per year. (Be careful with the units.)

(iii) Because of the extra mouths to feed, suppose that the price of
bananas rises to 16 pesos per kilogram. The money value of each
worker's banana consumption is _____ pesos per year.

(iv) Study Figure 3–2 carefully. How many of the 1,200 workers could be
withdrawn from agriculture before banana output begins to decline?
_____ workers.

(v) If this number of workers *plus* 100 more workers are withdrawn
from agriculture, then the level of banana production would drop to
_____ million kilograms, which is enough for each
worker in the economy to consume just _____ kilograms
of bananas per year.

(vi) The decline in production causes the price of bananas to rise to 20
pesos per kilogram. At this price, the money value of each worker's
banana consumption costs _____ pesos per year.

b. Now look at these conditions from the perspective of the industrial
sector. To attract workers from agriculture, industry has to pay an
annual wage high enough to permit urban workers to eat as well as their
kinfolk back on the farm.

(i) Starting with all 1,200 workers in agriculture, industry has to pay a
wage of _____ pesos per year to attract labor from
agriculture.

(ii) As many as _____ workers can be hired by industry
without causing banana production to drop. As these workers move
to industry, the production and consumption of bananas remain in
balance. So there is no upward pressure on banana prices or on
urban wages.

(iii) But if an *additional* 100 workers move to industry, then banana
output drops to _____ kilograms per worker (as you
calculated above) and the price of bananas rises to 20 pesos per
kilogram. Urban wages must rise to _____ pesos per year
to keep workers from moving back to the farm.

(iv) On the basis of your answers to the last three subsections, carefully
draw in Figure 3–3 the labor supply curve to the industrial sector;
and label it $S_1 S_1$. (Hint: the horizontal segment of $S_1 S_1$ lies above
the horizontal segment of $S_0 S_0$ and extends further to the right; do
you see why?)

c. Figure 3–3 now has two labor supply curves: $S_0 S_0$, showing conditions
with a total labor force of 1,000 workers; and $S_1 S_1$, showing conditions
with 1,200 workers but without any improvement in agricultural
productivity.

(i) Retaining the original demand for labor curve, *DD*, show the new
equilibrium in the industrial labor market. Label the equilibrium as
point *B'*. Comparing point *B* and point *B'*, how does the increase in

population from 1,000 to 1,200 workers affect Machismo's industrial sector in terms of

Job creation?

Output?

Real wages (cost per worker)?

Real standard of living per worker?

Profits for reinvestment?

(ii) Can you explain each of these outcomes with reference to the terms of trade between agriculture and industry?

d. Continue to assume that the labor force totals 1,200 workers. Suppose this time that productivity in agriculture increased by 50 percent. This means that banana output is 50 percent higher, for any given number of workers.

(i) Briefly state how this increase in productivity alters the agricultural production function as drawn in Figure 3–2, and the labor supply curve as drawn in Figure 3–3.

(ii) If the labor demand curve in industry (*DD*) remains unchanged, how would the increase in agricultural productivity affect conditions in Machismo's industrial sector?

Before going on, think about the lessons of the labor-surplus two-sector model concerning the balance between agriculture and industry, the role of relative prices, the effects of population growth, and the need for improved productivity to sustain economic development.

2. *Empirical patterns.* Figure 3–1B in the textbook shows how the share of GDP generated in the industrial sector varies with the level of per capita GNP in 1980, on average. Let's examine a variant of this relationship using more recent cross-section data. Table 3–1 shows the share of output produced by the manufacturing sector (MFG/GDP) in 12 developing countries in the population range of 15 to 50 million people in 1992. (If some of these countries aren't familiar, take a few minutes to look them up.) The table also shows per capita GNP (based on PPP conversions) for each country.

Table 3–1

Manufacturing and Per Capita Incomes, Selected Countries, 1992

Country	Per capita GNP (PPP$)	MFG share of GNP (%)
Ethiopia	340	8
Tanzania	630	5
Uganda	1,070	4
Nepal	1,100	8
Kenya	1,360	12
Ghana	1,890	9
Sri Lanka	2,810	15
Morocco	3,270	19
Egypt	3,670	12
Turkey	5,170	23
Colombia	5,760	20
Thailand	5,890	28

Source: World Development Report 1994, pp. 162–63, 166–67, 220–21.

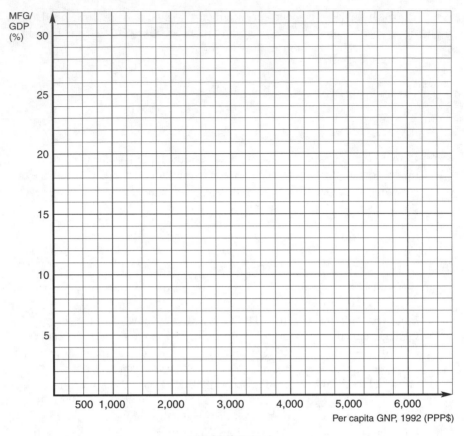

FIGURE 3–4

a. On Figure 3–4, carefully plot 12 points corresponding to the 12 data observations in Table 3–1. Then use a straight edge to draw the best-fit straight line showing the underlying pattern of changes in MFG/GDP as a function of per capita GNP for this class of countries. (Popular spreadsheet programs provide easy procedures for estimating statistical regression lines of this sort; consult the software manual for details.)

b. The observation for Ethiopia lies above the best-fit line, whereas the observation for Uganda lies well below the line. How can one explain these deviations in MFG/GDP from the underlying pattern? Is it fair to conclude from these observations that Ethiopia has performed well and Uganda has performed poorly relative to the normal structure of economic development? Explain briefly.

ANSWERS TO SELF-TEST

Completion

1. optimality
2. 0.40
3. social accounting matrix
4. unknowns; redundant
5. objective (or welfare)
6. labor
7. average
8. an early industry
9. computable general equilibrium (CGE)
10. fixed

True-False

1. F	6. T	11. T
2. T	7. F	12. T
3. F	8. F	13. T
4. T	9. F	14. T
5. T	10. F	15. T

Multiple Choice

1. d	8. b
2. b	9. b
3. c	10. c
4. d	11. b
5. b	12. a
6. a	13. c
7. b	14. b

CHAPTER 4 | Development and Human Welfare

OVERVIEW

The ultimate objective of economic development is to improve human welfare. More specifically, it is to reduce mass poverty and hold inequality to the minimum level necessary. Chapter 4 explains why economic growth is necessary but not sufficient for significant reductions in poverty, much less inequality. Measurement poses a serious problem. A simple measure of poverty is the proportion of the population whose income falls short of a predefined poverty line (head count ratio). Inequality, on the other hand, is a concept of relative standing, which can be gauged by the Gini concentration ratio (i.e., the ratio of the area between the Lorenz curve and the line of perfect equality to the area of the triangle below the perfect equality line). More comprehensive measures of development such as basic human needs and human development indicators are also discussed here.

One prominent generalization about human welfare trends is that, at least in some regions, income inequality worsens during the early stages of development before it shows a subsequent improvement (Kuznets's inverted-U hypothesis). The empirical evidence, however, shows diversity of experience (as between East Asia and Latin America), suggesting that trends in inequality are the result of complex interactions among historical, economic, social, and political conditions. Poverty also is a complex socioeconomic phenomenon that displays diversity in the composition of the poor by residence (more rural than urban), and demography (concentrated among the young, the aged, or women).

Following a brief survey of the major theories of inequality and poverty (classical, neoclassical, dualistic, and marxian), the authors explore alternative strategies for equitable development. These approaches include redistribution before growth, redistribution with growth, and basic human needs. A strong case is made for a strategy that focuses on policies that promote growth of productivity while ensuring short-term support in the form of well-targeted delivery of basic social services to all citizens.

MAIN LEARNING OBJECTIVES

After studying this chapter, you ought to understand and be able to explain

1. Why rising per capita income is necessary but not sufficient for broadly reducing poverty and improving human welfare.

2. How attitudes about inequality and poverty in developing countries have varied historically.

3. The distinction between income inequality, poverty, and equity.

4. The use of the head-count ratio to measure poverty.

5. The use of the Lorenz curve, the Gini concentration ratio, and income shares to measure the size distribution of income.

6. The use of social indicators to measure progress toward satisfying basic human needs.

7. Kuznets's inverted-U hypothesis describing changes in income inequality in the process of economic development.

8. How empirical evidence provides only weak support for Kuznets's hypothesis while strongly confirming the link between economic growth and poverty reduction.

9. The geography of world poverty, especially the concentration of poverty in rural areas.

10. The theoretical determinants of inequality and poverty in Ricardo's classical model, Marx' model, the neoclassical (marginal productivity) model, and the Lewis and Fei-Ranis labor-surplus models.

11. Four distinct strategies for growth with equity: grow first, then redistribute (traditional); redistribute first, then grow (socialist); redistribution with growth (reformist); and basic human needs (BHN).

12. Which policy approaches are most promising for achieving equitable growth.

ECONOMIC TOOLS AND TECHNIQUES

From what you have learned in this chapter, you should be able to

1. Construct a Lorenz curve from data on income shares and then calculate a Gini coefficient from the Lorenz curve.

2. Define and explain the limitations of the human development index (HDI) as an alternative to per capita income as an indicator of development.

3. Interpret empirical equations showing inequality and poverty as functions of per capita income.

4. Use the Lewis-Fei-Ranis model (from Chapter 3) to explain the inverted-U pattern of changes in income inequality.

5. Construct a head-count ratio from the data on poverty line and household income.

KEY TERMS AND CONCEPTS

basic human needs
dynamic redistribution of assets
equality of opportunity
human development index (HDI)
inequality
Kuznets's inverted-U hypothesis
labor-surplus model
Lorenz curve and Gini concentration
   ratio
marginal productivity theory

poverty head-count ratio
poverty line, global poverty line
redistribution first strategy
redistribution with growth (RWG)
   strategy
size distribution of income
social indicators
structural adjustment and adjustment
   with a human face
trickle down

SELF-TEST

Completion

1. The _____ distribution of income refers to how total income is divided among factors of production.

2. The _____ distribution refers to the pattern of differences in income across individuals or families.

3. The _____ curve is a graph showing what percentage of total income goes to any given percentage of households, which are ranked from poorest to richest in terms of per capita income).

4. The World Bank uses a _____ poverty line to measure the amount of poverty in the world, as distinct from using poverty lines defined by country-specific standards.

5. The United Nations Children's Fund (UNICEF) has criticized the standard structural adjustment policies in Africa and advocated "adjustment with _____ _____ _____."

6. Kuznets's inverted-U hypothesis states that income inequality _____ during the early stages of development and then _____ as per capita income rises further.

7. _____ contended that capitalist development held real wages down to the subsistence level by creating a "reserve army of _____."

8. According to _____ theory, each factor of production earns a return equal to its marginal product.

9. In the Fei-Ranis model, the most promising way to alleviate poverty and income inequality is to eliminate the labor surplus through policies that encourage _____ creation.

10. If Lewis's classical model can be characterized as "grow first, then redistribute," the socialist model can be characterized as "_____ first, then _____."

11. The inverted-U relationship identified by Kuznets holds up reasonably well when examined using cross-section data, but not with _____-_____ data for specific countries.

12. The head-count ratio does not measure _____ among the poor.

True-False

If false, you should be able to explain why.

_____ 1. Experience from the past 40 years confirms that economic growth yields a trickle down to the poor that is similar everywhere, regardless of government policies.

_____ 2. If two countries have the same Gini coefficient, then the share of income going to the poorest 20 percent of the households is necessarily the same in the two countries.

_____ 3. The Gini coefficients for South Korea (= 0.331) and Peru (= 0.443) reveal that income was distributed more equally in Korea.

_____ 4. In most LDCs, the poorest 20 percent of households receive roughly 12 percent of total income .

_____ 5. The rise in income inequality that often occurs at early stages of development indicates that the poor are getting poorer.

_____ 6. When countries are grouped by per capita income, countries in higher-income groups have better *average* performance than countries in lower-income groups on virtually every social indicator of development.

_____ 7. Most of the world's poor people live in rural areas, not urban areas.

_____ 8. In East Asia, rapid growth has been accompanied by dramatic declines in the extent and severity of poverty.

_____ 9. The poverty line is synonymous with the Lorenz curve.

_____ 10. In the Lewis and Fei-Ranis models, worsening income inequality is reversed only when governments begin to provide welfare benefits to the poor.

_____ 11. According to Lewis, rising inequality during the early stages of development helps to accelerate economic growth.

_____ 12. Burma, Ghana, and Jamaica are three examples of countries that successfully achieved equitable growth by pursuing the socialist approach of redistribution first.

Multiple Choice

1. Rising per capita GNP may not increase incomes for most citizens because
   a. the gains from growth may be used for expensive "glory" projects that provide *few* concrete benefits to the people.
   b. the gains from growth may be heavily reinvested, so improved consumption standards are deferred.
   c. those who are well-off already may capture the benefits.
   d. all the above.

2. To derive the Gini concentration ratio from the Lorenz curve drawn in Figure 4–1, one calculates the ratio
   a. $A/(A + B)$.   c. $C/(A + B)$.
   b. $B/(A + B)$.   d. A/B.

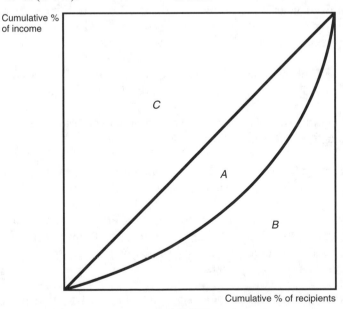

FIGURE 4–1

3. Most lists of basic human needs include all the following items *except*
   a. basic transportation such as bicycles.
   b. minimal levels of nutrition.
   c. minimal provision of shelter.
   d. basic health care.

4. The human development index (HDI) is an aggregate of several widely available indicators. Which of the following is *not* a component of the HDI?
   a. Life expectancy.
   b. Average years of schooling.
   c. Infant mortality rate.
   d. Literacy rate.

5. Research by Irma Adelman and Cynthia Taft Morris suggests that income inequality is relatively high in
   a. very poor countries dominated by small-scale farming.
   b. countries where well-entrenched elites control the most productive economic sectors.
   c. socialist and postsocialist economies.
   d. all the above.

6. From the case studies in Chapter 4, which country experienced rapid growth with high inequality?
   a. South Korea   c. Brazil
   b. India   d. All the above

7. Which of the following policy instruments is *not* a standard part of a redistribution with growth (RWG) strategy?
   a. Confiscation of property from the rich.
   b. Development of appropriate technologies to enhance the productivity of low-income workers.
   c. "Dynamic redistribution" by investing in small farms and small businesses.
   d. Measures to alter prices of labor and capital to encourage more employment of unskilled labor.

8. The main difference between the basic human needs (BHN) strategy and the redistribution with growth (RWG) strategy is that the BHN strategy
   a. is concerned with equity as well as growth.
   b. is concerned with equity rather than growth.
   c. is revolutionary rather than reformist.
   d. emphasizes *direct* provision of basic commodities and services for the poor.

9. Concern with problems of inequality and poverty in LDCs waned during the 1980s because
   a. the problem of restoring economic growth was more pressing.
   b. the Cold War drew to an end.
   c. problems of inequality and poverty diminished in importance following three decades of rapid economic growth.
   d. bitter experience showed that government policies have no significant effect on income inequality and poverty.

10. While there is no universally acceptable measure of human welfare, most people regard all but one of the following criteria to be essential for successful development. Which is the exception?
    a. Rising per capita income.   c. Improved health and longevity.
    b. Reduced poverty.   d. Rising income inequality.

11. The World Bank projects that between 1985 and 2000 the number of people living below the global poverty line will _____ in East Asia, _____ in South Asia, and _____ in sub-Saharan Africa.
    a. rise, rise, rise
    b. fall, rise, rise
    c. fall, fall, rise
    d. fall, fall, fall

12. David Ricardo's classical model predicted, incorrectly, that economic development would lead to
    a. stagnant real wages at a subsistence level.
    b. a growing share of national income going to landlords.
    c. shrinking profits for capitalists.
    d. all the above.

APPLICATIONS

Worked Example: The Lorenz Curve and the Gini Ratio

Table 4–1 presents data on the size distribution of income in Brazil and Hungary (both for 1989). The contrasts are unusually stark because Brazil is a world leader in inequality, whereas Hungary has one of the world's most equal income distributions.

Table 4–1

Percentage Share of Household Income Going to

	Poorest 20%	Second 20%	Third 20%	Fourth 20%	Richest 20%
Brazil	2.1	4.9	8.9	16.8	67.3
Hungary	10.9	14.8	18.0	22.0	34.3

Source: World Development Report 1994.

The Lorenz curve and Gini concentration ratio for Brazil are derived here. The corresponding derivations for Hungary are deferred to Exercise 1. The first step in constructing a Lorenz curve is to calculate the income share accruing to any given *cumulative* percentage of households. Taking data on income shares, starting with Brazil's poorest households, one finds

The poorest 20 percent receive		2.1 percent of total income.
The poorest 40 percent receive	2.1 + 4.9 =	7.0 percent of total income.
The poorest 60 percent receive	7.0 + 8.9 =	15.9 percent of total income.
The poorest 80 percent receive	15.9 + 16.8 =	32.7 percent of total income.
All 100 percent of the households receive		100.0 percent of total income.

The Lorenz curve is simply a graph showing these data points. The horizontal axis measures the cumulative percentage of recipient units (households here) covered, and the vertical axis shows the corresponding share of total income earned by those households. Figure 4–2 shows the Lorenz curve drawn from the Brazilian data.

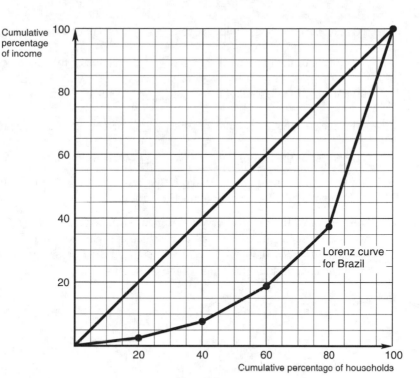

FIGURE 4-2

How can one calculate the Gini concentration ratio? Just apply the formula Gini = $A/(A + B)$, where B is the area under the Lorenz curve, and A is the area between the Lorenz curve and the diagonal line. As a first step, convert all the percentages into decimal units. In other words, consider 40 percent as 0.40. In this way the values on both axes range from 0.00 (that is, 0 percent) to 1.00 (that is, 100 percent). The box in which the Lorenz curve is drawn is thus a unit square, which always has an area of 1.00 (length times width = $1 \times 1 = 1$). The area under the diagonal must be half this. Thus, $A + B = 0.50$.

Area A can be computed geometrically using familiar formulas for the areas of rectangles and triangles, but the calculation is a bit messy. In this case, area AA works out as 0.285. (It is easiest to calculate area B and then take advantage of the equation $A = 0.5 - B$ to compute area A.). Then one can calculate the Gini ratio for Brazil from the formula

$$\text{Gini} = A/(A + B) = 0.285/0.50 = 0.57.$$

Exercises

1. It is your turn to derive a Lorenz curve and calculate a Gini concentration ratio.

   a. Use the data on income shares in Hungary from Table 4–1 to calculate the *cumulative* income shares. Start the cumulative calculation with the poorest households.

20 percent of the households receive _____ percent of total income.

40 percent of the households receive _____ percent of total income.

60 percent of the households receive _____ percent of total income.

80 percent of the households receive _____ percent of total income.

100 percent of the households receive _____ percent of total income.

b. Plot the points corresponding to these five data observations on Figure 4–2, and draw the Lorenz curve for Hungary.

c. The area under the Lorenz curve for Hungary can be calculated by marking off rectangles and triangles and then applying formulas from geometry. It is $B = 0.39$. Knowing the area under the Lorenz curve, find the value of area A and the value of the Gini ratio.

Area A = _____.

Gini concentration ratio = _____.

d. Study the Lorenz curve for Hungary in comparison with the one for Brazil. What do the curves reveal about the size distribution of income in these two countries.

e. Compare Gini ratios for Hungary and Brazil. Do the Gini ratios reflect the same differences that you observed in the Lorenz curves?

2. This exercise illustrates some of the problems encountered in measuring and interpreting income distribution statistics. The subject is Pauvritania, a very small country that uses the rupee as the national currency (as in India, Pakistan, and Nepal).

a. Pauvritania contains five households. A recent field census produced the following data on household incomes:

Household A   income =   500 rupees.
Household B   income =   700 rupees.
Household C   income =   900 rupees.
Household D   income = 1,100 rupees.
Household E   income = 3,000 rupees.
Total income, all households = 6,200 rupees.

(i) What share of total income goes to the following households in Pauvritania?

Poorest 20 percent: _____ percent of total income

Poorest 40 percent: _____ percent of total income

Richest 20 percent: _____ percent of total income

(ii) The government's national income accounts are derived from a wide variety of regular data reports on production, sales, earnings, and trade. According to these accounts, income in Pauvritania totals Rs8,000, which is nearly 30 percent higher than the total reported by the field census. What do you suppose is the reason for this difference?

b. The textbook says that the best ranking criterion is household income *per capita*. Let's see what difference this makes. The census data indicate that there are two people in household A, three people in B, four people in C, five people in D, and six people in E.

(i) Knowing income and the number of people in each household, you can calculate income *per capita* for each household:

Family A: per capita income = _____ rupees.

Family B: per capita income = _____ rupees.

Family C: per capita income = _____ rupees.

Family D: per capita income = _____ rupees.

Family E: per capita income = _____ rupees.

(ii) When the households are ranked by per capita income,

Household _____ is poorest.

Houschold _____ is second poorcst.

Household _____ is richest.

(iii) Has the ranking changed now that we are evaluating household income on a per capita basis?

c. The poverty line in Pauvritania is 250 rupees *per person*.

(i) Which households have incomes at or below the poverty line?

Households _____.

(ii) How many *individuals* are living in poverty? (Assume that each household member lives in poverty if the household's per capita income is at or below the poverty line.)

_____ individuals.

(iii) What percentage of the population lives in poverty?

_____% of the population.

(iv) A World Bank economist has just completed a study of poverty in Pauvritania. She concludes that the government has mismeasured the poverty line by using out-of-date statistics on the cost of living. The revised poverty line is 225 rupees. With this revised figure, what percentage of the population lives in poverty?

_____% of the population.

d. The textbook says that "lifetime income" would be an even better measure of the income distribution. Let's consider how life-cycle income patterns affect the measurement of inequality. In each household, just one person is out earning income. The five household heads are *absolutely identical* in terms of lifetime earnings patterns and demographic behavior. Specifically, each household head marries at age 20 and faces the following life cycle:

Age	Children	Household size	Income (rupees)
20	0	2	500
25	1	3	700
30	2	4	900
35	3	5	1,100
40	4	6	3,000

How does this information alter the meaning of the census data on income distribution and poverty in Pauvritania?

3. This exercise examines how economic development can produce an inverted-U pattern of changes in income inequality.

    a. Indozania is a country with a fixed population of five people. In the days before development began, all five people were dreadfully poor subsistence farmers, each with a subsistence income of $100 per year. The five incomes were 100, 100, 100, 100, and 100. Each number represents the income of one person. Under these initial conditions, what share of total income accrued to the poorest 40 percent of the population? The richest 20 percent?

        Poorest 40 percent: _____ percent of total income

        Richest 20 percent: _____ percent of total income

    b. Indozania then started on the path of growth and structural change. One foreign-owned factory opened up in the city, employing one worker. To lure the worker away from her farm, the factory paid twice the subsistence income, or $200. The income of the farmers stayed the same. At this point in the development process the income levels of the five people were 100, 100, 100, 100, and 200. What share of total income accrued to the poorest 40 percent of the population? The richest 20 percent?

        Poorest 40 percent: _____ percent of total income

        Richest 20 percent: _____ percent of total income

    c. Later a second factory opened up creating a second job at a wage of $200. This brought income levels to 100, 100, 100, 200, and 200.

        (i) At this stage of development, what share of total income accrued to the poorest 40 percent of the population? The richest 20 percent?

            Poorest 40 percent: _____ percent of total income

            Richest 20 percent: _____ percent of total income

(ii) To make a long story short, however, eventually there were five factories in operation providing five jobs, at $200 per worker. This brought the income distribution to 200, 200, 200, 200, and 200. What share of total income accrued to the poorest 40 percent of the population? The richest 20 percent?

Poorest 40 percent: _____ percent of total income

Richest 20 percent: _____ percent of total income

(iii) Review how income distribution changed during the course of economic development in Indozania. What happened to the income share of the poorest 40 percent? What happen to income inequality? What happened to the extent of poverty?

d. Let's add two details to make the model more realistic, at the cost of some extra complexity.

(i) First, let the factories be owned locally. One person is the capitalist. Suppose that each factory creates $600 of value added, of which the capitalist retains the residual after paying wages. With one factory operating, the incomes of the four workers plus the one capitalist are 100, 100, 100, 200, and 400. Note that the capitalist earns $600 – $200 from one factory. At this stage of development, what share of total income accrues to the poorest 40 percent of the population? The richest 20 percent?

Poorest 40 percent: _____ percent of total income

Richest 20 percent: _____ percent of total income

(ii) Next, recall (from the two-sector growth model in Chapter 3) that rural incomes ultimately rise as workers move off the farms. When the economy reaches this turning point, the wage in industry also rises. Figure 4–3 shows this as a rise in the supply curve of labor to industry once the third worker is drawn out of agriculture.

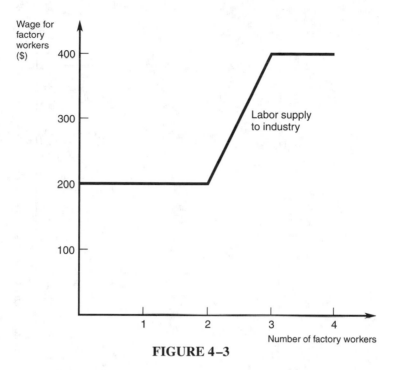

FIGURE 4–3

With three factories operating, the wage in industry is $400 per worker; the hardy soul who remains in agriculture now earns $200. The five income levels are 200, 400, 400, 400, and 600. What share of total income accrues to the poorest 40 percent of the population? The richest 20 percent?

Poorest 40 percent: _____ percent of total income

Richest 20 percent: _____ percent of total income

    (iii) Taking into account the income accruing to the capitalist as well as the rising wages once labor markets reach the turning point, explain how modern-sector growth generates an inverted-U pattern of income inequality in Indozania.

4. This exercise examines the relationship between per capita income and human development, as measured by the human development index (HDI). As noted in the textbook, the HDI is a composite of three basic elements: an index of life expectancy, an index of educational attainment, and an index of adjusted real income. Each component is scaled from 0.00 (worst) to 1.00 (best), so the HDI is also scaled from a minimum of 0.00 to a maximum of 1.00. Table 4–2 presents the HDI for 14 developing countries, along with per capita income (PPP measure, for 1992) and the Gini concentration ratio. The table also presents two dynamic indicators: the rate of growth of per capita income and the change in the HDI, in both cases for the period 1980 to 1992.

Table 4-2

Development Indicators, Selected Countries

Country	Human development index (1992)	Per capita income, 1992 (PPP$)	Gini concentration ratio	Per capita income growth, 1980–1992 (% per annum)	Change in HDI, 1980–1992
Ethiopia	0.249	340	0.312	–1.9	n.a.
Tanzania	0.306	630	0.572	0.0	0.024
India	0.352	1,010	0.311	3.1	0.086
Bangladesh	0.382	1,210	0.280	1.8	0.075
Kenya	0.309	1,230	0.551	0.2	0.094
Ghana	0.382	1,640	0.358	–0.1	0.059
China	0.644	1,910	0.351	7.6	0.169
Pakistan	0.393	2,130	0.301	3.1	0.106
Bolivia	0.530	2,270	0.411	–1.5	0.088
Sri Lanka	0.665	2,810	0.294	2.6	0.113
Indonesia	0.586	2,970	0.322	4.0	0.168
Peru	0.642	3,080	0.443	–2.8	0.052
Tunisia	0.690	5,130	0.391	1.3	0.191
Colombia	0.813	5,760	0.474	1.4	0.157

Sources: Tables 4–1 and 4–5 from textbook; World Bank, *World Development Report 1994;* and UNDP, *Human Development Report 1994* (New York: Oxford University Press, 1994).

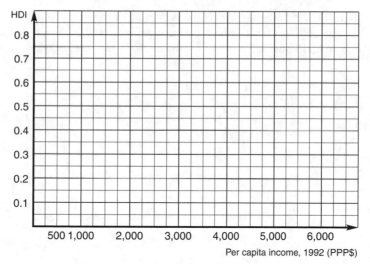

FIGURE 4–4

a. (i) In Figure 4–4, plot the 14 points representing the HDI and per capita income for each of the countries listed in Table 4–2.
   (ii) Generally, what does the graph reveal about the relationship between these two variables?

   (iii) For use in the next section, draw in a line representing the best approximation of the average pattern relating per capita income to the HDI. Label this the *Pattern line*.

b. One might reasonably suppose that higher income inequality produces relatively unfavorable performance in terms of human development. Let's check this hypothesis against the facts.
   (i) From Table 4–2, pick out the four countries that have the highest degree of income inequality, as measured by the Gini ratio.

            Country   Gini ratio

    _____   _____

    _____   _____

    _____   _____

    _____   _____

(ii) If the hypothesis stated at the beginning of this section is strictly valid, the HDI values for these four countries should lie well below the pattern line in Figure 4–4. How well do the facts bear this out?

(iii) Now pick out the four countries from Table 4–2 with the least income inequality.

Country	Gini ratio
_____	_____
_____	_____
_____	_____
_____	_____

(iv) If the hypothesis is strictly valid, these four countries should have HDI values lying well above the pattern line in Figure 4–4. How well do the facts bear this out?

(v) What do you conclude about the relationship between income inequality and HDI performance?

c. Next, look at the dynamic relationship to see whether economic growth is correlated with improvements in human development.

(i) In Figure 4–5, plot the points representing per capita income growth and the change in the HDI for each of the countries listed in Table 4–2.

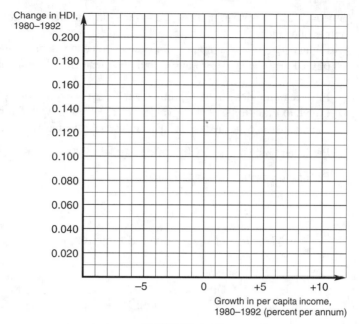

FIGURE 4–5

(ii) What can one conclude from this empirical analysis of the relationship between economic growth and changes in human development?

(Note: When analyzing data it is easy to forget about problems with the quality of the data. The textbook points out that the HDI is somewhat arbitrary in its selection of components, its definition of index values, and its weighting scheme. For example, the HDI yields relatively good scores for Zaire and Myanmar, two countries that are *not* paragons of virtue in terms of human development.)

5. *Advanced.* This exercise tests Kuznets's hypothesis that income inequality first rises and then falls during the process of economic development. The textbook presents an equation to show the empirical relationship between the Gini ratio and per capita GDP. The equation is repeated here.

$$\text{Gini} = -1.072 + 0.395 \log Y - 0.026 (\log Y)^2. \qquad [4-1]$$

Logarithms (base e) are used to convert per capita GDP into *proportional* differences. This is a statistical regression equation based on cross-section data for 65 countries. The regression equation traces the curve that most closely fits the data points. In this case, a quadratic term is introduced to generate a curvilinear relationship, since a simple linear equation cannot capture the pattern being tested. Numerous computer packages, including all the popular spreadsheets, can compute such regression equations.

a. Table 4–3 shows per capita income and the Gini ratio for the same
   sample of countries used in Exercise 4.
   (i) Fill in column 3 by computing for each country the natural logarithm
       of GDP per capita. Most hand calculators perform this computation
       easily.
   (ii) Fill in column 4 with the *square* of the log Y for each country.
   (iii) Plug into Equation 4–1 these values for log Y and $(\log Y)^2$ for each
       country to obtain the predicted Gini ratio. Taking Ethiopia as an example,

   Predicted Gini $= -1.072 + 0.395(\log 340) - 0.026(\log 340)^2 = 0.347$.

   Record the results of your calculations in column 5.

Table 4–3

Measures of Inequality and Income

	Gini ratio (1)	Per capita GDP, 1992 (PPP$) (2)	Log Y (3)	$(Log\ Y)^2$ (4)	Predicted Gini (5)
Ethiopia	0.312	340	5.829	33.977	0.35
Tanzania	0.572	630	_____	_____	_____
India	0.311	1,010	_____	_____	_____
Bangladesh	0.280	1,210	_____	_____	_____
Kenya	0.551	1,230	_____	_____	_____
Ghana	0.358	1,640	_____	_____	_____
China	0.351	1,910	_____	_____	_____
Pakistan	0.301	2,130	_____	_____	_____
Bolivia	0.411	2,270	_____	_____	_____
Sri Lanka	0.294	2,810	_____	_____	_____
Indonesia	0.322	2,970	_____	_____	_____
Peru	0.443	3,080	_____	_____	_____
Tunisia	0.391	5,130	_____	_____	_____
Colombia	0.474	5,760	_____	_____	_____

Source: Table 4–2.

b. Now examine the regression relationship graphically.
   (i) Plot the *predicted* Gini ratio for each country in Figure 4–6 and
       connect the points to form a graph of the regression equation.
   (ii) Describe the basic shape of this curve. Is it consistent with
       Kuznets's inverted-U hypothesis? Explain.

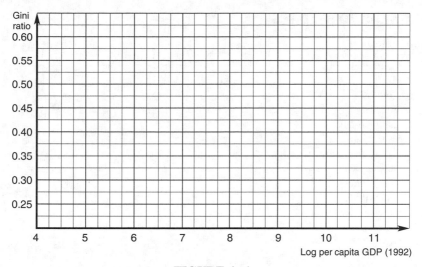

FIGURE 4–6

c. The text reports that $R^2 = 0.15$ for the regression equation. This means that differences in log Y explain just 15 percent of the observed variations in the Gini ratio across the sample. There is lots of *unexplained* variance in the data, so other country-specific factors strongly influence the degree of income inequality.

    (i) Plot the actual data point for the Gini ratio and per capita GDP for each country in Table 4–3.

    (ii) How well do the actual data points conform to the predicted values?

    (iii) Which countries have Gini ratios that are close to the predicted value, say, within plus or minus 0.05 of the predicted Gini? For which three countries are the actual Gini ratios farthest from the predicted value on the high side? On the low side? (Refer to your answers to Table 4–3 for exact figures.)

ANSWERS TO SELF-TEST

Completion

1. functional
2. size
3. Lorenz
4. global
5. a human face
6. rises, falls
7. Marx, unemployed
8. neoclassical
9. employment
10. redistribute, grow
11. time-series
12. inequality

True-False

1. F
2. F
3. T
4. F
5. F
6. T
7. T
8. T
9. F
10. F
11. T
12. F

Multiple Choice

1. d
2. a
3. a
4. c
5. b
6. c
7. a
8. d
9. a
10. d
11. c
12. d

Part II   Guiding Principles

CHAPTER 5

Guiding Development: Markets versus Controls

OVERVIEW

The past two decades of systemic reform in developing countries and the centrally planned economies have helped congeal the old debate on socialism versus capitalism. The emerging consensus is that both central plans and markets often fail in the absence of positive incentives and strong competition.

The chapter begins by discussing the circumstances under which markets and central plans can succeed or fail. It then examines the story of the march toward a well-functioning market economy by countries that tried for decades to supplant or to supplement it with government controls. In the postsocialist economies, the infrastructure of markets (private property rights, commercial codes, labor codes, regulatory systems, etc.) needed to be established anew. In many developing economies, where markets are underdeveloped, the task has been one of letting existing markets work more freely while creating missing ones.

The chapter examines extensively the economics of transition to a market economy: macroeconomic stabilization, liberalization, structural adjustment, and building new institutions. Market-oriented reform has proven quite complex: old rules of the game have to be replaced by new ones. The timing, speed, sequencing, and breadth of reforms continue to be intensely debated. The reform process also has exposed the intimate relationship between economics and politics: potential losers from the reforms often resist them successfully even though the benefits to the general population far outweigh the losses by the powerful few.

MAIN LEARNING OBJECTIVES

After studying this chapter, you ought to understand and be able to explain

1. The strengths of a market economy and the market failure problems that may justify various government interventions in a mixed economy.

2. The methods, strengths, and limitations of Soviet-style central planning.

3. Why strong government controls were so appealing to nearly all LDCs in the decades after World War II.

4. Why, more recently, many developing countries have been shedding controls in favor of harnessing market forces.

5. Five fundamental conditions needed for a well-functioning market system.

6. The substance of a typical stabilization program.

7. The main features of structural adjustment reforms.

8. The importance of property rights that are well defined, exclusive, transferable, and enforceable.

9. Why market-oriented reforms often spawn strong resistance.

10. The kinds of complications faced by former command economies in making the transition to a market system.

ECONOMIC TOOLS AND TECHNIQUES

From what you have learned in this chapter, you should be able to

1. Explain the basic theoretical argument in favor of a market economy and market-based prices.

2. Define *economic rent* and explain how rent-seeking spawns parallel (black) markets, corruption, and inefficiency.

3. Describe the empirical methods used by economists to evaluate how market orientation and macroeconomic stability affect growth.

KEY TERMS AND CONCEPTS

capitalism, socialism
conditionality
credibility
elasticity pessimists
export pessimism
external economies or diseconomies
factor productivity
import substitution
infant industry
International Monetary Fund
market economy, command economy,
    mixed economy

market failures
monopoly and oligopoly power
outward-looking strategy
parallel or black market
property rights
protective tariff
relative prices
rents (economic) and rent seeking
shock treatment
stabilization program
state-owned enterprises, privatization
structural adjustment and liberalization

SELF-TEST

Completion

1. Government ownership and control of the means of production is a

   defining attribute of the _____ economic system.

2. An _____ industry is one that is expected to become efficient

   after an initial period of learning by doing, during which time it may need

   protection against competition from imports.

3. Government controls and regulations create artificial opportunities for higher-than-necessary profits, which economists call _____.

4. While many developing countries experienced near stagnation during the 1970s and 1980s, Asia's "four tigers"—South Korea, Taiwan, Hong Kong, and Singapore—grew by 8 to 10 percent per year using _____- looking strategies of development.

5. The objective of a _____ _____ program is to reduce or remove price distortions generated by government interventions.

6. When it comes to raising factor _____, command economies have a notoriously poor record.

7. While successful in directing rapid and massive industrialization, Soviet-style planning was particularly ineffective in producing _____ goods.

8. In contrast to prior stabilization programs elsewhere in Latin America, _____ successfully ended hyperinflation in 1985 without applying price controls.

9. When a country's exchange rate becomes overvalued, this discourages production of _____ goods.

10. Success in reforming an economy depends vitally on the _____ of the entire reform package.

True-False

If false, you should be able to explain why.

_____ 1. Some national goals, such as equity goals, may not be achieved through market forces even with fully competitive markets.

_____ 2. In a standard structural adjustment program, government attempts to correct market failures by imposing minimum wage laws, interest rate ceilings, and food price controls.

_____ 3. Poland applied the shock treatment to hasten the transition to a market economy, whereas China and Vietnam chose more gradual approaches.

_____ 4. The import-substitution strategy entails government interventions to protect local manufacturers from import competition.

_____ 5. Development economists of the neoclassical school, such as Theodore Schultz, contend that small farmers in LDCs are too tradition bound to respond rationally to price signals.

_____ 6. In their empirical study of 75 countries, Jeffrey Sachs and Andrew Warner found that economic openness was strongly associated with rapid economic growth.

_____ 7. *Rent seeking* refers to special problems landlords face in developing countries when they try to enforce market-based leases with low-income tenants.

_____ 8. The economies of Eastern Europe and the former Soviet Union experienced long and deep recessions at the outset of their transition to a market system.

_____ 9. A mixed economy is one with a good balance between the development of agriculture and industry.

_____ 10. Markets usually prove to be more flexible than governments in reallocating resources as economic conditions change.

Multiple Choice

1. Which of the following conditions is *not* a clear example of a market failure?
   a. A few large firms dominate a particular market.
   b. Farm produce passes through the hands of private middle traders before reaching urban consumers.
   c. External economies are present, such as flood control downstream due to the construction of a dam.
   d. All the above.

2. Which of the following is *not* one of the three fundamental advantages of market allocations, as identified in the textbook?
   a. Unlike controls, the market does not favor the rich.
   b. By dispersing control over resources, markets provide an economic basis for individual liberty.
   c. Compared to controls, the market is a more efficient and less costly mechanism allocating resources.
   d. Markets adapt more flexibly than government allocations to changing economic conditions.

3. In Soviet-style economies, a one-year plan is used to control current _____ and a five-year plan is used for major _____ projects.
   a. prices, stabilization   c. consumption, infrastructure
   b. output, investment   d. harvests, industrial

4. The international organization with the main responsibility for helping to design and implement *stabilization* programs is
   a. the World Bank.
   b. OPEC.
   c. the United Nations.
   d. the International Monetary Fund.

5. A protective tariff or a subsidy to an infant industry could be justified only if the
   a. industry is state owned.
   b. protection or subsidy is phased out after a period of time.
   c. industry is a monopoly.
   d. industry involves external diseconomies such as pollution.

6. The liberalization trend in developing economies has been motivated by
   a. conditionality set by the World Bank and the IMF for developing countries to obtain loans and assistance.
   b. the difficulties encountered by developing countries in administering plans and controls.
   c. the observed success of a number of market-oriented developing countries.
   d. all the above.

7. The case study of Indonesia shows how one developing country successfully managed
   a. to make central planning work.
   b. stabilization but not structural adjustment.
   c. both stabilization and structural adjustment.
   d. to eliminate market failures.

8. Which of the following is *not* a typical conditionality requirement associated with IMF stabilization programs?
   a. Increase the tariff on imported goods.
   b. Reduce the government budget deficit.
   c. Set restrictive targets for central bank credits to the government and the commercial banks.
   d. Devalue the local currency.

9. Which of the following is *not* a common element of World Bank-sponsored structural adjustment programs?
   a. Privatize state-owned enterprises.
   b. Create an administrative mechanism to ration foreign exchange.
   c. Remove quotas on imports.
   d. Relax interest rate controls.

10. Which of the following is a valid argument for shock treatment reforms, Poland style, rather than gradualist reforms?
    a. Gradualism gives opponents a better chance to mobilize opposition to reforms.
    b. Supply and demand elasticities are so low that prices must be adjusted quickly.
    c. Gradualism works well in agriculture but not in the manufacturing sector.
    d. All the above.

APPLICATIONS

Worked Example: Rent-Seeking Behavior

The textbook explains that government interventions can create economic *rents*—abnormally high returns—that lead to parallel markets and rent-seeking behavior. You can see how this works by using simple supply-and-demand analysis. Figure 5–1 shows the supply and demand for flowers in Gardenia, per week. The government has imposed price controls to fix the price of flowers at $0.50 per bouquet, to benefit urban consumers. Flowers are sold at this price through state-owned flower shops. The supply curve shows that rural flower growers have an incentive, at this controlled price, to market only 100 bouquets per week (point *A*). Yet urban consumers demand 500 bouquets (point *A′*) per week. Because of the price controls, there is a serious shortage at the government shops.

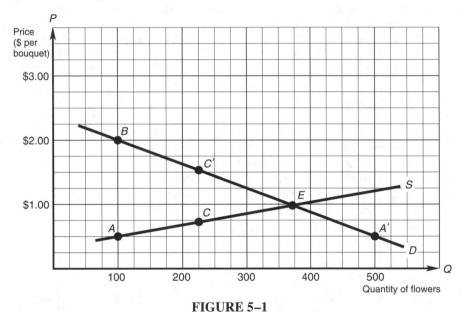

FIGURE 5–1

The shortage at the government shops breeds opportunities for traders to earn economic rents in the parallel (or black) market. If the shops only sell 100 bouquets per week, unsatisfied flower lovers would pay as much as $2 per bouquet (point *B* on the demand curve). The shortage creates an obvious opportunity for unauthorized traders to earn high profits. For example, traders can offer farmers $0.75 per bouquet, at which price production will rise to 225 bouquets per week (point *C* on the supply curve). The traders find consumers are willing to pay $1.50 per bouquet (point *C′* on the demand curve). Faced with an offer of $0.75 per bouquet, farmers divert their entire output to the parallel market; this leaves shelves bare at the government shops. The traders start to drive fancy cars, while government statistics—which exclude the parallel market—report that flower production shriveled to zero.

Then the government cracks down on "unscrupulous traders who fleece honest citizens" by charging high prices. Compelled again to deliver to official shops at the controlled price, flower growers reduce output to 100 bouquets per week. Before long, shelves in the shops are bare again. Why? This time it's the government officials who are diverting flower supplies to the parallel market, to capture economic rents created by the price controls. Some of the rents are shared with the police, who solicit bribes to look the other way.

The figure suggests that competition eventually can drive down the price to the free-market equilibrium of $1 per bouquet (point *E*), where excess profits disappear. This is possible. But the illegality of the parallel market in Gardenia—in some countries profiteers can be sentenced to death—and the cost of bribes will limit the extent of market activity and hold the price above $1. Ironically, removing price controls would cause the average price paid by consumers to *fall* to point *E*.

The price-control policy is highly inefficient: The government runs a chain of flower shops with bare shelves while in furtive parallel markets flowers sell at inflated prices. Moreover, flower production wilts relative to the free-market equilibrium outcome. Why, then, did the government impose the price controls? The intention was to promote the urban industrial sector by holding down the cost of living for urban workers, and for government officials, who happen to be very fond of flowers. Why is the policy not reversed when the side effects appear? Maybe the answer has something to do with government officials who are sharing in the rents.

Exercises

1. It is your turn to analyze how government interventions create rents that lead to parallel markets and corruption. In Figure 5–2 the supply and demand curves are the same as in the Worked Example. This time, however, the supply curve (*S*) represents flowers that are *imported* into Gardenia from a neighboring country. Gardenia initially has no domestic flower industry.

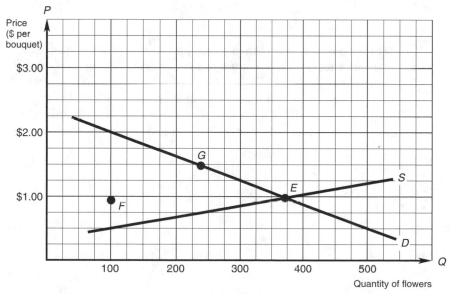

FIGURE 5–2

a. What is the equilibrium market price and quantity of flowers in Gardenia (at point E)?

$$P_E = \$_____.$$

$$Q_E = _____ \text{ bouquets per week.}$$

b. The government of Gardenia views flower growing as an infant industry, which should become competitive after a learning period. Initially, however, domestic production costs will be very high. The government concludes that the industry will not develop without protection.
   (i) Draw a straight line through points F and G in Figure 5–2. Label this line S'. This line indicates the *domestic* supply curve (that is, supply from domestic producers).
   (ii) To nurture domestic production, the government bans flower imports. The market equilibrium is now determined by the demand curve and the *domestic* supply curve S'. What is the equilibrium price and quantity after the ban on imports takes effect?

$$P' = \$_____.$$

$$Q' = _____ \text{ bouquets per week.}$$

   (iii) The ban on imports succeeds in cultivating a new industry of flower production in Gardenia. But how does the import ban affect flower *consumers*?

c. This government intervention breeds opportunities for traders to earn economic rents—above-normal profits—in the parallel market through smuggling.
   (i) With reference to Figure 5–2, explain how the potential **rents** arise as a result of the ban on flower imports. (Hint: Examine the import supply curve S in relation to the new equilibrium price P'.)

(ii) As an example, calculate the amount of rent that can be earned by smuggling in 100 bouquets per week. Supply curve *S* shows that smugglers can procure 100 bouquets at a price of

$_____ per bouquet.

To ensure a quick sale, the smugglers sell the contraband supplies in Gardenia for $1.40 per bouquet. This allow them to clear a profit of

$_____ per bouquet or

$_____ for the full 100 bouquets.

d. How does the smuggling activity affect development of the domestic flower industry in Gardenia? Explain.

e. What rent-seeking behavior might arise among government personnel in response to the profit opportunities created by import controls?

Think about how prevalent rent-seeking activities can be in an economy where prices and allocation decisions are widely subject to controls. In such an environment, business executives may devote more energy to lobbying for favors than to improving their products or controlling their costs!

2. This exercise presents a case study relating to controls, stabilization, structural adjustment, and growth. The textbook states that notable reforms in Africa have occurred in countries with stagnating economies. Let's see what the situation was like in Ghana from 1963 to 1992.

a. Until 1983, when comprehensive reforms were introduced, Ghana's record exemplifies the sad legacy of widespread controls and political instability. On gaining independence in 1960, Ghana embarked on a state-controlled development strategy, as was in vogue at the time. The macroeconomic results are summarized in the first two columns of Table 5–1.

Table 5–1

Macroeconomic Conditions in Ghana

	1963	1983	1992
1. Real GDP (millions of Cedis, constant 1985 prices)	258,700	318,000	474,500
2. Population (millions)	7.0	11.9	16.0
3. Index of production in manufacturing sector (1965 = 100)	100*	76	152
4. Export earnings (millions of U.S.$)	307	439	986
5. Index of production in agriculture (1965 = 100)	100*	117	147
6. Ghana consumer price index (1985 = 100)	0.3	64.9	511.4
7. Investment (millions of Cedis)	218	6,922	386,100
8. Nominal GDP (millions of Cedis)	1,101	184,038	3,008,800

*The initial year is 1965 instead of 1963.

Sources: Derived from IMF, *International Financial Statistics Yearbook 1994*
(Washington, D.C.: International Monetary Fund, 1994), and World Bank, *World
Tables 1994* and *1983* (Baltimore: Johns Hopkins University Press, 1994 and 1983).

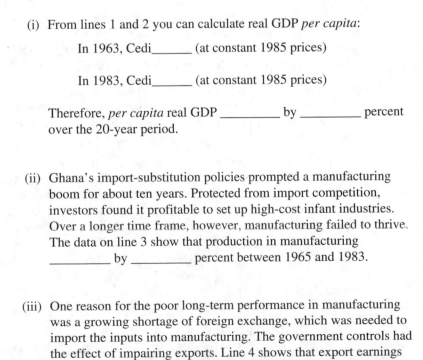

(i)   From lines 1 and 2 you can calculate real GDP *per capita*:

In 1963, Cedi_____ (at constant 1985 prices)

In 1983, Cedi_____ (at constant 1985 prices)

Therefore, *per capita* real GDP _____ by _____ percent
over the 20-year period.

(ii) Ghana's import-substitution policies prompted a manufacturing
boom for about ten years. Protected from import competition,
investors found it profitable to set up high-cost infant industries.
Over a longer time frame, however, manufacturing failed to thrive.
The data on line 3 show that production in manufacturing
_____ by _____ percent between 1965 and 1983.

(iii) One reason for the poor long-term performance in manufacturing
was a growing shortage of foreign exchange, which was needed to
import the inputs into manufacturing. The government controls had
the effect of impairing exports. Line 4 shows that export earnings
rose _____ percent between 1963 and 1983 in nominal U.S.

dollars. But dollar prices in 1983 were 225 percent higher than in 1963 due to inflation in the United States. Adjusting for dollar inflation, Ghana's *real* export earnings _____ by _____ percent between 1963 and 1983. [Hint: (1 + real growth) = (1 + nominal growth)/(1 + price growth), where growth factors are expressed as decimals rather than as percentages.]

(iv) Agriculture also languished because the controls favored the industrial sector. The data on lines 5 and 2 show that agricultural production rose _____ percent between 1965 and 1985 while population grew by _____ percent. What happened to agricultural production *per capita*? [Hint: (1 + per capita growth) = (1 + total growth)/(1 + population growth), where growth factors are expressed as decimals rather than as percentages.]

(v) Ghana's real economy was withering, but inflation was in full bloom. Line 6 indicates that average price level in 1983 was _____ times higher than 20 years earlier.

(vi) Under the circumstances, it is not surprising that investment crashed and so dimmed the hopes for subsequent growth. The data on lines 7 and 8 indicate that the ratio of investment to GDP fell from _____ percent in 1963 to just _____ percent in 1983.

Of course, the full story is more complex. For example, Ghana made great progress on education and health. Long-term prospects for further improvements would be grim, however, without economic growth. External shocks certainly hurt Ghana's economic health after 1974. But then other developing countries managed to adjust to equally severe shocks. Also, the official statistics overstate the collapse to the extent that part of the lost output simply went into the black market where it was not counted.

b. What was the effect of the structural adjustment program that was introduced in 1983? Compare columns 2 and 3 in Table 5–1. Compute the following outcomes for the period 1983 to 1992.
   (i) Per capita real GDP _____ by _____ percent.

   (ii) Production in manufacturing _____ by _____ percent.

(iii) Production in agriculture _____ by _____ percent.

(iv) Dollar export earnings _____ by _____ percent. Taking into account the fact that dollar prices in 1992 averaged 41 percent higher than in 1983, Ghana's real export earnings _____ by _____ percent.

(v) Ghana still suffered from inflation, but less severely. Consumer prices rose by _____ percent over the nine-year period 1983 to 1992.

(vi) Investment rose to _____ percent of GDP.

c. *More difficult.* Many observers contend that Ghana's reforms failed to deliver benefits to the people. The textbook points out that the public often judges reforms by comparing the situations before and after, when the proper comparison for analyzing the effectiveness of a reform program is with and without. Let's see what this means.
   (i) In exercise 2b(i) you should have found that per capita real GDP rose 11 percent between 1983 and 1992. Calculate the corresponding *annual* rate of growth (R) during this nine-year period.

$$R = \underline{\hspace{1cm}} \% \text{ per annum.}$$

[Hint: When a variable grows G percent in nine years, the *annual* growth rate (R percent per annum) can be obtained from the formula $(1 + r) = (1 + g)^{(1/9)}$, where r and g are the same as R and G but in decimal units rather than percentage units.]

   You can see that per capita income grew quite slowly after 1983. No wonder many people are not applauding Ghana's postreform performance, especially considering how poor the country had become by the start of the reform period.
   (ii) Yet the postreform performance compares favorably with the two prior decades, when per capita income _____ by _____ percent per year.

   (iii) If the economy continued on this same growth trend, then from 1983 to 1992 per capita real GDP would have _____ by _____ percent. This hypothetical projection is called the *counterfactual*.

   (iv) Compare the value of per capita income in 1993, with reforms, to the counterfactual projection of what would have occurred *without* reforms. Using a with-and-without comparison, the reforms raised real per capita income by what percentage as of 1993?

(v) Performance after 1983 *without* the reforms might have been even worse than what was calculated above. We assumed that the trend from the previous two decades would have continued in the absence of reforms. In fact, the trend was worsening markedly at the time the reforms were adopted. How does this information affect your with-and-without evaluation of Ghana's reform program?

On balance, Ghana's reform program was effective in transforming a worsening downtrend into an uptrend. But no one should be satisfied with slow growth. Further gains in efficiency and investment are needed to achieve a true success story.

3. Let's look at how markets and controls function in Pumpernickel, a poor country where 70 percent of the people are farmers and 30 percent live in urban areas. The farmers eat nothing but maize (the traditional crop), whereas the urban households eat nothing but bread (the main industrial product). Farmers grow maize for personal consumption, and they grow rye as a cash crop to sell to urban bakers.

   a. Initially, the free market allocates cropland between maize and rye.
      (i) Explain in general terms how the free market determines the allocation of cropland to maize and to rye.

      (ii) If farmers were subjected to a heavy tax in order to finance a doubling of salaries for urban workers, who eat bread, then the demand curves for maize and bread would shift in obvious ways. How would this alter the market allocation of cropland to maize and rye?

b. Various *market failure* problems can distort the allocation of cropland, in Pumpernickel, relative to the social optimum. Consider each of the following problems.

   (i) While urban households represent 30 percent of the population, they earn 80 percent of national income. One *national goal* is to reduce income inequality. Judged relative to this goal, does the market allocate too much or too little cropland to rye production? Why?

   (ii) A monopolist gains control of the bakery industry. Compared to a competitive market outcome, he produces less bread in order to charge a higher price. How does this *monopoly power* in the bakery industry affect the market allocation of cropland between maize and rye? Why?

   (iii) Wood-fired ovens used by bakers are a major cause of air pollution and deforestation in Pumpernickel. Considering these *external diseconomies*, does the market allocate too much or too little cropland to rye production? Explain.

c. A populist coup brings to power a government committed to helping poor farmers. To improve rural nutrition, the new regime wants to reallocate cropland toward more maize production. The regime adopts direct controls requiring each farmer to reduce rye production by 20 percent. At the same time, the government imposes price controls to prevent profiteers from charging high prices for rye or bread, as supplies decline.

   (i) Although intended to help farmers, the farmers turn out to suffer as a result of the controls. How can such an adverse effect come about? (Hint: Think supply and demand, with Q held 20 percent below equilibrium and no increase in P.)

    (ii) Do the controls on rye production create opportunities for rent-seeking activities, such as the emergence of a black market or corruption of officials? Explain.

    (iii) Ten years after the coup, Pumpernickelian economists estimate that maize output is lower than it would have been under the free-market system. How can controls that *increase* maize output possibly lead to a *decline* in maize output in the long run?

4. The textbook identifies five basic conditions for a "well-functioning market system." This exercise checks your understanding of these conditions by examining a host of problems that plague the Republic of Bejeebers.

  a. *Macroeconomic environment.* Bejeebers has a fixed exchange rate despite high inflation and a large trade deficit. This creates an unstable macroeconomic environment because everyone expects the currency to be devalued sharply, but no one knows when.

    (i) A currency devaluation would cause imports to become more expensive. How does this unstable macroeconomic environment distort business decisions about importing inventory stocks?

    (ii) A devaluation would increase the local-currency value of foreign currency. How does the macroeconomic instability distort the choice made by savers between placing funds in foreign banks versus investing in Bejeebers?

(iii) On the basis of the two previous questions, briefly summarize how the unstable macroeconomic environment impairs the "well functioning" of markets in Bejeebers.

b. *Controls and the scope for market forces.* Getting a license to open a new business or expand an existing business requires 17 signatures from officials in five different ministries. Dedicated entrepreneurs can complete the process in six months. Briefly explain how this red tape impairs the "well functioning" of markets in Bejeebers.

c. *Competition.* Imports of textiles are prohibited in Bejeebers because local production is viewed as an infant industry. To avoid wasteful competition, only one textile company is permitted to operate in the country. The company happens to be owned by the president's daughter.
   (i) Briefly summarize how the lack of competition impairs the "well functioning" of the market for textiles.

   (ii) Would your answer change if there were still just one domestic producer, but with *unrestricted* imports of textiles?

d. *Relative prices reflecting relative scarcities.* Family cars that are imported into Bejeebers suffer a 200 percent tariff, which triples the price. Dune buggies, though, are imported tariff free.
   (i) Would you expect to see more family cars or dune buggies on the streets of Bejeebers? Why?

(ii) Imports of vehicle components are duty free. Dune buggies can be assembled locally from imported components at a cost 50 percent higher than the world price of the vehicles. Family cars can be assembled locally at double the world price of the vehicles. Given the tariff on competing imports and the cost of local assembly, is it profitable to assemble either vehicle in Bejeebers? Explain.

(iii) Briefly summarize how the relative price distortions due to tariffs impair the "well functioning" of the market for vehicles.

e. *Response to profit signals.* The government of Bejeebers owns all the steel mills. The managers of the state-owned companies know that the national treasury will cover all losses. How does the lack of accountability for making profits impair the "well functioning" of the market for steel in Bejeebers?

The conditions described above may seem mildly outlandish, but similar conditions have been prevalent in many developing countries. No wonder structural adjustment programs are so complex and so important.

ANSWERS TO SELF-TEST

Completion

1. socialist
2. infant
3. rents
4. outward
5. structural adjustment
6. productivity
7. consumer
8. Bolivia
9. export
10. credibility

True-False

1.	T	6.	T
2.	F	7.	F
3.	T	8.	T
4.	T	9.	F
5.	F	10.	T

Multiple Choice

1.	b	6.	d
2.	a	7.	c
3.	b	8.	a
4.	d	9.	b
5.	b	10.	a

CHAPTER 6 | Sustainable Development

OVERVIEW

Chapter 6 examines the management of natural resources, including environmental quality. Many developing countries are richly endowed with natural resources, but few have been able to convert this wealth into rapid economic growth. Too often, resources are degraded or depleted without yielding sustainable development. The inefficiencies stem in part from market failures. Where there is open access to common resources—whether forests, fishing stocks, wildlife, aquifers, soils, rangeland, or the air we breathe—it leads to excessive depletion. More broadly, the exploitation of natural resources creates external diseconomies, including congestion, erosion, and pollution. In such cases, competitive markets exploit the resources beyond the point that maximizes net benefits to society.

Economic analysis provides clear rules for the sustainable harvest of renewable resources and for the optimal rate of depletion of nonrenewable resources. The general rule is to maximize the discounted present value of resource rents (net revenues). This implies that the present generation can exploit nonrenewable resources and reinvest, without sacrificing the welfare of future generations. The higher is the real return on alternative investments (and thus the discount rate), the greater the warranted rate of exploitation.

The fact that externalities cause markets to overexploit resources suggests that government interventions are needed to produce an efficient outcome. Most countries respond with arbitrary regulations, but it is difficult for any government to establish regulations that produce efficient, minimum-cost outcomes. A better solution is to *internalize* the externalities so that market participants take the costs fully into account. One way to do this is to confer long-term, transferable property rights. A second device is to impose taxes that approximate the external costs. A more efficient device is to introduce marketable permits that entitle the holder to use the resource. The permit is a virtual property right with a market value; use of the permit therefore entails an opportunity cost, which internalizes the externality. All three of these devices are ways to correct the market rather than regulate it. Minimizing government intrusion is desirable, because *policy* failures are another major cause of resource mismanagement. Through protectionist trade measures, tax breaks, energy subsidies, and poorly appraised infrastructure investments, government interventions often accentuate the wasteful use of scarce resources.

Standard measures of national income and product contribute to poor management of resources by neglecting the depletion of natural capital or the degradation of the environment. Thus, national accounts overstate consumable output and growth, particularly for resource-rich developing countries. To correct this, economists have devised a measure of *adjusted net national product* (ANNP), but the adjusted accounts are not yet widely used.

The final issue is *global* sustainability of development. While many uncertainties remain concerning the long-term effects of pollution, history consistently has disproved simple Malthusian views that the world is running out of resources. One reason is that technology has more than kept pace with population growth. More to the point, neoclassical economics shows that markets respond to scarcity by inducing substitutions, conservation, exploration for new reserves, and development of alternative materials. Hence, a sound strategy for global sustainability is to promote efficient markets, effective property rights, and a minimum of distortionary interventions. Since poverty is a powerful impediment to conservation and prudent management of resources, economic development itself is part of the solution. In this regard, the rich nations have a great stake in development of the poor nations.

MAIN LEARNING OBJECTIVES

After studying this chapter, you ought to understand and be able to explain

1. The problems caused by open access to common resources.

2. How external diseconomies distort market outcomes.

3. The concept of resource rent.

4. The implications of the rule for optimizing the harvest of a renewable resource and the rule for optimal depletion of a nonrenewable resource.

5. How secure, long-term, transferable property rights can reduce the market failures that cause overexploitation of natural resources.

6. The information requirements for regulating externalities efficiently.

7. How taxes or marketable permits (rights to pollute) can internalize external costs and lead to an efficient market outcome for natural resources.

8. How government interventions and policy failures have contributed to the wasteful use of resources.

9. How national accounts can be adjusted to incorporate the depletion of natural capital.

10. The neoclassical analysis of how markets respond to scarcity, and its implications for global sustainability of development.

11. Why widespread poverty is a threat to the global environment, and economic development is part of the solution.

12. How rich nations and poor nations differ with regard to global resource management, so room exists for a bargain that can benefit all nations.

ECONOMIC TOOLS AND TECHNIQUES

From what you have learned in this chapter, you should be able to

1. Use supply-and-demand analysis to show how external diseconomies drive a wedge between private and social marginal costs and distort the market outcome.

2. Analyze the net benefit of different rates of exploiting a renewable resource, like a fishery, and apply the rule for maximizing resource rents from a sustainable harvest (marginal cost equals marginal revenue).

3. Apply the intertemporal optimization rule for a resource like copper, equating the present value of marginal net benefits each year.

4. Determine the optimal level of pollution and explain how the market could reach the optimum with an appropriate tax or marketable permits.

5. Calculate the economic value of natural capital and the value of resource depletion, using the net present value of future resource rents.

6. Apply the definitions for *adjusted net national product* (ANNP) and *net saving*.

KEY TERMS AND CONCEPTS

adjusted net national product (ANNP),
   nct saving
common resources
debt-for-nature swap
discount ratc, discounting, present
   value
energy pricing
externalities
internalize external costs
Malthusian trap
marginal abatement cost

marginal net benefit
marketable permits
natural capital
open access
optimal level of pollution
private and social marginal cost
property rights
renewable and nonrenewable
   resources
resource rent
sustainability

SELF-TEST

Completion

1. When forests are public property and people have open access, the timber is overcut and the forests deteriorate rapidly. This exemplifies the problem of managing _____ resources.

2. Pollution is a form of external _____.

3. The difference between the rate of harvest and the rate of growth for a renewable resource is called the *rate of* _____.

4. When *total cost* is defined to include the necessary return to capital, then the term *net revenue* is synonymous with *resource* _____.

5. The higher is the _____ rate, the lower the present value of future benefits or costs.

6. When a _____ right to a scarce resource is auctioned, potential owners bid up the price to the point where they still earn a reasonable profit but most of the resource rents are paid to the government.

7. The optimal level of pollution is the level at which the _____ external cost equals the _____ abatement cost.

8. Some environmental groups have helped to finance conservation programs in developing countries through debt-for-_____ swaps.

9. Many economists advocate that the government issue _____ permits granting holders licenses to pollute up to specified amounts.

10. Net national product (NNP) = gross national product (GNP) *minus* _____.

11. To obtain the *adjusted* net national product (ANNP), one also deducts the annual depletion of _____ capital.

12. According to the _____ view of development, the growing world population will exhaust the earth's capacity to produce food.

True-False

If false, you should be able to explain why.

_____ 1. On average, the developing countries having rich endowments of natural resources grow more rapidly than other developing countries.

_____ 2. The central theme of Chapter 6 is that external diseconomies make it impossible for the market to manage natural resources efficiently without direct government controls.

_____ 3 In a polluting industry, the social marginal cost of production exceeds the private marginal cost.

_____ 4. The *optimal* harvest in a fishery is the maximum that can be achieved without causing extinction of the fish stock.

_____ 5. For any positive discount rate, benefits realized in future years have less present value than comparable benefits realized immediately.

_____ 6. One implication of the rule for optimal depletion of a natural resource is that the higher is the discount rate, the more a resource should be exploited by the present generation.

_____ 7. The regulatory approach to reducing pollution generally is inefficient because it creates higher-than-necessary abatement costs.

_____ 8. The Brazilian government subsidizes ranchers who encroach on the Amazon rainforests, even though the yield to the economy from the subsidized investments is negative.

_____ 9. Taxes on environmentally damaging activities cannot achieve an efficient market outcome because they allow some pollution to continue.

_____ 10. In 1990, the world's proven reserves of fuel were five times higher than in 1950, and ultimately recoverable reserves were sufficient to last hundreds of years.

_____ 11. The incentive to conserve forest land is greater if property rights to the forest land are *not* transferable.

_____ 12. By increasing an economy's reliance on markets, economic reform programs generally sacrifice sustainability of development.

Multiple Choice

1. resource wealth into rapid economic growth?
   a. Zambia
   b. Malaysia
   c. South Korea
   d. India

2. The test of sustainable development is that
   a. nonrenewable resources are not depleted.
   b. a high value is placed on conservation for its own sake.
   c. pollution is prohibited above an absolute minimum level.
   d. consumption can be maintained indefinitely at a constant level or better.

3. The example of soil erosion in Java demonstrates that
   a. poor farmers do not understand how to prevent soil erosion.
   b. farmers in low-lying areas should pay upland farmers to control soil erosion.
   c. bearing additional costs to conserve soil is not economically sound for upland farmers.
   d. poor farmers do not have enough time between rains to maintain the terraces needed for soil conservation.

4. For a renewable resource such as a teak forest, what is the relationship between the harvest that maximizes the *total* sustainable revenue and the harvest that maximizes the *net* sustainable revenue?
   a. Maximizing total revenue involves a smaller annual harvest.
   b. Maximizing total revenue involves a larger annual harvest.
   c. The two are identical.
   d. The relationship depends on the world price of teak.

5. If the discount rate is 12 percent, what is the present value of a marginal net benefit equal to $1,000 earned five years hence?
   a. Present value = $1,000(0.12/5)$.
   b. Present value = $1,000(1.12)/5$.
   c. Present value = $1,000/(1.12)^5$.
   d. Present value = $1,000/(1 + .12/5)$.

6. To be effective in conveying incentives for efficient management of scarce resources, property rights must be
   a. transferable.   c. long term.
   b. secure.   d. all the above.

7. Using a high discount rate, rather than a low discount rate,
   a. makes tropical reforestation projects less profitable.
   b. makes long-lived dam projects more attractive.
   c. makes current mineral extraction less worthwhile.
   d. all the above.

8. In designing regulations to control pollution, the government's objective should be to
   a. minimize the sum of the abatement cost and the external cost.
   b. reduce the external cost to zero.
   c. maximize the difference between the marginal abatement cost and the marginal external cost.
   d. minimize the marginal abatement cost.

9. Malaysia has had success with using emission fees to cope with pollution from
   a. automobile traffic.
   b. palm-oil processing.
   c. human waste in urban areas.
   d. all the above.

10. A policy of controlling fuel and energy prices at artificially low levels causes which of the following adverse effects?
   a. It encourages the use of vehicles that add to congestion and pollution.
   b. It discourages efforts to adopt energy-saving technologies.
   c. It encourages the development of industries that are excessively energy intensive.
   d. All the above.

11. The example of Lumpinee Public Park in Bangkok shows that
    a. no monetary value can be placed on environmental amenities unless users are somehow charged a market price.
    b. the valuation of amenities depends critically on the methodology used.
    c. one can obtain a reasonable value for the park amenities by tabulating travel costs incurred by park users.
    d. the government of Thailand prefers controls to markets.

12. A country's *natural* capital includes all the following *except*
    a. forests.   c. mineral deposits.
    b. water.   d. roads.

APPLICATIONS

Worked Example: The Valuation and Management of Copper Resources in Zambia

The date is 1995 and Zambia's Nchanga open-pit copper mine is widely regarded as having only five years worth of exploitable ore. Suppose that the production plan entails extracting 100,000 metric tons of copper each year for five years. Assume that the state-owned mining company expects world copper prices to be stable at $2,500 per metric ton (after adjusting for inflation). The cost of mining, smelting, refining, and delivering copper, including a normal return on capital, is a steady $1,900 per metric ton. Therefore, the resource rent is $600 per metric ton.

The *economic value of the copper deposit* is the present value of expected resource rents from the deposit. If the discount rate is 12 percent, then the resource rent in each year t must be multiplied by $1/(1.12)^t$ to obtain the present value, where $t = 0$ for 1995. Under the stated conditions, the copper deposit is worth $242.2 million in 1995, as shown in the following table. (Check the right-hand column to make sure you understand how to calculate present values.)

Year	Production (metric tons)	Resource rent (million $, at $600/metric ton)	Present value (million $, at $r = 12\%$)
1995 ($t = 0$)	100,000	60.0	60.0
1996	100,000	60.0	53.6
1997	100,000	60.0	47.8
1998	100,000	60.0	42.7
1999	100,000	60.0	38.1
Total	500,000		**242.2**

Gross revenue in 1995 is $250 million (100,000 metric tons × $2,500 per metric ton). To generate this revenue, Zambia has to *deplete* its natural capital by $60 million, which is the resource rent on the tonnage produced in 1995. Unless Zambia reinvests $60 million of the gross income, the *total* capital stock will fall and the income stream will be unsustainable. As explained in the text, standard national accounting methods neglect such resource depletion. Thus, the national accounts for 1995 overstate the *net* product from the Nchanga mine by $60 million.

You may have noticed that something is wrong with this scenario: It violates the maximizing rule for exploiting a natural resource over time. To maximize the present value of the resource rents, extraction should be managed so that the marginal net benefit (MNB) for any year t is equal to the discounted value of the MNB for year $t + 1$. In algebraic terms, $MNB_t = MNB_{t+1}/(1 + r)$. In the example, a ton of copper produced in 1995 generates a marginal resource rent of $600, whereas the discounted value of a marginal ton produced in 1996 is $600/1.12 = $536. Zambia could gain by shifting production at the margin from 1996 back to 1995. A similar adjustment would pay off in later pairs of years.

For example, let copper production rise to 140,000 tons in 1995, matched by reductions of 10,000 tons in years 1996 through 1999. Suppose that this reallocation does not affect price or cost. Although total extraction remains unchanged, the present value of the resource rents rises by more than $5 million, to $247.9 million (see Exercise 1). To be more realistic, large changes in the extraction rate could affect costs and perhaps world market prices. Also, the presence of fixed costs sets a floor on the feasible level of production in any year. So there is a limit to the gains from such rescheduling. Nonetheless, the stable-output production plan shown above would be far from optimal.

Exercises

1. It is your turn to analyze the copper resources at Zambia's Nchanga mine. As in the Worked Example, the date is 1995. The state-owned mining company expects the world price of copper to remain at $2,500 per metric ton. Company economists anticipate that the cost of production, inclusive of a normal return on capital, will remain at $1,900 per ton.

   a. (i) Calculate the present value of resource rents, on the basis of the schedule of copper production shown in Table 6–1. Using a 12 percent discount rate, fill in all of the blanks in the table.

Table 6–1

Year	Production (metric tons)	Resource rent (million $, at $600/metric ton)	Present value (million $, at $r = 12\%$)
1995	140,000	_____	_____
1996	90,000	_____	_____
1997	90,000	_____	_____
1998	90,000	_____	_____
1999	90,000	_____	_____
Total	500,000	_____	_____

(ii) What is the economic value of the natural resource deposit at Nchanga mine?

$_____ million.

What is value of resource depletion from production in 1995?

$_____ million.

To what extent will the standard national accounts overstate the net product in 1995 from the Nchanga mine?

$_____ million.

(iii) If the discount rate rises to 15 percent, then the economic value of the natural resource deposit _____ to $_____ million.

(iv) What is the *economic logic* of valuing the resource *less* when the discount rate rises? (An answer that simply refers back to the formula is insufficient.)

b. With the extraction pattern as in Table 6–1, the company economists revise their projection of copper prices. They now foresee real copper prices rising by 10 percent per year, while costs remain stable at $1,900 per metric ton.

(i) Under this scenario the price of copper will be

$2,500 per metric ton in 1995

$_____ in 1996

$_____ in 1997

$_____ in 1998

$_____ in 1999

(ii) The real resource rent per ton (equal to price minus cost) will rise from $600 in 1995 to

$_____ in 1996

$_____ in 1997

$_____ in 1998

$_____ in 1999

(iii) With the 12 percent discount rate, what is the economic value of the natural capital lying underground at Nchanga now? (Don't forget to multiply the resource rent per ton by the number of tons per year.)

$_____ million.

c. Given the new projection of rising copper prices (from part b), let's see if the production plan in Table 6–1 is optimal.
   (i) The resource rent earned on copper in 1995 is $_____ per ton.
   (ii) With the discount rate still at 12 percent, the discounted value of the resource rent per ton of copper in 1996 is $_____ per ton.

(iii) If prices and costs would remain as stated, would Zambia benefit from producing more in 1995 and less in 1996 or vice versa?

Explain why.

(iv) The present production plan for 1995 and 1996 would be optimal if the company expected copper prices to rise to $_____ per metric ton in 1996. (Hint: apply the maximizing rule and remember that MNB is the difference between price and cost.)

d. Return to the original price and cost estimates from the opening paragraph. The government is thinking of selling the mine to Monzanium Monopoly Corporation (MMC). MMC does not share the government's projections.

  (i) In particular, MMC believes that costs would drop to $1,500 per metric ton if the mine were privately owned and managed. The resource rent then would be $_____ per ton, each year.

 (ii) For simplicity, assume that production plan remains as shown in Table 6–1 and that the discount rate is still 12 percent. What is the *present value* of the resource rents expected by MMC over the five-year period?

$_____ million.

(Of course, an optimal production plan would allow MMC to do even better than this.)

(iii) The government negotiators insist that the mine will not be sold for less than its own valuation (from part a) *plus* $100 million. Will MMC accept this deal? At this price, how will the government of Zambia and MMC split the resource rents arising from the privatized operation of the mine? Do both parties come out ahead? Explain.

2. The optimal harvest of a *renewable* resource is defined by equating marginal benefits and costs. In Madagascar, most families rely on firewood or charcoal made from firewood, for cooking and keeping warm in chilly weather. Firewood, of course, is a renewable resource since limbs and trees grow back. But the woodlands are a common resource with open access.

a. Curve *TV* in Figure 6–1 shows how the *sustainable* total value of the annual harvest, in francs, varies as a function of the effort, *E*, in person-days, to gather firewood. (When firewood does not pass through the market, the value is imputed.)

  (i) Up to point *A* the *TV* curve rises at a decreasing rate. The sustainable harvest value rises in smaller and smaller increments as successive units of effort are devoted to gathering firewood. What ecological and economic factors explain the declining payoff per unit of extra effort?

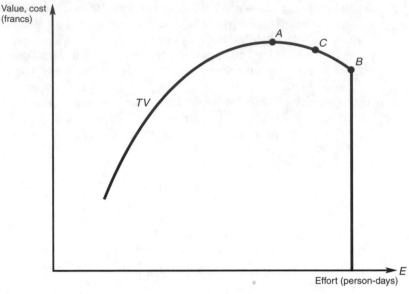

FIGURE 6–1

(ii) The *TV* curve reaches a peak at point *A*. Additional effort reduces the annual harvest value. Explain how this is possible.

(iii) At point *B* the sustainable harvest abruptly drops to zero. What is the environmental meaning of this outcome?

b. For simplicity, suppose that firewood is gathered exclusively by children, who otherwise have no gainful work to do. Their parents attribute zero cost to each unit of effort

(i) Mark on the horizontal axis the level of effort that produces the maximum sustainable *net* benefit, which is defined as the difference between the annual harvest value and the harvest cost (zero here). Label this point *E1*.

(ii) In terms of effort level, how does the maximum *net* benefit compare with the *maximum* total harvest value? Explain.

c. Now allow for a fixed cost per unit of effort. In Figure 6–1, draw a straight line from the origin through point C; label this line TC, for total cost of gathering firewood.

(i) Mark on the horizontal axis the level of effort that produces the maximum sustainable *net* benefit. Label this point $E2$.

(ii) In terms of effort level, how does the maximum *net* benefit in this case compare with the *maximum* total harvest value? Explain.

d. With open access to the woodlands, individual family decisions determine the actual amount of harvest effort. Assume here that effort costs remain as in part c.

(i) With the effort level at $E2$, individual families have an incentive to gather more firewood. How can this be when the curves show that the marginal cost exceeds the marginal value?

(ii) Even when effort is at $E1$, some families still have an incentive to gather more firewood. How can this be when the marginal value is negative beyond $E1$?

(iii) In the absence of irrational behavior, can individual decisions lead to point B, where the sustainable harvest falls to zero? Explain.

(iv) In general, will the free market produce the efficient level of firewood harvest in Madagascar? Explain.

3. Indonesia needs to expand electricity production. The country has abundant reserves of relatively inexpensive coal. However, coal burning creates pollution in the form of soot and ash, as well as nitrogen and sulfur oxides, which contribute to smog and acid rain. These costs are *externalities* because they are borne by parties other than those engaged in the sale and purchase of coal.

Figure 6–2 summarizes conditions in the market for coal. Coal is available in virtually unlimited amounts for $35 per ton; this is shown by the supply curve. Since the supply curve is horizontal, the private marginal cost of coal equals the average cost per ton. Each ton of coal burned, however, imposes $10 worth of external costs on society; this is shown by the curve labeled *MEC*, for marginal external cost. The competitive equilibrium, which disregards the external cost, is at point *A*.

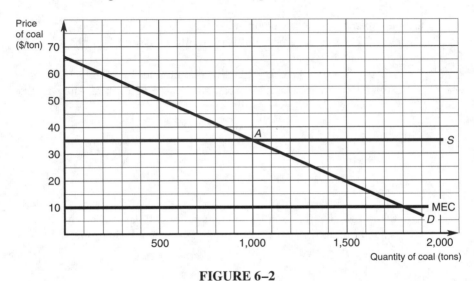

FIGURE 6–2

a. (i) In Figure 6–2, draw the *social marginal cost* curve by adding together vertically the supply curve and the MEC curve. Label it *SMC*. This curve combines the private and external costs of using coal.

(ii) Label the intersection of the SMC curve and the demand curve point *B*. Label the corresponding output Q_B.

(iii) At the competitive market equilibrium (point *A*), buyers value the last units of coal at $_____ per ton. Private supply costs are $_____ per ton. External costs are $_____ per ton. On balance, the last units of coal yield a *net* loss to society of $_____ per ton. Because of the external diseconomy, the market does *not* achieve an efficient level of coal production.

(iv) If output is at Q_B, what is the *net* benefit or cost to society from the last units of coal produced?

(v) At the efficient output level Q_B is there any pollution? Explain.

b. To achieve the efficient outcome, where social marginal cost equals the marginal benefit to coal users, the government can directly regulate coal transactions. Or it can impose a tax on coal—a *green tax*. This shifts the market supply curve upward at each point by the amount of the tax per ton.
   (i) A tax of $____ per ton will shift the supply curve for coal just enough to achieve a market equilibrium at the efficient output level Q_B.
   (ii) In what sense does the green tax *internalize* the external cost?

c. A technological change allows the power company to eliminate pollution entirely at a cost of $5 per ton of coal. Thus, adding $5 per ton to the *private* cost would reduce the *external* cost to zero.
   (i) Now that this pollution-abatement technology is available, is Q_B still the *efficient* output level? Explain.

   (ii) With the green tax defined above, does the power company have an incentive to adopt the new technology? Explain.

   (iii) Suppose the tax is restructured as a charge per unit of *pollution* rather than per ton of coal. This entails levying a $10 tax on the volume of pollutants produced initially per ton of coal, to achieve the outcome at point B. With this new tax structure, does the power company have an incentive to adopt the new pollution-control technology? Explain.

d. The exercise has been concerned with how government can *correct* a market failure created by external diseconomies. But government policies often make market outcomes *worse*. For each situation below, explain how an external diseconomy arises and state whether the government policy moves the market closer to or further from the efficient outcome.

   (i) Cattle ranchers clear land for grazing in Brazil's Amazon basin; the government has subsidized the ranching operations through tax breaks and low-interest loans.

   (ii) Cotton growers in Uzbekistan divert large volumes of water from the Amu Darya River for irrigation; the government has supplied the irrigation water at a heavily subsidized price.

   (iii) The government of Nigeria increases the price of gasoline, which has been fixed at far below the market equilibrium level.

4. Exercise 3 assumed that the marginal external cost of pollution and the marginal abatement cost both were constant. Letting these costs vary allows us to examine the concept of optimal pollution and the rationale for marketable permits. Consider the case of water pollution from palm-oil mills in Malaysia.

   a. External cost rises with the amount of effluent discharged into the rivers; in fact, the external cost rises at an increasing rate. Suppose that the *marginal* external cost (MEC, measured in Ringgit) is related to the discharge of effluent (DIS, in tons per palm-oil mill per year) according to the equation MEC = 10 + 4DIS.

      (i) Draw the line showing this relationship in Figure 6–3; label it *MEC*.

      (ii) The prevailing level of discharge is 100 tons per palm-oil mill per year. The *marginal* external cost imposed by the last ton of discharge is M$_____. (M$ is the symbol for the Malaysian Ringgit.)

      (iii) The *total* external cost of pollution (TEC) is related to the level of discharge by the equation TEC = 10DIS + 2DIS^2. (Note that *MEC* is the slope of the TEC function at each point.) The total external cost from the prevailing level of discharge is M$_____ per palm-oil mill.

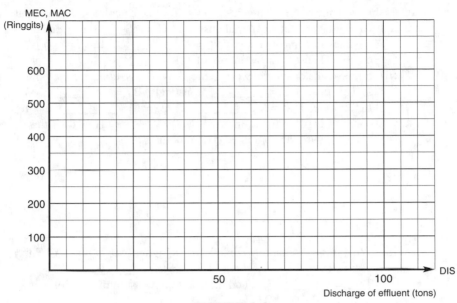

FIGURE 6–3

b. Abatement costs rise with the extent of the clean-up; in fact, abatement costs rise at an increasing rate since easy and cheap measures can reduce pollution up to a point, but further abatement is increasingly expensive. The relationship between the marginal abatement cost (MAC, in Ringgit) and the amount abated (ABT, in tons) is MAC = 10 + 4ABT.

(i) The minimum level of abatement is none, in which case DIS = 100 and ABT = _____. The theoretical maximum abatement eliminates all the pollution, in which case DIS = 0 and ABT = _____. In general, the amount abated is ABT = 100 – DIS.

(ii) In Figure 6–3, draw in and label the line representing MAC. Be careful to draw it so that the minimum value occurs at DIS = 100.

(iii) For the theoretical maximum abatement, the marginal cost of eliminating the last ton of discharge is M\$_____.

(iv) The *total* abatement cost is TAC = 10ABT + 2ABT². For the theoretical maximum abatement, the total cost of cleaning up pollution is M\$_____ per palm-oil mill.

(v) Which creates a larger cost to the Malaysian economy: zero abatement or full abatement?

c. Something in between these extremes is to be preferred in the interest of minimizing the overall cost. The rule is to equate MEC and MAC. On the graph, this is the point where the two lines cross.

(i) Identify in Figure 6–3 the optimal level of pollution, as point X on the horizontal axis.

(ii) At point X, the discharge of effluents remains at DIS = _____ tons.

d. Is this truly the optimal outcome? Let's do some calculations to find out.

   (i) At point X the total external cost is TEC = M\$_____ and the total abatement cost is TAC = M\$_____; this gives a combined cost to the economy of M\$_____.

   (ii) Suppose the discharge were reduced by 5 tons, compared to point X. This gives DIS = _____ tons and ABT = _____ tons. In this case, TEC = M\$_____, TAC = M\$_____, and the combined cost to the economy is M\$_____. How does this compare with the combined cost at point X?

   (iii) What if the discharge were left 5 tons higher than at point X? This gives DIS = _____ tons, TEC = M\$_____, TAC = M\$_____, and the combined cost to the economy is M\$_____.

   (iv) If the welfare criterion is to minimize the total cost to society, what do you conclude?

e. Finally, consider the issue of marketable permits. A permit grants the holder the right to discharge 1 ton per year. As awful as this may sound, let's judge the scheme on its merits.

   (i) The government issues X permits to each mill, where X is the optimal discharge level per mill that you identified above. Assuming that the permits can be enforced (which is no harder than enforcing direct controls), how does the total amount of pollution compare with the optimum found above?

   (ii) After receiving the initial allotment of permits, you discover a way to clean up effluents at your mill for M\$150 per unit of DIS, while at my mill it costs M$210. Explain why there is an incentive now for us to trade permits. Will you sell permits to me, or vice versa?

(iii) What is the effect of our transaction on the total discharge of effluents? What is the effect on total costs to society?

(iv) Does the presence of marketable permits provide a profit incentive for you to seek out less expensive means to reduce pollution to the allowable level? Explain.

5. *Net national product* (NNP) is defined as gross national product (GNP) less depreciation of what the textbook calls *made* capital, as distinct from human capital or natural capital. Depreciation is also the difference between gross and net *domestic* product (GDP and NDP), as well as gross and net investment. Depreciation is an accounting measure of the extent to which assets wear out and need to be replaced to sustain production capacity. It is often measured using the straight-line method, which means that an asset lasting 15 years wears out at a rate of 1/15 per year. This is a simple approximation to the true rate of depreciation.

a. You buy a truck for $30,000 and estimate that it has a useful life of 10 years. Under the straight-line method, the depreciation rate is _____ percent per year and the annual value of depreciation is $_____.

b. Suppose that GNP per capita in Bangweulu is $400.
   (i) If the capital-output ratio for the economy is 2.0, then the capital stock is $_____ per capita.
   (ii) The capital stock has an estimated average life of 20 years. Using straight-line depreciation, this means that the depreciation rate is _____ percent per year.
   (iii) The annual value of depreciation is $_____ per capita. So *net* national product (NNP) per capita is $_____. NNP is _____ percent of GNP. This is fairly typical.

(iv) To produce this output, the economy digs up mineral resources equivalent in value to 6 percent of GDP, and soil loss from agriculture is estimated at 4 percent of GDP. Deducting this depletion of natural capital, the adjusted net national product (ANNP) is $_____ per capita.

(v) To maintain its capital stock and ensure the sustainability of the economy's capacity to generate income, total investment in Bangweulu must be no less than _____ percent of GNP.

c. Economist Robert Repetto and associates estimated resource depletion and degradation in Indonesia during the early 1980s. Table 6–2 shows their results, with line 3 added to account for depreciation of made capital (assuming conservatively that this depreciation amounts to 5 percent of GDP).
(i) Calculate the growth rate of GDP and fill in line 2 in the table.

(ii) Subtract depreciation from GDP to get net domestic product (NDP), and fill in line 3.

Table 6–2

Gross and Net Domestic Product in Indonesia, 1982–1984
(billions of constant 1973 rupiah)

	1982	1983	1984
1. GDP	12,325	12,842	13,520
2. Growth rate of GDP		_____%	_____%
3. *Less* depreciation	–616	–642	–676
4. Net domestic product (NDP)	_____	_____	_____
5. *Less* net change in natural resources:			
a. Petroleum	–1,158	–1,825	–1,765
b. Forests	–551	–974	–493
c. Soils	–55	–71	–76
d. Total depletion	_____	_____	_____
6. *Adjusted* net domestic product (ANDP)	_____	_____	_____
7. Growth rate of ANDP		_____%	_____%
8. Gross domestic investment (GDI)	2,783	3,776	3,551
9. Net domestic investment (NDI)	_____	_____	_____
10. *Adjusted* net domestic investment (ANDI)	_____	_____	_____
11. GDI as percent of GDP	_____%	_____%	_____%
12. ANDI as percent of ANDP (net investment rate)	_____%	_____%	_____%

Source: World Resources Institute, *World Resources 1990–91* (New York: Oxford University Press, 1992), with line 3 added based on the assumption that depreciation = 5 percent of GDP.

(iii) Find the sum of lines 5a, 5b, and 5c to obtain total depletion of natural capital, and fill in line 5d.

(iv) Deduct the depletion of natural capital from NDP to get adjusted net domestic product (ANDP); fill in line 6.

(v) Then calculate the growth rate of ANDP and fill in line 7.

(vi) How does the growth rate of ANDP relate to the growth rate of GDP? Explain.

d. Look at Indonesia's investment performance, before and after taking into account depreciation and depletion.

(i) In Table 6–2, deduct depreciation from gross domestic investment (GDI) to get net domestic investment (NDI). Then deduct depletion of natural capital to get the *adjusted* net domestic investment (ANDI). Fill in lines 9 and 10.

(ii) To gain perspective, compute GDI and ANDI as percentages of GDP and ANDP, respectively. Fill in lines 11 and 12.

(iii) Compare the stories told by lines 11 and 12. What do you conclude about investment performance in Indonesia, relative to gross domestic product?

(Note: Keep in mind that the exercise has used an arbitrary basis for determining the depreciation of made capital.)

6. How does a debt-for-nature swap work? In 1987 Bolivia had just conquered hyperinflation, but one legacy of previous mismanagement was an external debt of $5.8 billion, or $875 per capita (compared to per capita GNP of $530). Because of Bolivia's poverty and the austerity required to curb inflation, the government could not afford the luxury of funding national park services. Enter an international conservation organization (ICO) that is interested in preserving Bolivian forests. The ICO sees room for a deal.

   a. Since the country was virtually insolvent, international creditors were selling Bolivian debt obligations for about 15 cents on the dollar.
      (i) Therefore, the ICO can purchase $20 million of Bolivian debt from an overseas bank for $_____ million.

      (ii) The $20 million debt obligation bears an interest rate of 9 percent, so Bolivia owes $_____ million *per year* in interest payments to whomever holds the debt paper. (If a payment is missed, the interest charge still accrues as additional debt which Bolivia would have to deal with in the future.)

      (iii) At the prevailing exchange rate of 2.05 Bolivianos per dollar, the government's annual interest charge for this debt obligation equals B_____ million.

   b. The ICO approaches the government of Bolivia with the following deal.
      (i) We will buy your $20 million debt obligation, feed the legal documents through a shredder, recycle the scraps of paper, and forgive the debt. This will save you $____ million per year, or B_____ million, in interest charges alone.

      (ii) In return, we ask you to commit B2 million per year to pay for management of a designated national park. Compared to the interest charges on the debt, you save B_____ million per year.

      (iii) By shredding your debt obligation, we also reduce the debt principal that you owe by the equivalent of B_____ million—not to mention future legal fees for negotiating with the bank on possible debt relief. Of course, the deal also leaves you with a well-managed national park for future generations to enjoy.

c. This is a debt-for-nature swap. Why does the ICO prefer the swap over simply *giving* an equal dollar amount to Bolivia to finance management of the national park? (Hint: The yield on dollar investments is less than the interest rate on Bolivian debt, which the ICO purchases at a deep discount. Second hint: Local responsibility.)

ANSWERS TO SELF-TEST

Completion

1. common
2. diseconomy
3. *depletion*
4. *rent*
5. discount
6. property
7. marginal, marginal
8. nature
9. marketable
10. depreciation
11. natural
12. Malthusian

True-False

1.	F	7.	T
2.	F	8.	T
3.	T	9.	F
4.	F	10.	T
5.	T	11.	F
6.	T	12.	F

Multiple Choice

1.	b	7.	a
2.	d	8.	a
3.	c	9.	b
4.	b	10.	d
5.	c	11.	c
6.	d	12.	d

Part III Human Resources

CHAPTER 7 | Population

OVERVIEW

This is the first of four chapters to examine the role of human resources in development. After defining and explaining some basic demographic concepts, the chapter surveys the history of world population growth. Of particular importance is the acceleration of population growth since World War II. As industrial countries passed through a demographic transition to low rates of population growth, developing countries experienced a rapid decline in death rates that was not matched by an equal drop in birthrates. Only recently have widespread declines in fertility become evident. The result has been rapid population growth, which will continue well into the century.

Birthrates largely are determined by the age and sex structure of the population, by marriage practices, and by marital fertility rates. Fertility undoubtedly is a product of social customs and personal passions, but fertility rates also respond to economic costs and benefits. Economic development changes the costs and benefits in ways that encourage lower fertility.

While development leads ultimately to declining birthrates, population growth in turn can affect economic development. Given the supply of nonlabor resources, there is a particular population size that maximizes per capita income; relative to this standard a country may be either overpopulated or underpopulated. But more important is the dynamic relationship between population *growth* and economic *growth*. Most economic models lead one to conclude that slower population growth would enhance economic development in many countries. This conclusion is controversial, because empirical patterns do *not* reveal a clear relationship. The data suggest that economic growth is determined mainly by factors other than population growth.

Most LDC governments favor slower population growth. But why should governments have any involvement in the intensely personal decisions about fertility? There are two main rationales. First, public-sector programs can provide information and access to contraceptives to help couples achieve their preferred family outcomes. Second, the purpose is to correct for external diseconomies, but it is difficult to measure the external costs. The main policy tools are family planning programs and measures that affect incentives by altering the costs and benefits of having children. Examples include policies to improve education opportunities for girls and job opportunities for women, social security schemes, bans on child labor, and health policies that reduce infant mortality.

MAIN LEARNING OBJECTIVES

After studying this chapter, you ought to understand and be able to explain

1. Demographic terms such as the *birthrate*, the *death rate*, *life expectancy*, and the *total fertility rate*.

2. Major features of world population history, including the demographic transition.

3. Current demographic conditions in developing countries, including high dependency ratios, rapid urbanization, and strong demographic momentum despite declining fertility rates.

4. The main determinants of the crude birthrate and the theories of fertility that relate family size to the economic costs and benefits of having children.

5. Why most economists and demographers conclude that many developing countries would achieve more rapid gains in per capita income if population growth were less rapid and how the empirical evidence makes this a controversial proposition.

6. The rationale for government intervention of any kind to influence individual fertility outcomes.

7. The range of policies used in developing countries to slow down population growth, including family planning programs and measures that alter incentives to have children.

8. The fundamental point that population policy and development policy are mutually supportive—development facilitates declining fertility and slower population growth promotes development.

ECONOMIC TOOLS AND TECHNIQUES

From what you have learned in this chapter, you should be able to

1. Find the population doubling time for a given rate of natural increase, which can be computed from the crude birth and death rates.

2. Explain the concepts and implications of Gary Becker's new household economics theory of fertility and distinguish Becker's model from the views of Richard Easterlin and John Caldwell.

3. Explain what determines a country's optimum population and how the optimum changes over time.

4. Outline the main characteristics and implications of the Coale-Hoover model of population growth and development.

KEY TERMS AND CONCEPTS

age-specific fertility and death rates, infant death rate

capital widening versus capital deepening

child replacement thesis

child quality

Coale-Hoover model

crude birthrate, crude death rate

demographic momentum

demographic transition

demography

dependency ratio

family planning program

incentives to have children

life expectancy at birth

Malthusian theory

new household economics

optimum population

population redistribution

positive checks and preventive checks

rate of natural increase

replacement level of fertility

total fertility rate

"ultimate resource" of Julian Simon

wan xi shao campaign and "one child" campaign of China

SELF-TEST

Completion

1. The rate of natural increase of the population is the difference between the _____ _____ and the _____ _____ rate, converted to percentage units.

2. The number of children the average woman would bear during her lifetime, given prevailing age specific fertility rates, is called the _____ *fertility rate*.

3. The doubling time for a population growing at 2.5 percent per year is approximately _____ years.

4. The historical shift from slow population growth with high birth and death rates to slow population growth with low birth and death rates is called the _____ _____.

5. The case study of _____ shows how a low-income country succeeded in reducing the total fertility rate from 5.5 to 2.9 between 1970 and 1992.

6. Even if fertility rates were to drop immediately to the replacement level, population would continue to grow for decades due to demographic _____.

7. According to Becker's new household economics, the fall in fertility as incomes rise can be explained primarily by the rising opportunity cost of parents' _____.

8. Empirical research tends to support the view that rapid population growth _____ private savings.

9. The study of population is called _____.

10. _____ _____ programs work by making contraceptives more readily available and by educating people about the use of contraceptives.

11. According to Caldwell, parents will opt to have _____ children as extended-family ties weaken and nuclear families become more common.

12. Rati Ram and Theodore Schultz point out that longer _____ spans (due to falling death rates) increase the incentive for investment in _____ capital.

True-False

If false, you should be able to explain why.

_____ 1. The crude birthrate is defined as the number of births in a given year per 1,000 women of child bearing age.

_____ 2. Some LDCs have crude death rates as low as those in the industrialized counties, despite much higher age-specific death rates.

_____ 3. Continued growth at 1.7 percent per year would bring world population from 5.5 billion in 1992 to over 14.5 billion by 2050.

_____ 4. Studies have found that rural-urban migrants, on average, improve their standard of living when they move to the cities.

_____ 5. Changing tastes are a major determinant of fertility in Easterlin's model of childbearing decisions.

_____ 6. The empirical record, in fact, does not establish a clearcut negative correlation between population growth and the growth of per capita income.

_____ 7. In a country where the population is growing rapidly, there may be no capital deepening even though the capital stock is increasing.

_____ 8. The slogan "take care of the people and the population will take care of itself" aptly expresses the consensus view on population policy as presented in the text.

_____ 9. Even with no change in age-specific fertility rates, a shift in age structure can cause the crude birthrate to rise.

_____ 10. Studies show that most couples in LDCs desire no more than two children, so large families primarily are the result of inadequate birth control methods.

_____ 11. The child replacement thesis implies that health programs to lower child death rates will cause fertility rates to decline.

_____ 12. In Simon's view, population growth hinders development by increasing the cost of higher education, which is the "ultimate resource."

Multiple Choice

1. In a country of 1 million people, 40,000 babies are born in a year. Of these, 4,000 die within their first year of life. The infant mortality rate is
   a. 100.   c. 4.
   b. 10.   d. 4,000.

2. At the beginning of the Industrial Revolution, the population of the world was a bit under
   a. 100 million people.   c. 400 million people.
   b. 2 billion people.   d. 10 million people.

3. In 1987 the world's population surpassed
   a. 5 billion people.   c. 15 billion people.
   b. 2 billion people.   d. 40 billion people.

4. Over the period 1980 to 1992, the annual rate of population growth averaged 3.0 percent in _____ and 1.8 percent in _____.
   a. Latin America, Africa
   b. Latin America, Asia and the Pacific
   c. Asia and the Pacific
   d. Africa, Asia and the Pacific

5. The dependency ratio is defined as the ratio of
   a. imports to GDP.
   b. children to adults in the population.
   c. unemployed to employed workers in the labor force.
   d. non-working-age population to working-age population.

6. The model of childbearing as an economic decision generates several implications that have been confirmed empirically. For example, fertility rates tend to be
   a. higher where primary school attendance is compulsory.
   b. higher where family incomes are higher.
   c. lower where better opportunities exist for women to work outside the home.
   d. lower where child survival rates are low.

7. According to the modern theory of fertility, what is the most important factor in lowering age-specific fertility rates?
   a. Increased availability of modern birth control methods.
   b. Improved understanding of social problems caused by rapid population growth.
   c. Changes in the age structure of the population.
   d. Changes in the balance of benefits and costs of childbearing at the family level.

8. Which of the following changes would reduce a country's "optimum" population?
   a. Capital accumulation.
   b. Increased labor productivity.
   c. Depletion of natural resources.
   d. Establishment of an effective social security system.

9. Family planning programs tend to work best in countries where
   a. infant death rates are low and opportunities are widespread for women to work outside the home.
   b. social norms inhibit what Malthus called "passion between the sexes."
   c. the population is largely rural and there is little opportunity for rural-urban migration.
   d. incomes are low.

10. Malthus's theory included all but one of the following elements. Which is the exception?
    a. Population grows geometrically while food supplies grow arithmetically.
    b. Population is controlled largely by positive checks, such as famines, wars, and epidemics.
    c. Preventive checks, such as birth control, are strongly advocated.
    d. Improved living standards can only be temporary, because they stimulate higher birthrates.

11. Which of the following statements best summarizes China's policy on population since 1971?
    a. No action is needed since "revolution plus production" can solve all problems.
    b. The government has adopted strong and fairly successful policies to reduce the population growth rate.
    c. The government has tried to slow the population growth rate, with no success.
    d. No action is needed since there is still a large amount of unused arable land in China.

12. In 1988, Tanzania's crude birthrate was 48, while the crude death rate was 13. The rate of natural increase of Tanzania's population was
    a. 35 percent.   c. 3.7 percent.
    b. 3.5 percent.   d. 37 percent.

APPLICATIONS

Worked Example: Effects of Population Growth on Development, a Coale-Hoover Analysis

Let's see how rapid population growth can reduce the growth of per capita income, using the simple Harrod-Domar model from Chapter 2. Recall that the GDP growth rate (g) can be expressed as $g = s/k$, where s is the savings rate and k is the incremental capital-output ratio (ICOR). For simplicity, the ICOR is fixed at $k = 4$ here, so $g = s/4$.

Consider Hobbitshire, a placid country with a population in year 0 of 1,000 workers (over age 10) and 1,000 children (under age 10); this gives a dependency rate of $1,000/1,000 = 1.0$. Total GDP is $Y = $ BB1 million (BB stands for Bilbo, the currency). Hence, per capita income is BB500. Deaths, births, and children reaching age 10 are equal in number each year, so the population is constant in terms of both size and structure. The savings rate is $s = 28$ percent, so GDP grows by $g = 28/4 = 7$ percent per year. Because population is constant, per capita income also grows by 7 percent per year and reaches BB983 [$= 500(1.07)^{10}$] by year 10.

Suppose, instead, that the population grew by 4 percent per annum beginning year 0. In year 1, Hobbitshire would have 80 extra people, all of whom would be children. In year 10 there would be an extra 960 people, all still children. What would be the effects on per capita income? First, the "more-mouths-to-feed" effect would precede the "more-hands-to-work" effect by 10 years. During this period, the extra people would not add to output. They would simply reduce income per capita. If output were to continue to grow by 7 percent a year while the population grew by 4 percent per year, per capita income would increase by only 3 percent per year.

Second, with more and more children around, the *dependency rate* would increase steadily. As workers would now have more mouths to feed, the savings rate would drop by, say, 1 percentage point each year and hit 18 percent in year 10. This would cause GDP to grow more and more slowly. Table 7–1 summarizes the trend. Third, when the population bulge did enter the labor force, investment would be lower (due to lower values for both s and Y, compared to the case of zero population growth) and the available capital stock would be spread among more workers. Consequently, worker productivity would grow more slowly. More of the available investment would be used for *capital widening* (that is, simply equipping the additional workforce) and less for *capital deepening*.

As the textbook notes, this kind of analysis, pioneered by the Coale-Hoover model for India, is simplistic. The outlook for Hobbitshire would brighten if population pressure induced workers to work harder or if necessity stimulated more rapid technical progress.

Table 7–1

Hobbitshire, with 4 Percent Population Growth*

Year	s (%)	g = s/4 (%)	Y (million BB)	Population	Y/pop. (BB)	Dependency rate
0	28	7.0	1.00	2,000	500	1.00
1	27	6.75	1.07	2,080	514	1.08
2	26	6.50	1.14	2,163	527	1.16
3	25	6.25	1.22	2,250	542	1.25
.	.	.	.	.	.	.
.	.	.	.	.	.	.
.	.	.	.	.	.	.
10	18	4.50	1.77	2,960	597	1.96

*An ICOR of 4 is assumed, and s declines by 1 percentage point per year.

Exercises

1. *Demographic transition.* Table 7–2 shows crude birthrates (CBR) and crude death rates (CDR) in 1970 and 1992 for all developing countries with populations of 20 million or more (in 1992). Rather than showing the individual observations, countries are grouped into categories by level of per capita income (1992, PPP$). There are seven groups, one of which happens to be an empty set, so we have six observations for each date. One obersvation represents the simple average of the group.

   a. Fill in the last two columns of Table 7–2 by calculating the natural rate of population increase (NRI) from the CBR and CDR data. (Pay attention to units: CBR and SDR are measured *per 1,000* population; NRI is a *percent* growth rate.)

Table 7-2

Demographic Data

Group	Income range (PPP$)	PPP$, 1992	CBR (per 1,000) 1970	CBR (per 1,000) 1992	CDR (per 1,000) 1970	CDR (per 1,000) 1992	Rate of natural increase (%) 1970	Rate of natural increase (%) 1992
1	Less than $1,000	485	46	48	21	17		
2	$1,000–$2,000	1378	44	32	18	11		
3	$2,000–$3,000	2527	43	32	16	9		
4	$3,000–$4,000	3340	43	28	16	8		
5	$4,000–$5,000	No large-country observations in this income range						
6	$5,000–$6,000	5515	40	27	12	7		
7	Over $6,000	7828	34	24	9	6		

Source: Calculated from *World Development Report 1994*, Tables 26 and 30.

b. (i) On Figure 7–1, plot the six data points for crude birthrates in 1970. Connect the points and label this line CBR70. Similarly plot the six points for crude death rates in 1970. Connect the points and label this line CDR70.

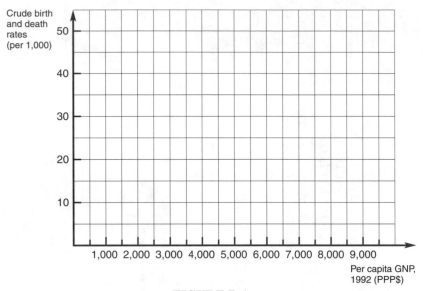

FIGURE 7–1

(ii) These two lines show the average cross-section relationship between demographic conditions and income. Does the graph reveal any sign of the demographic transition among these large developing countries in 1970? Explain.

c. (i) Now plot the six crude brithrates for 1992. Connect the points and label the line CBR92. Then plot the six crude death rates for 1992. Connect the points and label the line CDR92.

   (ii) Ignore the 1970 data for a moment. Does the cross-section graph for 1992 reveal a demographic transition? Explain.

    (iii) Now compare the graphs for 1970 and 1992. Is there any indication of a demographic transition's taking place over *time*? Explain.

  d. Suppose countries that are poor in 1992 simply followed the pattern shown by lines CBR92 and CDR92 in Figure 7–1.

    (i) What level of per capita income will they have to attain before the crude birthrate falls below 30?

$$\$\underline{\hspace{2cm}}.$$

    (ii) What level of per capita income will they have to attain before the rate of natural increase of the population falls below 2.0 percent per year?

$$\$\underline{\hspace{2cm}}.$$

    (iii) If per capita income grows by 2 percent per year, then a country where per capita income is presently PPP\$500 would need _____ years to reach the income level consistent with population growth below 2 percent per year. (Hint: Use the exponential growth formula from footnote 1 in Chapter 7.)

The last calculation shows that it would take a long time for population growth to slow down in countries that are poor today if they just waited for economic development to influence fertility. To reduce population growth more quickly, countries can adopt policy measures that accelerate the process.

2. According to the economic theory of fertility, a couple's desired family size is influenced significantly by economic conditions that determine the private benefits and costs of childbearing and child raising.

  a. In Becker's economic theory of fertility, how will each of the following changes affect fertility? Let + denote a rise in fertility, – denote a decline in fertility, and 0 denote no effect, and mark the effect in the Effect column.

Change	Effect
(i) Primary school made compulsory	_____
(ii) Reliable social security system introduced	_____
(iii) Migration from farms to urban areas	_____
(iv) Improved opportunities for women to work outside the home	_____
(v) Redistribution of farmland to poor families	_____
(vi) A campaign to educate people about social congestion effects of high fertility	_____

b. If fertility behavior is the result of fairly rational individual responses to benefits and costs, how is it possible for family planning programs and provision of birth control devices to alter fertility behavior to any significant extent?

c. Consider the following statement: "If parents perceive net benefits from having children (including the pleasure of raising them), then there is no justification for government action to modify individual fertility behavior." Strictly in terms of economic analysis, how would most development economists rebut this contention?

d. According to standard microeconomic theory, higher income leads to higher demand for everything except inferior goods, *ceteris paribus*. Children are *not* inferior goods. Therefore, the desired number of children should rise with family income. In reality, however, the average number of children *declines* with family income. How do economic models of fertility resolve this apparent inconsistency?

3. This exercise explores the relationship between infant mortality rates, the population age structure, and demographic momentum. Table 7–3 provides a worksheet for tracking demographic conditions in Fecund, a country where quadruplets are common. (A few blanks already are filled in to help you with your calculations.) Here are the facts you need to know. Each person lives one year as a child, one year as a middle-age adult, and one year as a senior citizen. (Think of one year in Fecund as a metaphor for 20 years of real life.) Only working-age adults produce babies. Death strikes down half all newborns shortly after birth, and all senior citizens pass away just before their fourth birthday.

a. Examine the first two lines of Table 7–3. The table assumes that each *pair* of middle-age adults bears four babies. Even so, the population remains stable because the death rate is high: each year, 100 newborns plus 100 seniors die. Be sure you understand how the conditions in 1995 determine the numbers appearing in columns 1 to 5 for 1996.

(i) Fill in columns 1 to 5 for 1997, on the basis of the conditions prevailing in 1996.

(ii) With these initial demographic conditions, what is the population grow rate in 1997 (relative to 1996)?

b. Beginning in 1997, improvements in the primary health care system cause the infant mortality rate to drop from 50 to 20 percent. Fertility remains unchanged: there still are four births per middle-age couple, but now 80 percent of the newborns survive.

(i) Given these conditions, fill in the last two entries for 1997; then fill in columns 1 to 5 for 1998.

(ii) What is the population grow rate in 1998 (relative to 1997)?

(iii) During 1998 the birthrate remains unchanged. So does the infant mortality rate. Fill in the last two entries for 1998, and columns 1 to 5 for 1999.

(iv) What is the population grow rate in 1999 (relative to 1998)?

c. In 1999, fertility in Fecund drops to 2.5 births per middle-age couple. Since one fifth of the newborns do not survive, the new fertility rate produces exactly two surviving children per middle-age couple. Fertility has fallen to the *replacement level* in Fecund.

(i) Does achieving replacement-level fertility stop population growth? To find out, fill in the remaining columns for 1999 and columns 1 to 5 for 2000.

(ii) You should find that the population is still growing at the millennium. Briefly explain how this is so.

d. The World Bank estimates that *even if* fertility rates drop immediately to the replacement level (where each pair of adults rears just two babies), the population in many LDCs would continue to grow for about 50 years. By that time the population would nearly double before stabilizing. In view of the lesson from Fecund, what causes this *demographic momentum* to occur?

Table 7–3

Demographic Worksheet for Fecund, 1995–2000*

Year	Number of children (1)	Number of middle-age adults (2)	Number of older adults (3)	Total population (4)	Rate of pop. growth (%) (5)	Number of births (6)	Number of infant deaths (7)
1995	100	100	100	300	0	200	100
1996	100	100	100	300	0	200	100
1997	___	___	___	___	___	___	___
1998	___	100	___	___	___	___	___
1999	___	___	___	___	16.7	___	___
2000	___	___	___	___	___	___	___

*Columns 1 to 4 refer to population at the beginning of the year, column 5 is the rate of growth over the previous year, and columns 6 and 7 are the number of births and infant deaths *during* the year.

4. Now consider the economic effects of the demographic changes taking place in Fecund, from Exercise 3.

   a. Review the numbers in Table 7–3, with particular attention to the population growth rate and age structure.

      (i) The reduction in infant mortality in 1997 caused Fecund's population growth rate to _____ by _____ percent between 1997 and 1998.

     (ii) The *dependency ratio* is the ratio of non-working-age population (children plus seniors) to working-age population. What was the dependency ratio in Fecund,

              In 1996: _____

              In 1997: _____

              In 1998: _____

   b. Will faster population growth rate and the higher dependency ratio in 1998 tend to *increase* or *decrease* each of the following items? Briefly explain why. (The first four are covered in the Worked Example, whereas the fifth requires some thought.)

      (i) The level of per capita income in 1998.

     (ii) The domestic savings rate in 1998.

    (iii) The education services provided per child in 1998 (which determines human capital, per worker, the following year).

    (iv) The extent of capital deepening in 1999.

     (v) The GNP growth rate in 1999.

   c. The government of Fecund is concerned about adverse economic effects of the demographic changes caused by the drop in infant mortality.

      (i) What *demographic* policies could be implemented to slow down the population growth rate?

     (ii) What *economic* policies could be implemented to slow down the population growth rate?

(iii) Could other economic policies be used to ameliorate the adverse economic effects of population growth?

5. This exercise examines the concept of optimum population. Table 7–4 shows the relationship between the size of a country's labor force (LF) and the level of GNP, given the initial stock of capital and natural resources and the initial level of technology.

Table 7–4

Population and Per Capita Income

Labor force	GNP	Population	Per capita income
10	10,000	_____	_____
20	28,000	_____	_____
30	48,000	_____	_____
40	72,000	_____	_____
50	98,000	_____	_____
60	118,000	_____	_____
70	134,000	_____	_____
80	148,000	_____	_____

a. Assume for simplicity that the labor force equals exactly one half the population (POP). Therefore, POP = LF × 2. Per capita income (PCI) simply equals GNP/POP. Using these two formulas, fill in the values for POP and PCI in the last two columns of Table 7–4.

b. On Figure 7–2, draw in the curve showing the relationship between population size and per capita income. Label this curve *PP*. Label the optimum population as *POP*∗ and label the corresponding level of per capita income as *PCI*∗.

c. Suppose that the actual population size (call it POP⁰) currently is below the optimal population POP∗. Can there be any reason for the government to be concerned about reducing the population growth rate? (Hint: Refer to the Worked Example and Exercise 3d.)

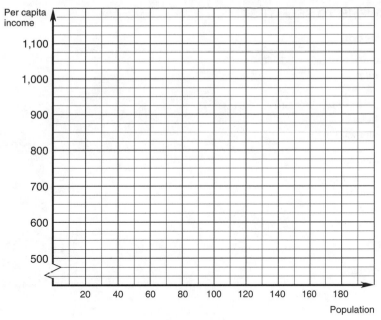

FIGURE 7–2

d. For each of the economic changes listed below, what is the effect (*ceteris paribus*) on optimum POP and optimum PCI? Use the symbol + to designate a positive effect and the symbol – to designate a negative effect.

	Effect on optimum	
Change	POP	PCI
(i) Increase in capital stock	_____	_____
(ii) Increase in labor-force participation rate	_____	_____
(iii) Major natural resource discovery	_____	_____
(iv) Widespread introduction of production robots	_____	_____

ANSWERS TO SELF-TEST

Completion

1. crude birthrate, crude death
2. *total*
3. 28
4. *demographic transition*
5. Indonesia
6. momentum
7. time
8. reduces
9. *demography*
10. Family planning
11. fewer
12. life, human

True-False

1.	F	7.	T
2.	T	8.	F
3.	T	9.	T
4.	T	10.	F
5.	T	11.	T
6.	T	12.	F

Multiple Choice

1.	a	7.	d
2.	b	8.	c
3.	a	9.	a
4.	d	10.	c
5.	d	11	b
6.	c	12.	b

| Labor's Role

OVERVIEW

With a lag of 15 to 20 years, rapid population growth generates rapid labor force growth—adding to existing problems of labor underutilization in developing countries. Labor is underutilized through overt unemployment and disguised unemployment, in which people are occupied with jobs that pay very little and contribute little to the national product. To cope with labor-force growth and to improve real wages broadly, developing countries face a pressing need to expand *productive* employment opportunity. Make-work schemes are not the answer, since labor has a positive opportunity cost. One rarely finds surplus labor, in the sense of zero marginal productivity, even in densely populated low-income countries.

Labor markets in developing countries consist of three segments: a relatively high-wage urban formal sector, with a queue of job seekers; a competitive urban informal sector; and a low-income rural labor market. Wage differentials between the urban and rural labor markets stimulate rural-to-urban migration, though reverse migration and rural-to-rural migration also occur. International migration is important if highly skilled workers depart (the brain drain) or if unskilled workers send home large remittances of income earned abroad.

In most developing countries, modern industry absorbs only a small share of the expanding labor force. The contribution of modern industry is particularly disappointing where factor prices are distorted by protectionism and controls that encourage capital-intensive development. Productive employment opportunities could expand more quickly if countries reduced these factor price distortions and opened their markets to more competition. Other policies to promote more labor-intensive industry include developing more appropriate technologies, eliminating barriers to small-scale industries, seeking investments that *complement* labor productivity, and instituting labor-intensive infrastructure programs such as food for work. Fundamentally, achieving *equitable* growth hinges on more-rapid creation of productive employment.

MAIN LEARNING OBJECTIVES

After studying this chapter, you ought to understand and be able to explain

1. The main characteristic features of the labor force and wage structure in developing countries.

2. The segmentation of labor markets into the formal and informal urban markets and the rural labor market.

3. The problems of defining and measuring labor underutilization in economies where disguised unemployment predominates over visible unemployment.

4. The costs and benefits of reallocating labor to urban jobs and the economic factors that motivate internal migration.

5. Why employment in the industrial sector absorbs only a small fraction of the growing workforce in most developing countries.

6. How government can accelerate employment creation with policies such as correcting factor price distortions, opening markets to competition, and promoting the use of more appropriate technology.

7. The underlying theme that the creation of productive employment is a crucial objective of development policy for achieving equitable growth.

ECONOMIC TOOLS AND TECHNIQUES

From what you have learned in this chapter, you should be able to

1. Use supply-and-demand analysis to analyze the three-tiered structure of developing-country labor markets.

2. Apply the Harris-Todaro model to show how the rate of rural-to-urban migration is determined by conditions in the rural and urban labor markets.

3. Analyze the factors that determine ΔE_i, the annual growth of industrial-sector employment as a percentage of the labor force.

4. Use the elasticity of substitution and isoquant analysis to evaluate the extent to which factor price distortions affect employment.

KEY TERMS AND CONCEPTS

appropriate technology
brain drain
capital-intensive and labor-intensive
   technologies
costs of urbanization
efficiency wage theory
elasticity of substitution
elasticity optimists and pessimists
expected urban wage
factor proportions
food-for-work programs
Harris-Todaro model

indirect and secondary job creation
labor force
opportunity cost of labor
price incentive school, technologist
   school, radical reform school
rural-urban migration
small-scale industry
unemployment, disguised
   unemployment, underemployment
urban formal sector, urban informal
   sector, rural labor market
wage-rental ratio

SELF-TEST

Completion

1. In most low-income countries more than 60 percent of the labor force works in the _____ sector of the economy.

2. The urban _____ sector in most low-income countries nearly always has a queue of workers looking for jobs at wages above the market clearing level.

3. _____ unemployment consists of workers who are employed, but in jobs of low productivity and pay.

4. _____ unemployment includes people who are not in the _____ _____ because they have no expectation of finding a job (discouraged workers).

5. The elasticity of substitution shows the percentage change in the _____-_____ ratio resulting from a given percentage change in the _____-_____ ratio.

6. An elasticity pessimist believes that the elasticity of substitution is very _____.

7. For many low-income countries, international migration of _____ labor has a low opportunity cost and generates benefits in the form of remittances and training.

8. The emigration of highly educated, skilled workers from developing countries is often referred to as the _____ _____.

9. An increase in the wage-rental ratio causes labor intensity in industry to _____.

10. The social cost of a development project includes the loss of what workers could produce in their next best alternative use; this is called the _____ _____ of labor.

11. Acceleration of a country's _____ growth rate causes the labor-force growth rate to accelerate 15 to 20 years later.

12. If the daily wage for unskilled urban labor is 40 rupees and the probability of finding work is 80 percent, then the *expected* urban wage is _____ rupees.

True-False

If false, you should be able to explain why.

_____ 1. Wage differentials across skill and education levels are generally wider in low-income countries than in developed countries.

_____ 2. By the definition of *unemployment*, all those with jobs in the urban informal sector are counted as unemployed.

_____ 3. Underutilized labor represents a pool of resources that can be put to work on development projects at virtually zero cost to the economy.

_____ 4. A consensus has emerged that the marginal product of labor in developing-country agriculture is nearly always zero in densely populated, low-income countries.

_____ 5. Minimum-wage policies generally benefit those with modern-sector jobs while hurting the much larger group of workers in the informal sector.

_____ 6. Domestic producers are more likely to use inappropriate, capital-intensive factor proportions when insulated from import competition by trade barriers.

_____ 7. If the elasticity of substitution is very low, then factor price distortions have a large adverse effect on labor intensity.

_____ 8. Simulation studies have revealed that the redistribution of income to the poor can create many jobs as a result of changes that take place in demand patterns.

_____ 9. Irrigation infrastructure is one example of investment that may complement labor, rather than substitute for it.

_____ 10. Economists generally agree that creating appropriate technologies and using appropriate factor proportions requires a political and social revolution.

_____ 11. The main lesson from the case study of Jakarta, Indonesia, is that urban informal-sector activities represent an enormous waste of human resources.

_____ 12. Since the 1980s, labor-force growth has begun to slow down in Asia and Latin America but not in Africa.

Multiple Choice

1. It has been observed that unemployment is a "luxury" in poor countries. This remark refers to the fact that
   a. many people in poor countries prefer not to work.
   b. only the relatively well-off can afford to be without work for an extended period while searching for a job.
   c. high-paying jobs are more difficult to find than low-paying jobs.
   d. for poor people a period of unemployment is a relief from working long hours at strenuous jobs.

2. Which of the following remarks about voluntary internal migration in developing countries is correct?
   a. Migration from urban areas back to rural areas is virtually nonexistent.
   b. Migrants generally end up being worse off in the city than they would have been in the rural area.
   c. Economic factors have little effect on migration decisions.
   d. Where large wage distortions and congestion effects are present, the social costs of migration can exceed the social benefits.

3. "Inappropriate" technology is commonly characterized by all the following conditions *except*
   a. excessive labor intensity.
   b. large-scale production operations.
   c. need for technical skills that are very scarce in low-income countries.
   d. products that are not designed for developing-country market conditions.

4. Of the two isoquants in the accompanying figure, isoquant A is the one that has the _____ elasticity of substitution, which means that factor proportions are _____ responsive to changes in the wage-rental ratio.
   a. higher, more
   b. lower, more
   c. higher, less
   d. lower, less

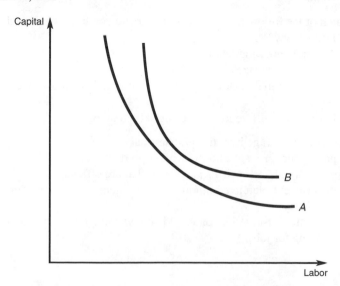

5. Which of the following policies discourages the use of more labor-intensive production technologies?
    a. Protecting domestic industry from import competition.
    b. Holding minimum wages above the market-clearing level.
    c. Lowering interest rates on bank loans.
    d. All the above.

6. If unskilled workers perceive a 10 percent chance of obtaining an urban job paying 20 shillings per day when the rural wage is 5 shillings per day, the Harris-Todaro model would predict
    a. rural-to-urban migration of workers.
    b. no internal migration; this is an equilibrium.
    c. urban-to-rural migration of discouraged urban workers.
    d. none of the above; additional information is needed.

7. As an empirical average, when value added in the industrial sector of a low-income country increases by 10 percent, industrial employment increases by about _____
    a. 16 percent.   c. 0.6 percent.
    b. 6 percent.   d. 60 percent.

8. Which of the following countries has achieved rapid growth of industrial employment through rapid expansion of labor-intensive industrial exports?
    a. Republic of Korea.   c. Nigeria.
    b. Pakistan.   d. Venezuela.

9. In the debate about employment creation, the technologist school claims that developing-country governments should
    a. simply "get prices right" to solve the problem of inappropriate technologies.
    b. protect domestic producers from high-technology import competition.
    c. seek out the most modern technologies in order to create high-productivity jobs.
    d. invest directly in research and development of more appropriate technologies.

10. Which of the following is *not* a characteristic condition of most developing countries today?
    a. A rapidly growing labor force.
    b. Low average wages and productivity levels.
    c. Urban informal-sector wages that are well below rural wages in real terms.
    d. Large wage differentials favoring skilled labor.

11. The efficiency wage hypothesis states that
    a. paying higher wages boosts worker productivity.
    b. only formal-sector firms pay wages that are efficient.
    c. government-mandated minimum wages generally enhance industrial efficiency.
    d. wages for unskilled labor should be low enough to eliminate inefficient queuing for jobs.

12. Industrial development leads to secondary job creation in developing countries because
    a. industry requires office workers as well as production-line workers.
    b. workers employed in high-paying industrial jobs spend their incomes on consumer goods and services.
    c. most industrial workers are paid so little that they must work second jobs.
    d. workers consider obligations at home to be their primary responsibility.

APPLICATIONS

Worked Example: Factor Prices and Labor Intensity

Urban formal sector employees in Dynamique are paid the legal minimum wage of $w = \$60$ per month. The cost of capital services is $r = \$40$ per month. This cost of capital depends on the purchase price of capital goods, the finance costs, and tax rates. Given these factor prices, the wage-rental rate is $w/r = \$60/\$40 = 1.5$. Knowing the factor prices, one can identify the various combinations of labor (L) and capital (K) that exhaust any given budget (B). For example, with $B = \$900$ a firm can purchase any combination of K and L satisfying the equation $900 = 40K + 60L$. For any given level of B, one can draw a budget line in Figure 8–1. All such lines have a slope equal to $-w/r$. In the present case, the slope equals -1.5; because $6K$ can be traded for $4L$ (or vice versa) at the prevailing factor prices.

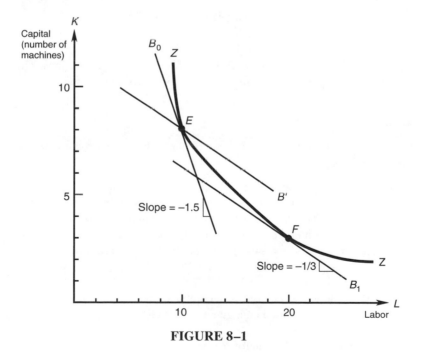

FIGURE 8–1

A Dynamiquan zipper producer is considering investing in a new factory to produce 1,000 boxes of zippers per month. Isoquant ZZ in Figure 8–1 shows the alternative combinations of K and L that can be used to produce this output. The least-cost production method of production is indicated by the point on ZZ that lies on the lowest possible budget line, in this case B_0. The firm chooses point E, at which 1,000 boxes of zippers are produced with eight machines and ten workers, for a monthly cost of $B = \$920$. The factory will operate with a capital-labor ratio of $K/L = 8/10 = 0.8$.

Subsequently, the government of Dynamique becomes concerned about the need to create more jobs for the growing labor force. The government decides to reduce the minimum wage to $w = \$50$ and to eliminate capital subsidies; this raises the firm's cost of capital to $r = \$150$. Now the wage-rental ratio is $w/r = 50/150 = 1/3$. With these factor prices, the budget line through point E will now has a slop of $-1/3$, as shown by line B'. Obviously, point E no longer minimizes production costs. Instead point F, which is tangent to budget line B_1, is the least-cost production technique. The same output of zippers will now be produced using $K = 3$ and $L = 20$; the firm's capital-labor ratio is $K/L = 3/20 = 0.15$. Reducing factor price distortions has resulted in more jobs per unit of capital, and more jobs per box of zippers produced.

The policy reform reduced the wage-rental ratio from 1.5 to 0.33. This represents a 78 percent decline, since $(0.33/1.5) - 1 = -0.78$. As a result, the capital-labor ratio dropped from 0.8 to 0.15. This is a decline of 81.25 percent, since $(0.15/0.80) - 1 = -0.8125 = -81.25$ percent. The elasticity of substitution in Dynamique's zipper industry therefore is

$$\sigma = \frac{\text{percentage change in } K/L}{\text{percentage change in } w/r} = \frac{-81.25}{-78} = 1.04.$$

The elasticity pessimists in the Ministry of Industries lose their jobs. They are replaced by elasticity optimists from the University of Dynamique.

Exercises

1. Now it is your turn to examine the effect of relative factor prices on factor proportions.

   a. In Figure 8–2, isoquant SS shows alternative combinations of capital and labor that can be used to produce 100,000 polyester shirts per month in Travail, a country with an abundance of labor. The wage rate in Travail's modern sector is $w = \$400$ per month (per worker), and the cost of capital is $r = \$400$ per month (per unit of capital).
      (i) The wage-rental ratio is $w/r =$ _____.

      (ii) Each budget line showing combinations of labor and capital that can be purchased on a given budget (B) will have a slope = _____.

      (iii) Draw a budget line for $B = \$40,000$ in Figure 8–2 and label it B_0. (Hint: Given the prevailing factor prices, B_0 must go through the point $K = 100, L = 0$.)

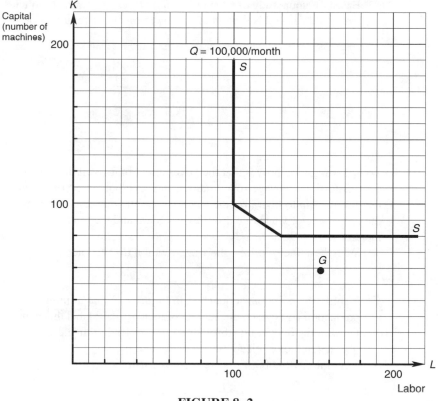

FIGURE 8–2

b. At the prevailing wage-rental ratio, a whole family of lines parallel to B_0 can be drawn—one for each possible budget sum. Taking this into account

   (i) Identify the *minimum cost point* on isoquant *SS* in Figure 8–2; label it point *X*.

   (ii) Draw in the appropriate budget line through point *X*, and label it B_X. (Hint: B_X is parallel to B_0, and it just touches *SS*.)

   (iii) At point *X*, *L* = _____ workers are employed and *K* = _____ units of capital are used to produce 100,000 polyester shirts.

   (iv) At point *X*, the capital-labor ratio used to produce polyester shirts is $K/L =$ _____.

c. You are hired by the government of Travail to explore policy changes that might increase labor intensity in the industrial sector. Immediately your thoughts turn to factor price distortions.

   (i) You know that industrial production tends to be excessively capital intensive if existing policies cause the wage-rental ratio to be too

   _____.

(ii) Based on your study of Chapter 8, name *three* government policies that could cause this kind of distortion in the wage-rental ratio.

d. Your investigation proves that the government of Travail indeed has been distorting the wage-rental ratio, using such policies. You convince the government to liberalize the labor and capital markets. As a result the formal-sector wage rate drops to $w = \$300$ and the rental rate increases to $r = \$600$.

   (i) With these factor prices, the wage-rental ratio becomes

$$w/r = \underline{\hspace{1cm}}.$$

   (ii) Identify the point on isoquant SS in Figure 8–2 that minimizes production costs given the new set of factor prices; label this point Y.

   (iii) Draw in the budget line through point Y reflecting the new, liberalized factor price ratio; label the line B_Y.

   (iv) At point Y, 100,000 shirts are produced using

$$L = \underline{\hspace{1cm}},$$

$$K = \underline{\hspace{1cm}},$$

$$K/L = \underline{\hspace{1cm}}.$$

e. Compare the situation before liberalization of the factor markets ($w = \$400$ and $r = \$400$) with the outcome after liberalization (pard d).

   (i) As a result of the policy change, the wage-rental ratio declined by \underline{\hspace{1cm}}percent.

   (ii) The capital-labor ratio declined by \underline{\hspace{1cm}}percent.

   (iii) The observed elasticity of substitution is $\sigma = \underline{\hspace{1cm}}$.

   (iv) The same output is produced using \underline{\hspace{1cm}} percent less capital and \underline{\hspace{1cm}} percent more labor.

   Take a moment to reflect on the lesson: Polyester shirt producers in Travail respond to the reform of relative factor prices by altering production methods, increasing labor intensity, and creating jobs.

2. Factor prices influence not just factor proportions in a particular industry, but also the mix of goods produced, as well as the nature of induced technical change. This exercise explores these broader repercussions. (Note: it is important that you complete Exercise 1 first.)

a. Factor prices affect production costs. Look back at your analysis of polyester shirt production in Exercise 1.

(i) When factor prices were $w = \$400$ and $r = \$400$ in Travail, you found that 100,000 polyester shirts would be produced using $L = \underline{\hspace{1cm}}$ workers and $K = \underline{\hspace{1cm}}$ units of capital (point X in Figure 8–2).

(ii) Under these conditions the factor cost for producing 100,000 polyester shirts was $C_P = \$\underline{\hspace{1cm}}$. (Hint: $wL + rK$.)

(iii) After factor prices changed to $w = \$300$ and $r = \$600$, you found that the same output would be produced using $L = \underline{\hspace{1cm}}$ and $K = \underline{\hspace{1cm}}$ (your point Y in Figure 8–2).

(iv) At these new factor prices, the factor cost for producing 100,000 polyester shirts became $C'_P = \$\underline{\hspace{1cm}}$.

(v) Hence, the factor price reforms led to a $\underline{\hspace{1cm}}$ in factor costs for polyester shirt producers.

b. Polyester, though, is not the only shirt material around. There is competition from *cotton* shirts. For simplicity, assume that the cotton shirt industry is characterized by fixed factor proportions: The isoquants are L-shaped and the elasticity of substitution is zero. To be specific, each lot of 100,000 cotton shirts requires $50K$ and $150L$.

(i) The capital-labor ratio in cotton shirt production is fixed at $K/L = \underline{\hspace{1cm}}$.

(ii) When factor prices were held at $w = \$400$ and $r = \$400$, the factor cost per 100,000 cotton shirts amounted to $C_c = \$\underline{\hspace{1cm}}$.

(iii) After factor prices changed to $w = \$300$ and $r = \$600$, the factor cost per 100,000 cotton shirts became $C'_c = \$\underline{\hspace{1cm}}$.

(iv) For *cotton* shirt producers, the liberalization of factor prices led to a $\underline{\hspace{1cm}}$ in factor costs per shirt.

c. (i) Which type of shirt (polyester or cotton) is produced using the more *labor*-intensive process? $\underline{\hspace{1cm}}$ shirts.

(ii) Which shirt producers benefit from lower production costs when the wage-rental ratio declines due to liberalization of the factor markets in Travail? $\underline{\hspace{1cm}}$ shirts.

      (iii) Retail market prices for the two kinds of shirts reflect the respective factor costs. Therefore, liberalization of factor prices causes the retail price of _____ shirts to decline, relative to the price of _____ shirts. (Note: The mechanism is that the supply curves shift when the production costs change.)

      (iv) This change in relative prices will cause sales of cotton shirts to _____; meanwhile, sales of polyester shirts will _____.

      (v) How will these adjustments in the pattern of sales in the product market affect employment in the shirt industry? Explain briefly.

d. You should have reached the conclusion that polyester shirt producers who use capital-intensive methods see their market share fall after liberalization of factor prices in Travail. The story does not end there. Competitive pressures provide the polyester trade association with a strong incentive to develop new production techniques that are more labor intensive.

      (i) The industry's research leads to the development of point G in Figure 8–2 as a feasible process for producing 100,000 polyester shirts per month. Point G has a low capital-labor ratio. At postreform factor prices, is point G more profitable than point Y for producing polyester shirts? Explain.

      (ii) For polyester shirt production in Travail, which is the more appropriate technology: point Y or point G? Explain. (Assume that the post-reform factor prices properly reflect the opportunity costs of labor and capital.)

    The Worked Example in Exercise 1 show how relative factor prices can influence the mix of labor and capital used to produce a particular product. Exercise 2 demonstrates that liberalizing factor prices also can induce substitutions by consumers in favor of labor-intensive products. All these effects stimulate more rapid employment creation.

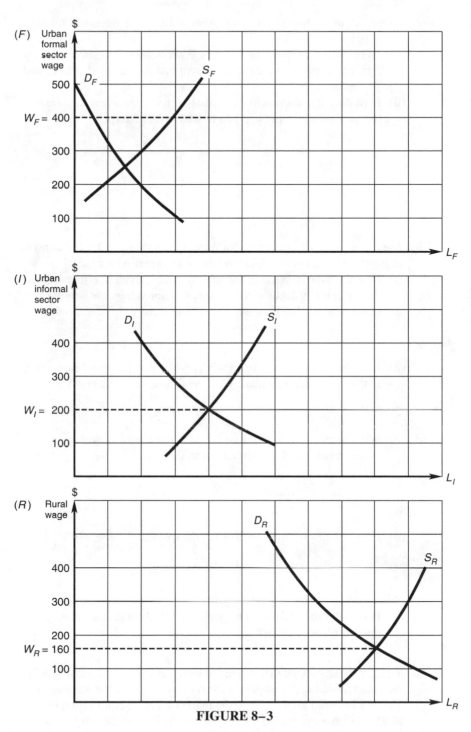

FIGURE 8–3

3. Now let's use supply-and-demand analysis to trace the impact of Travail's liberalization policies (from Exercises 1 and 2) on the country's labor markets. The three panels in Figure 8–3 show initial conditions in each of the three labor markets—the urban formal market (F), the urban informal market (I), and the rural market (R). Prior to the reforms, the minimum wage in the urban formal sector was $w_F = \$400$.

a. As a result of the liberalization program, the wage in the urban formal sector falls to $w_F' = \$300$.

   (i) Draw a line in panel F of Figure 8–3 showing this postreform wage rate. Label the quantities of labor supplied and demanded as L_s' and L_d', respectively.

   (ii) How does this decline in the formal-sector wage affect the size of the queue for jobs in the urban formal market? Explain.

b. The queue of people searching for formal-sector jobs in Travail consists of people who are meanwhile working at informal-sector jobs.

   (i) How does the increase in formal-sector employment affect the supply curve of labor in the *informal* sector? Draw the new supply curve in panel I of Figure 8–3 and label it S_I'.

   (ii) How does this shift in the supply curve affect the equilibrium wage in the urban informal market? In the figure, label the new wage W_I'.

c. (i) Will the changes that have occurred in the urban labor markets induce *migration* from rural areas to the cities? Explain.

   (ii) How would such migration affect the two urban labor markets?

   (iii) How will this rural-urban migration affect the equilibrium wage in the *rural* labor market?

d. You may have noticed that, when the government liberalized wages in the urban formal sector as part of the reform program, the wage in this sector did not fall all the way to the market-clearing equilibrium of $260. Yet labor unions are not very strong in Travail. So why would employers chose to pay more than the market equilibrium wage?

This exercise shows that the policy reforms directly effected just the urban formal sector, but the favorable adjustments spread through all three segments of the labor market.

4. This exercise applies the analysis of industrial employment growth, using Equation 8–5 from the textbook.

   a. The Republic of Kita in 1996 has a labor force of 1,000 workers, of whom 150 work in the industrial sector. Because industrial policy favors growth of capital-intensive activities, on average a 10 percent increase in industrial value added brings about only 4 percent growth in industrial employment on average.

      (i) This means that the elasticity of industrial employment with respect to value added in industry equals _____. Call this the *employment elasticity*, for short.

      (ii) Value added in the industrial sector is expected to increase by 15 percent in 1997. If so, then employment in the industrial sector will increase by _____ percent.

   b. The minister of industries is pleased to hear how quickly industrial employment will be growing. She remarks, "Since the labor force is growing only 2 percent per year, industrial-sector growth should take care of the employment problem in Kita."

      (i) She is wrong. In fact, only _____ new jobs will be opening up in the industrial sector in 1997, while the labor force will grow by _____ workers.

      (ii) Using Equation 8–5 from the text, 1997 industrial employment growth in Kita can be analyzed as follows:

      η = _____ (the employment elasticity).

      $g(V_i)$ = _____ % (growth of industrial value added).

      S_i = _____ (industrial employment share of total employment, in *decimal* units).

      (iii) So employment growth in industry, as a percentage of the initial labor force, will be only

      $$\Delta E_i = \underline{\hspace{2cm}}\%.$$

      Evidently, industrial job creation amounts to less than 1 percent of the labor force.

      (iv) Only _____ percent of the *additional* workers entering the labor force in 1997 will be able to find jobs in industry. More than half the new workers will have to find jobs elsewhere.

   c. (i) Given S_i and η, value added in the industrial sector would have to grow how fast to provide jobs for all 20 new members of the labor force in 1997?

      $$g(V_i) = \underline{\hspace{2cm}}\%.$$

    (ii) Alternatively, taking S_i and $g(V_i)$ as given, the industrial sector could provide jobs for all 20 new members of the labor force in 1997 if the employment elasticity is

$$\eta = \underline{\hspace{2cm}}.$$

    (Hint: Find the value of n such that $\Delta E_i = 2$ percent.)

    (iii) What policies could the government of Kita use to raise the employment elasticity and thereby promote more-rapid job creation in industry?

d. The neighboring Republic of Chikita is identical to Kita in all respects except that 35 percent of the labor force already is employed in industry by 1996. Chikita has 1,000 workers. The labor force is growing by 2 percent per year. Industrial value added is expected to grow by 15 percent in 1997. And the industrial employment elasticity is the same as the one you calculated for Kita.

    (i) Under these conditions, calculate the employment growth in Chikita's industrial sector, as a percentage of the country's initial labor force.

$$\Delta E_i = \underline{\hspace{2cm}}\%.$$

    (ii) The growth of the industrial sector in Chikita will create _____ new jobs, which are more than enough to cover all the new entrants to the labor force in 1997.

    (iii) Chikita is identical to Kita in most respects. How come the number of jobs created in the industrial sector exceeds the number of entrants to the labor force in Chikita. but not in Kita Explain.

e. How is your analysis of Kita's 1997 employment problem affected when you take into account *indirect and secondary* job creation resulting from the growth of the industrial sector?

5. In this exercise you will analyze internal migration using the Harris-Todaro model.

   a. In Samudra the urban wage is fixed by the government at Rp1,500 per day (Rp stands for rupiahs). Rural workers earn Rp1,000 per day (so the opportunity cost of rural labor equals Rp1,000). The Harris-Todaro model predicts that rural-urban migration takes place as long as the *probability* of finding an urban job is greater than _____. (Give a numerical answer.)

   b. There are 165 urban workers competing for 150 urban-sector jobs in Samudra.

     (i) Using Equation 8–3 from the textbook, the probability of finding an urban job is

$$p = \text{_____}.$$

     (ii) The *expected* urban wage is thus

$$w_u^* - \text{_____} \text{ rupiah.}$$

     (iii) The response rate of potential migrants is $h = 0.1$ (see textbook Equation 8–4). Given the rural wage and the expected urban wage, how many people will migrate to the urban area to search for jobs each year?

$$M = \text{_____} \text{ migrants.}$$

     (Round your answer to the nearest whole person.)

   c. Let's look at a variation of the textbook model. Suppose that the initial 165 urban workers fall into two groups: 150 workers already have jobs that they intend to keep and 15 workers are unemployed and looking for jobs. In this context the probability of finding an urban job should be defined as

     p = (number of new jobs opening up)/(number unemployed).

     (i) If nine new urban jobs open up, then the probability of a job seeker finding a job is

$$p = \text{_____}.$$

   (ii) In this case the *expected* urban wage is

$$w_u^* = \underline{\hspace{2cm}} \text{ rupiah.}$$

   (iii) What pattern of migration would be induced by these labor market conditions?

ANSWERS TO SELF-TEST

Completion

1. agricultural
2. formal
3. Disguised
4. Invisible, labor force
5. capital-labor, wage-rental
6. low
7. unskilled
8. *brain drain*
9. decline
10. *opportunity cost*
11. population
12. 32

True-False

1.	T	7.	F
2.	F	8.	F
3.	F	9.	T
4.	F	10.	F
5.	T	11.	F
6.	T	12.	T

Multiple Choice

1.	b	7.	b
2.	d	8.	a
3.	a	9.	d
4.	a	10.	c
5.	d	11.	a
6.	c	12.	b

| Education

OVERVIEW

This chapter on education and the following chapter on health examine *investment in human capital*, which is investment to improve labor productivity and earnings. The relationship between economic development and investment in human capital is mutually supportive: an expanding economy can afford to devote more resources to human capital investment, while human capital investment contributes to economic growth and development. Indeed, education itself is a growth industry. In general, there is a strong empirical correlation between income and education, for both individuals and countries.

Developing countries have accorded a high priority to investing in education. Government intervention is easily justified since education yields important economic and social external benefits. Therefore, relying solely on market forces would underallocate resources to these investments. Throughout the world, great progress has been made in expanding educational opportunities, particularly for primary school. Rapid growth of primary enrollments has created other problems, though, such as teacher shortages, high dropout and repeat rates due to economic necessity, educational inequalities, and "educated unemployment."

As with any investments, criteria are needed to decide on the volume and pattern of investment in education. Chapter 9 explains how formal tools like manpower planning and cost-benefit analysis can be used to evaluate education investments. Neither tool, however, provides mechanical solutions to determine policy choices. Yet economic analysis can lead to better-informed decisions about the allocation of resources to education. For example, studies generally find that investment in primary education produces the highest returns in low-income countries. Economic analysis also reveals that private returns to schooling often exceed social returns because of large subsidies to education; therefore, popular demand is not necessarily a sign of high social returns.

The chapter concludes with a survey of critiques and reform proposals for education policy in developing countries. These include the radical critique of education as a process for bolstering class structures and the market-based critique favoring decentralization and vouchers, as well as reformist proposals that emphasize vocational and nonformal education.

MAIN LEARNING OBJECTIVES

After studying this chapter, you ought to understand and be able to explain

1. The concept of investment in human capital and its contribution to growth.

2. Why governments in developing countries have accorded high priority to investment in education.

3. The main trends and characteristics of education in developing countries.

4. The uses and limitations of manpower planning as a tool for determining the education investment requirements.

5. The uses and limitations of cost-benefit analysis for educational planning.

6. How the private rate of return can diverge from the social rate of return to education and the implications of this divergence for education policy.

7. The range of critiques and proposals for reforming education policy in developing countries.

ECONOMIC TOOLS AND TECHNIQUES

From what you have learned in this chapter, you should be able to

1. Apply cost-benefit analysis to calculate private and social rates of return to investment in education.

2. Explain how the Tinbergen-Parnes manpower-planning methodology has been used to determine educational investment requirements.

KEY TERMS AND CONCEPTS

cost-benefit analysis
discounting present value
dropouts and repeaters
educational deepening
educational vouchers
explicit and implicit costs of education
formal, nonformal, and informal
   education

internal rate of return
investment in human capital
lifetime earnings curves
manpower planning
social versus private rate of return
unemployment among the educated
vocational schools

SELF-TEST

Completion

1. The use of scarce resources to improve the productivity of human beings is called investment in _____ _____.

2. Organized learning programs that take place outside of schools can be called _____ *education*.

3. When benefits are measured by before-tax earnings, the _____ rate of return to education necessarily exceeds the _____ rate of return.

4. Over time, people with more schooling fill jobs that were previously filled by people with less schooling. This process is termed *educational* _____.

5. Empirical studies show that the highest social rates of return in low-income countries are earned on _____ education.

6. Some countries where school enrollments expanded rapidly have experienced severe problems of _____ among educated people.

7. A common proposal for reforming developing-country educational systems is to promote _____ schools that emphasize practical skills.

8. In many low-income countries, enrollment ratios for _____ education are still below 3 percent.

9. Learning that takes place outside any institutional framework or organized program is called _____ *education*.

10. Rapid expansion of school systems often creates _____ shortages, which leads to very large class sizes.

11. The heart of the _____-_____ approach to education policy is estimating impending gaps between the demand and supply for workers with specific educational qualifications.

12. When large numbers of people base their demand for education on current earnings differentials, they may find that the return to education is _____ than expected.

True-False

If false, you should be able to explain why.

_____ 1. Age-earnings studies confirm that individual earnings are positively correlated with years of schooling in developing countries.

_____ 2. Most low-income countries had achieved adult illiteracy rates below 25 percent by 1990.

_____ 3. Empirical studies in developing countries consistently show that the rate of return on investment in education is lower than the rate of return on investments in physical capital.

_____ 4. In most developing countries, central governments allocate between 10 percent and 15 percent of their budget to education.

_____ 5. Until the 1980s, primary school enrollments expanded slowly in most developing countries because policy makers were not aware of the importance of human capital investment.

_____ 6. Education specialists generally agree that manpower planning techniques should be used more widely to determine educational investment requirements in developing countries.

_____ 7. The case study of Indonesia illustrates that expanding primary education to the rural masses is a very slow process in low-income countries.

_____ 8. Most of the countries that emerged from colonialism after World War II started off with poor primary education systems.

_____ 9. Standardized arithmetic, science, and reading tests show that fourth and eighth graders in most low-income countries score as well as students in middle-income countries.

_____ 10. In applying cost-benefit analysis, one takes into account all the explicit costs but not the implicit costs of education.

_____ 11. Where education is heavily subsidized, investments in education can yield high private rates of return even though the social rate of return is low.

_____ 12. Technical tools like manpower planning and cost-benefit analysis play a large practical role in educational planning in most developing countries.

Multiple Choice

1. Public expenditure on education in developing countries typically accounts for _____ percent of GNP.
   a. 3 to 6   c. less than 1
   b. 8 to 10   d. 20 to 30

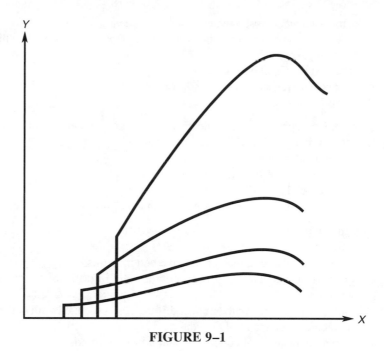

FIGURE 9–1

2. The axes in Figure 9–1 are labeled as X and Y. The corresponding variable names are
   a. X = years of schooling and Y = age.
   b. X = years of schooling and Y = earnings.
   c. X = earnings and Y = age.
   d. X = age and Y = earnings.

3. The discount rate that equates the discounted present value of net benefit to zero is called the
   a. opportunity cost of capital.
   b. social rate of return.
   c. private rate of return.
   d. internal rate of return.

4. To determine education requirements using the manpower planning methodology, the first step is to
   a. estimate the target growth rate of GNP for the planning period.
   b. conduct a sample survey of education plans at the household level.
   c. evaluate the social and economic rates of return to different forms of education.
   d. find out how many school graduates are unemployed.

5. Lifetime earnings curves for developing countries generally show all but one of the following results. Which one is the exception?
   a. People with more schooling achieve higher earnings.
   b. The earnings curve rises more steeply for people with more schooling.
   c. The earnings curve reaches a peak at a younger age for people with more schooling.
   d. People with more schooling begin earning at a later age.

6. Which is an *implicit* cost of education for a student's family?
   a. The earnings or productive household work that is foregone when the student attends school.
   b. The cost of school books.
   c. The cost of transportation to and from school.
   d. All of the above.

7. From the standpoint of economic efficiency, a government should expand investment in those forms of education that
   a. are in greatest demand.
   b. lead to increased productivity and earnings.
   c. have a social rate of return greater than zero.
   d. have a social rate of return greater than the opportunity cost of capital.

8. Which is *not* a valid criticism of using cost-benefit analysis to evaluate investment in education?
   a. Manpower-planning techniques give better results.
   b. Data on current earnings do not provide valid information on future earnings.
   c. One cannot assume that earnings differences associated with education are actually the result of the education.
   d. Important benefits of education cannot be quantified.

9. According to the textbook, a child who fails to complete at least _____ years of education gains little from attending school.
   a. 2   c. 5 or 6
   b. 12   d. 8

10. Textbook Table 9–3 shows that secondary and tertiary enrollment ratios declined between 1980 and 1990 for which major group of developing countries?
    a. Latin America and the Caribbean.
    b. Severely indebted countries.
    c. All developing countries.
    d. None.

11. The case study on educational policy in Kenya and Tanzania illustrates the point that
    a. manpower planning is deeply flawed as a basis for educational policy.
    b. the public demand for secondary schooling proved to be quite limited in low-income African countries.
    c. vocational schools are more productive than standard secondary schools.
    d. all the above.

12. Experience with vocational schools in developing countries is summarized best by which statement?
    a. The merits of vocational education are largely untested.
    b. Many vocational schools make valuable contributions, but many others have failed.
    c. Experiments with vocational education have generally failed.
    d. The private rate of return on vocational education is high, but the social rate of return is low.

APPLICATIONS

Worked Example: Private versus Social Rates of Return

To evaluate the rate of return to education, one must calculate the discounted present value of lifetime earnings. To simplify this cumbersome task, let us assume that people live for only two "years": youth (year 1) and adulthood (year 2). Youths either go to school or work. If they go to school then they earn zero, but if they work they earn $1,000. As adults, everyone works. An educated adult earns $3,500, while an uneducated adult earns only $2,000. Individuals therefore choose between two alternative lifetime earnings profiles:

	Earnings ($)	
	Year 1	Year 2
A. Earnings profile: No school	$1,000	$2,000
B. Earnings profile: With school	0	3,500
C. Earnings gain from schooling	−1,000	+1,500

The benefit of going to school is the present discounted value of the earnings stream so generated. Note that the relevant figure consists of *incremental* earnings that accrue from going to school. In year 2, this amounts to $1,500. In year 1 the earnings "gain" is actually −$1,000. The foregone earnings in year 1 can be treated as an implicit cost, or it can be incorporated in the calculation of the earnings gain from schooling as a negative gain. The overall result is the same either way. Here, we use the latter approach in order to be consistent in defining the benefit each year as incremental earnings.

To avoid ambiguity and simplify the calculation, let earnings be paid at the beginning of each year; thus, earnings for year 1 do not need to be discounted, while earnings for year 2 are discounted by a factor of $(1 + r)$. The present discounted value of the benefits of schooling is

$$V = -1,000 + \frac{1,500}{1+r},$$

where r is an appropriate discount rate, in decimal units. For example, if $r = 0.10$, then

$$V = -1,000 + \frac{1,500}{1.10} = \$364.$$

Now what about costs of schooling? There are both *implicit* and *explicit* costs to consider. The implicit cost consists of the earnings foregone by going to school instead of working. This *opportunity cost* was taken into account above. As for the explicit cost, we will assume that the cost of providing schooling is $400 per student per year and that the government provides a subsidy to cover this full amount. Under these conditions the net benefit of schooling, as far as the individual is concerned, is V as defined above.

The private *rate of return* is defined as the discount rate for which the present value of net benefits equals zero. This is the effective yield earned on the investment in education. It is not hard to see that the private rate of return in this case is 50 percent. You "invest" $1,000 (in foregone earnings) to get back

$1,500 a year later. In terms of the mathematics, $V = 0$ can be solved to find $r = 0.5 = 50$ percent.

To calculate the *social* rate of return, all the costs must be taken into account, whether borne by the individual or by the government. Factoring in the explicit cost of $400, the net social benefit in year 1 equals –$1,400. For year 2, the net social benefit is +$1,500, representing the *extra* national product generated by the investment in education. To calculate the social rate of return, one finds the value of r such that:

$$V = -1,000 + \frac{1,500}{1 + r} = 0.$$

Looking at the *social* costs and benefits, an investment of $1,400 pays off $1,500 the following year. Solving the equation gives $r = 0.0714 = 7.14$ percent. This is the social rate of return. Since the social rate of return is only 7.14 percent, there are probably alternative investments that would be more productive than education in this case. Yet because of the subsidies, the private rate of return is 50 percent. Hence, the demand for education is likely to be very strong, despite the low social rate of return.

Exercises

1. It is your turn to calculate private and social rates of return on education. In Baccalauria, primary school is compulsory; further education is not. For simplicity, assume that people live for four "years": a year in primary school (age 1), a year when they could be going to secondary school (age 2), a year when they could be in college (age 3), and a year where everyone is in the labor force (age 4). Each Baccalaurian chooses one of three alternative lifetime earnings options, summarized in Table 9–1.

Table 9–1

Lifetime Earnings Options (Baccalaurian $)

		Earnings at			
Options		Age 1	Age 2	Age 3	Age 4
A. Primary school only	→	0	800	1,000	1,200
B. Secondary school	→	0	0	1,500	2,000
C. College	→	0	0	0	5,000

a. In Figure 9–2 draw the three lifetime earnings curves corresponding to the three options shown in the Table. Label the three curves A, B, and C, respectively.

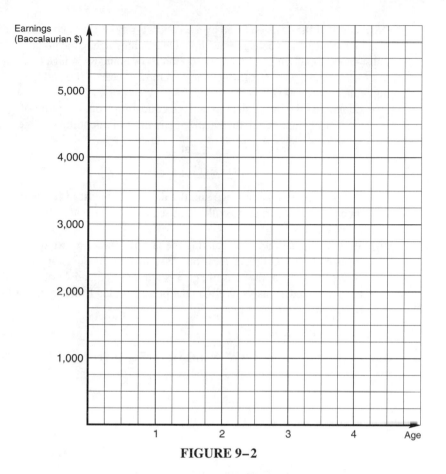

FIGURE 9–2

b. Consider the choice of whether or not to attend secondary school.
   (i) What are the *incremental* earnings one can expect from attending secondary school, compared to joining the labor market straight out of primary school?

   Incremental earnings at age 2 = $_____.

   Incremental earnings at age 3 = $_____.

   Incremental earnings at age 4 = $_____.

   (ii) Would someone with a very high discount rate, say 40 percent, choose to go to secondary school? Explain. (Note that a high discount rate is characteristic of people in dire poverty, for whom deferment of income is very costly.)

c. Now consider the decision faced by a secondary-school graduate about whether to invest in a college education. On reaching age 3, the graduate must choose between going to work (option *B*) or going to college (option *C*). College costs $1,000, of which the government bears $500 and the individual pays $500.

(i) Looking at the investment in college education from the point of view of the individual, the *net private* benefit of attending college is

$$\$\underline{\hspace{1.5cm}} \text{ at age 3}$$

$$\$\underline{\hspace{1.5cm}} \text{ at age 4.}$$

Don't forget to take into account the opportunity cost of foregoing income in year 3 to go to college, as well as the individual's share of the explicit costs.

(ii) Write the equation for calculating the private rate of return to investment in a college education. Assume that the decision on college is made at the start of age 3, so that ages 3 and 4 correspond to years 0 and 1, respectively, in the present-value formula. Use *r* to represent the discount rate.

$$V = \underline{\hspace{3cm}}.$$

(iii) What is the *private rate* of return to investing in a college education? Remember, this is defined as the value of *r* for which $V = 0$.

$$\underline{\hspace{2cm}}\%.$$

d. Now evaluate the investment in college education from the point of view of society.

(i) Taking into account the $500 cost that is borne by the government, in addition to the $500 cost to the individual, the *net social* benefit of a college education is

$$\$\underline{\hspace{1.5cm}} \text{ at age 3}$$

$$\$\underline{\hspace{1.5cm}} \text{ at age 4.}$$

(ii) Write the equation for calculating the *social rate* of return to investment in a college education? Again use *r* to represent the discount rate.

$$V' = \underline{\hspace{3cm}}.$$

(iii) What is the *social rate* of return to investing in a college education?

$$\underline{\hspace{2cm}}\%.$$

2. There are pitfalls in using earnings data for cost-benefit analysis of investments in education. First, current data may not be a good indicator of future payoffs. In fact, the figures in Table 9–1 were published on the sports page of the *Baccalaurian Times*. This information convinced many high-school graduates to attend college that year. After all, the private rate of return to investment in higher education looked quite high. A year later, though, the flood of college graduates hit the labor market. This increase in supply caused average earnings for college graduates to fall to $4,500. All other earnings figures remained unchanged.

a. The drop in earnings for graduates meant that an investment in college education produced less of a benefit than people had expected.

   (i) The net private benefit at age 4 of having a college education turned out to be just

$$\$_____ .$$

   (ii) The private rate of return on a college education turned out to be

$$_____\% .$$

   (iii) And the social rate of return on investment in a college education was

$$_____\% .$$

   (Hint: For the social rate of return you should get a very round number.)

b. A second problem is that it may be incorrect to infer from the data that education is the *cause* of higher earnings. An astute economist discovered that people who attend college are more industrious than people who don't attend. He surmised that part of the observed wage differential is caused by the "screening" effect of a college degree, not a genuine productivity gain. The economist calculated that the same people, if they skipped college, would earn more anyway than the amounts shown for option *B* in Table 9–1. They would earn $1,600 at age 3 and $2,400 at age 4 without a degree, compared to $0 at age 3 and $4,500 at age 4 if they do attend college.

   (i) If this analysis is valid, the net *private* benefit of a college education to these industrious citizens is actually

$$\$_____ \text{ at age 3}$$

$$\$_____ \text{ at age 4.}$$

   (Don't forget to include the explicit costs at age 3.)

   (ii) The net *social* benefit of investing in a college education for these industrious citizens is

$$\$_____ \text{ at age 3}$$

$$\$_____ \text{ at age 4.}$$

      (iii) What are the true private and social rates of return to investment in a college education in this case?

Private rate of return = _____%.

Social rate of return = _____%.

  c. Compare the private and social rates of return calculated in part b above with the returns that you calculated in Exercise 1. What do the differences imply about the accuracy of cost-benefit *analysis*? What do you conclude about the efficiency of investing in higher education in Baccalauria?

3. This exercise works through an application of the Tinbergen-Parnes methodology for manpower planning. The case in point is planning undertaken in 1995 to fulfill *skilled* labor requirements in the year 2000 for the economy of Sinecure. The exercise follows the step-by-step estimation procedure outlined in the text.

Step 1 is to establish a target growth rate of GNP. The government of Sinecure has targeted 6 percent per annum growth during the five-year planning period. At this growth rate, GNP will rise from P1,000 in 1995 to P1,338 by 2000.

Step 2 is to estimate structural changes in output, by sector, to achieve the target growth rate. Government economists have used input-output analysis (see Chapter 3) to estimate that output by sector will grow as shown in Table 9–2.

Table 9–2

Output by Sector (thousands of 1995 pesos)

Sector	1995	2000	Increase (%)
Agriculture	700	800	14.3
Manufacturing	300	538	79.3
Total GNP	1,000	1,338	33.8

a. *Step 3* is to estimate employment by sector. In 1995 the labor force in Sinecure totals 1,000 workers, of whom 800 work in agriculture and 200 work in manufacturing. Define the labor coefficient as the number of workers per thousand pesos of output in each sector.

   (i) From the information provided, the labor coefficient in agriculture is _____ workers per thousand pesos of output.

  (ii) The labor coefficient in manufacturing is _____ workers per thousand pesos of output.

 (iii) In which sector is labor productivity (defined as output per worker) highest in 1995? _____.

 (iv) If the labor coefficients remain unchanged, how many workers will be required in 2000 to produce the projected output levels?

              _____ workers in agriculture.

              _____ workers in manufacturing.

b. Life isn't so simple. The labor coefficients will not remain fixed. Planners expect productivity gains to reduce the labor requirement per thousand pesos of output by 5 percent in agriculture and by 15 percent in manufacturing.

   (i) Productivity gains will reduce the labor coefficient in agriculture to _____ workers per thousand pesos of output, and the labor coefficient in manufacturing will become _____ workers per thousand pesos of output. [Hint: to reduce a number by x percent, multiply the number by the quantity $1 - (x/100)$.]

  (ii) Taking into account productivity gains, in 2000 agriculture will require _____ workers and manufacturing will require _____ workers.

 (iii) The total labor force requirement in 1997 will be _____ workers.

c. *Step 4* is to convert the labor-force projections into occupational categories. Table 9–3 shows the structure of Sinecure's labor force in 1995 by occupational category for each sector.

Table 9–3

Labor Force (numbers of workers)

Sector	Unskilled	Skilled	Total
Agriculture	800	0	800
Manufacturing	150	50	200

(i) Skilled workers represent _____ percent of the agricultural labor force and _____ percent of the labor force in manufacturing. These figures define the occupational structure of the workforce in each sector.

(ii) Assuming that the occupational structures remain unchanged, how many *skilled* workers will be required in 2000?

_____ in agriculture.

_____ in manufacturing.

_____ total for the economy.

(iii) *Step 5* is to convert the occupational requirements into educational terms. All skilled workers need vocational education. Unskilled workers need only primary education, which already is universal in Sinecure. In view of these projections, the economy will require a total of _____ vocational-school graduates in 2000.

d. You have completed the demand side of the manpower-planning problem. What about the supply side? Each year the labor force in Sinecure will increase by 35 workers, so by 2000 there will be 1,175 workers in the labor force—more than enough to satisfy the total labor requirement. The *skilled* labor force, however, will grow by only 4 workers per year (ignore retirements and deaths) because of the limited capacity of vocational schools in Sinecure.

(i) The economy starts with 50 skilled workers. After 5 years this number will rise _____ skilled workers in the country, by present trends.

      (ii) The manpower-planning projections showed that the economy will require _____ skilled workers by 2000.

      (iii) Hence, you forecast a skilled-labor shortage of _____ workers by 1997.

      (iv) On the basis of this calculation, what is your recommendation about investment in vocational education?

e. Is this recommendation valid? Suppose the government ignores the manpower analysis, so that skilled labor grows by only 4 workers per year, as expected.

      (i) The supply of skilled labor falls short of the number "required," in terms of the forecast; therefore, market forces naturally cause real wages for skilled workers to _____.

      (ii) This market-driven change in the real wages for skilled workers induces manufacturers to their use of skilled labor. If the skilled-labor "requirement" drops to _____ workers, then the anticipated shortage becomes a mirage.

      (iii) As to the forecast that _____ skilled workers would be needed in 2000, demand for skilled workers only has to drop by _____ percent to eliminate the anticipated shortage.

f. Part (e) identified one problem with manpower-planning analysis: Future labor requirements are not necessarily fixed coefficients. Identify three other problems with using manpower planning as a tool for determining educational investment priorities.

ANSWERS TO SELF-TEST

Completion

1. human capital
2. *nonformal*
3. private, social
4. *deepening*
5. primary
6. unemployment
7. vocational
8. tertiary (higher)
9. *informal*
10. teacher
11. manpower-planning
12. lower

True-False

1.	T	7.	F
2.	F	8.	T
3.	F	9.	F
4.	T	10.	F
5.	F	11.	T
6.	F	12.	F

Multiple Choice

1.	a	7.	d
2.	d	8.	a
3.	d	9.	c
4.	a	10.	d
5.	c	11.	a
6.	a	12.	b

CHAPTER 10 | Health and Nutrition

OVERVIEW

Health care is both a basic human need and a productive investment in human capital. Virtually all developing countries have made great strides in improving health outcomes, yet health programs too often remain tragically underfunded and poorly designed. Crude death rates in many developing countries have fallen to levels not much above those in the industrialized countries, but this crude measure of health is largely an artifact of differences in age distribution. Other health indicators, such as life expectancy, remain far below the levels observed in developed countries. The main reason for the shorter life expectancy in developing countries is the high mortality rate among infants and children due to inadequate health care and poverty. The most prevalent causes of premature death—infectious, parasitic, and respiratory diseases—generally are preventable.

Considered as an investment, health care can increase labor productivity and also lengthen the productive life span of workers. The rate of return to such investments, however, is very hard to quantify, even before tackling the question of how to value health as an end in itself. Health status typically improves with per capita income, but even low-income countries can achieve major health gains by addressing the causes of sickness and premature death: (1) poor environmental sanitation; (2) malnutrition; and (3) inadequate and inappropriate medical care. Protein-calorie malnutrition among infants and children is widespread.

In general terms, a household's nutrition status depends on its income, on food prices, and on tastes or preferences. Ensuring food security for any nation requires that even poor families have the means (entitlements) to obtain nutritious foods, and that adequate supplies are available. Policy options include food distribution through maternal and child health programs, nutritional education, food fortification, targeted subsidies, and policies to increase food production.

Government expenditures on medical care can be made more effective by focusing on preventative and primary care delivered by nonphysicians and by improving the distribution of medical services. Charging fees could be a useful device to increase funds for medical care, especially for curative services that are supplied primarily to higher-income groups. But fees are of questionable value when they block poor families from gaining access to health care. In general, health care is one area where poor countries cannot afford to rely on the price system. This reinforces the concern with improving the efficacy of public health care.

MAIN LEARNING OBJECTIVES

After studying this chapter, you ought to understand and be able to explain

1. The empirical record on health conditions and health expenditures in developing countries, including patterns and trends in life expectancy and the main causes of high mortality.

2. The positive effects on development from improved health and the role of health care expenditure as an investment in human capital.

3. How environmental conditions such as poor water quality, poor air quality, and inadequate waste disposal contribute to health problems in developing countries.

4. The extent and character of malnutrition in developing countries.

5. The advantages and disadvantages of various nutrition interventions and food subsidy programs for promoting food security.

6. The inadequacy of the medical services in many developing countries and the nature of reforms that can enhance the effectiveness of health care systems.

7. The pros and cons of charging user fees to recover a portion of health care costs.

ECONOMIC TOOLS AND TECHNIQUES

From what you have learned in this chapter, you should be able to

1. Discuss the difficulties faced in quantifying the returns to investment in health.

2. Outline the tabulation of a national food balance sheet to measure calorie supplies and explain the weaknesses of such statistics.

3. Explain how nutritional status is related to income, relative prices, and tastes.

KEY TERMS AND CONCEPTS

"barefoot doctors"
cost effectiveness
crude death rate (CDR)
environmental sanitation
food entitlements
food security
food supplementation (fortification)
infectious, parasitic, and respiratory
    diseases
life expectancy

maternal and child health (MCH)
    programs
morbidity and mortality
nutrition intervention
oral rehydration therapy (ORT)
preventative versus curative health
    services
protein-calorie malnutrition (PCM)
substitution effects
user fees
World Health Organization (WHO)

SELF-TEST

Completion

1. The health statistic that measures the incidence of illness is the
   _____ rate.

2. The United Nations agency responsible for health programs generally is
   referred to by the initials _____, which stand for _____
   _____ _____.

3. Typhoid, dysentery, and cholera are examples of _____ diseases
   that are prevalent in many developing countries.

4. Health conditions in China improved dramatically when the _____
   doctors began providing both preventative and curative health care in the
   countryside.

5. The most prevalent form of malnutrition is _____-
   _____ malnutrition, often referred to as PCM.

6. _____ _____ therapy (ORT) is a simple, effective,
   and inexpensive treatment that can prevent most deaths from diarrhea.

7. One of the most effective ways to reduce malnutrition is to link food
   distribution to _____ and child health (MCH) programs.

8. An increase in life expectancy should _____ the rate of return
   on investment in education.

9. Funds devoted to improving health conditions serve as investments in
   _____ capital.

10. Dramatic success in preventing goiter has been achieved by adding iodine
    to the _____ supply in goiter-prone areas.

11. Egypt and Sri Lanka are two countries where food _____ grew
    so expensive that they became a threat to fiscal stability.

12. Some experts propose that developing countries should finance a portion of
    health care costs through _____ _____, rather than
    provide free care for all.

True-False

If false, you should be able to explain why.

_____ 1. To improve rural health care for the poor in low-income countries,
training nurses and paramedics is more effective than training doctors.

_____ 2. In 1992, the crude death rate in middle-income countries was lower than the crude death rate in high-income countries.

_____ 3. Government spending on health care in low-income countries amounted to slightly over $100 per capita in 1990.

_____ 4. In low-income countries, the average life expectancy has not increased since 1960.

_____ 5. Malnutrition can be widespread even if available calorie supplies, per capita, exceed 100 percent of the recommended requirements.

_____ 6. When poor families earn higher incomes, the nutritional content of their diet generally declines.

_____ 7. Life expectancy and infant mortality rates are determined largely by per capita income; government health and nutrition policies appear to have little effect.

_____ 8. During the first ten years after Castro gained power in Cuba, the ratio of doctors-to-population more than doubled.

_____ 9. Health care systems in most developing countries have been distorted by urban bias.

_____ 10. When poor families face a shortage of food, it is often the young children and the elderly who suffer disproportionate cuts in their rations.

_____ 11. Most developing countries consider investment in health care to be so important that health ministries receive one of the largest budget shares.

_____ 12. The average male in developed countries lives 19 years longer than the average male in low-income countries other than China and India.

Multiple Choice

1. The most important cause of death in low-income countries is
   a. cancer and heart disease.
   b. infectious, parasitic, and respiratory diseases.
   c. warfare.
   d. famine.

2. The single most pressing nutrition problem in developing countries is
   a. calorie deficiency.   c. iron deficiency.
   b. vitamin A deficiency.   d. all the above equally.

3. The prevalence of malnutrition is greatest among
   a. young adults.   c. the elderly.
   b. children.   d. the newborn.

4. The textbook states that the most prevalent malnutrition in the world today
   is the type known as protein-calorie malnutrition (PCM). PCM entails
   a. inadequate caloric intake or undernutrition.
   b. inadequate protein and caloric intake.
   c. inadequate protein intake only.
   d. inadequate intake of all necessary nutrients.

5. Food supplementation programs are designed to
   a. fortify widely consumed foods with extra nutrients.
   b. supply imported foods where domestic production is insufficient to
      meet demand.
   c. provide extra food to target groups such as children and pregnant
      women.
   d. expand agricultural production.

6. Amartya Sen's study of famines revealed that the main problem is not a
   general shortage of food supplies, but rather that
   a. many poor people lacked effective entitlements to food.
   b. too much food was exported.
   c. the food being consumed was not nutritious.
   d. the food was hoarded by speculators.

7. Which of the following statements accurately describes health conditions in
   Sri Lanka?
   a. At independence in 1948, health and life expectancy were unusually
      low for a poor country.
   b. Malaria control was primarily responsible for the dramatic improvements
      in health status.
   c. Medical care was free and the network of health facilities reached all
      parts of the island.
   d. Health conditions improved despite a high incidence of malnutrition.

8. The term *indigenous health practitioner* refers to
   a. native-born doctors, nurses, and paramedics.
   b. doctors who studied medicine at local medical schools.
   c. health workers who deal with preventative rather than curative medical
      services.
   d. those, like herbalists or exorcists, who practice traditional healing rather
      than modern medicine.

9. Economists point out that an increase in food prices has an income effect.
   The point is that higher food prices
   a. increase farmers' incomes.
   b. reduce the purchasing power of poor families' incomes.
   c. incite demands for higher wages.
   d. raise the income of government food marketing agencies.

10. When food policy experts use the term *food security*, they are referring to the goal of
    a. assuring that all people have access to enough food to lead active, healthy lives.
    b. maintaining adequate military strength to protect food supplies and vital routes for food distribution.
    c. achieving self-sufficiency in food production.
    d. stabilizing farmers' incomes.

11. The textbook authors support the imposition of user fees for public-health services in situations in which
    a. there are large external benefits from improved health care.
    b. the fees would generate revenues that are earmarked for further investments in health care.
    c. the funds can be used to support other development programs.
    d. the fees are limited to curative services that primarily benefit the rich.

12. The cost effectiveness of food subsidy programs can be improved by
    a. eliminating special eligibility criteria.
    b. paying farmers less for their food products.
    c. targeting subsidies to high-need groups.
    d. applying subsidies only to food produced domestically.

APPLICATIONS

Worked Example: National Food Balance Sheet

A national food balance sheet is a double-entry accounting system that identifies the sources and uses of various food groups, and the net balances available for human consumption in a given country. Table 10–1 shows the 1991 national food balance sheet for Tapioca, a small island country with a population of 1,000, of which 600 live in poverty. The table shows only the foods that are important dietary items for the poor. Study the table closely. In rows 1 to 4, you can see that total domestic supply of each food equals the amount produced plus the amount imported, less the amount exported. The balance sheet shows that Tapioca depends on imports for almost one fourth (50/210) of its rice supplies, while over one fifth (40/180) of the fish output gets exported.

Rows 5 to 9 show that all available food supplies do not end up on the dinner table. For example, almost 5 percent of the 210,000 kg of rice (10/210) is held by the government to add to the stockpile for meeting future food emergencies. Also, nearly one fourth (50/210) is wasted due to spoilage and rodents. Overall, just 71 percent (150/210) of the available rice reaches consumers. For cassava, only 55 percent of the total supply gets eaten; large proportions are used for animal feed or industrial processing.

Rows 10 to 12 tabulate per capita supplies, and then per capita calorie equivalents. The calculation is straightforward. For each food, divide the total amount consumed by the population (1,000). Then multiply the per capita food supply (kilograms per year) by the appropriate nutritional factor (calories per kilogram) shown in row 11. The result is per capita nutrition supply (calories per year). Dividing by 365 gives the final figure, per capita calories per day, as shown in row 12 for each food.

Table 10-1

National Food Balance Sheet for Tapioca, 1995

	Rice	Cassava	Fish
Sources (kg)			
1. Production	160,000	360,000	180,000
2. Imports	50,000	0	0
3. Exports	0	0	40,000
4. Total domestic supply	210,000	360,000	140,000
Uses (kg)			
5. Accumulation of stocks	100,000	0	0
6. Animal feed	0	50,000	20,000
7. Waste	50,000	10,000	20,000
8. Processed as nonfood product	0	100,000	0
9. Food consumption	150,000	200,000	100,000
10. Per capita kg/year	150	200	100
11. Calories/kg	3,660	980	640
12. Per capita calories/day	1,504	536	175

Total per capita calories/day = 2,215

Source: Derived from 1976 food balance sheet for Indonesia presented in C. Peter
   Timmer et al., *Food Policy Analysis* (Baltimore: Johns Hopkins Press, 1983).

Together, the three foods shown in Table 10-1 provide an average of 2,215
calories per person per day (= 1,504 + 536 + 175, from row 12). Given the average body size and work regimen of the population, nutritionists estimate that the
average Tapiocan requires 2,100 calories per day to maintain good health. Hence,
daily per capita calorie supplies equal 105 percent of the requirement for Tapioca
(2,215/2,100, times 100 to convert to percentage units).

Notice that with few exceptions, such as the increase in government rice
stocks, virtually every number in this calculation is difficult to measure with
precision. Suppose the average caloric requirement is underestimated by 10 percent (so the true figure is $2,100 \times 1.1 = 2,310$), and official data overestimate
calorie consumption by 10 percent (so the true figure is 2,215/1.1 = 2,013). Then
the correct figure for the daily calorie supplies as a percentage of requirements
would be 87 percent (2,013/2,310), not 105 percent.

Above all, even if the numbers were accurate, the fact that calorie supplies
exceed 100 percent of requirements doesn't mean that everyone has an adequate
diet. The national average of 150 kilograms of rice per year per person hides
differences between the rich and the poor. For example, the average poor person
may subsist on a diet of just 100 kilograms per year, while the average rich person
eats 225 kilograms per year. [Check: 60 percent of the population is poor, so
average consumption would be $(100 \times 0.6) + (225 \times 0.4) = 150$.] In this case,
poor people eat 1,002 (= 100 x 3,660/365) calories of rice per day—far less than
required. With national food balance sheets, as with other statistics, averages
must be interpreted with care.

Exercises

1. Now it's your turn to examine a national food balance sheet.

   a. The 1 million citizens of Sucrose live on a diet of coconuts with sugar. Table 10–2 shows the 1995 food balance sheet for Sucrose, but some numbers are missing. Fill in the blanks in the table.

   b. Nutritionists estimate that the average Sucrosian requires 2,400 calories per day for good health.
      (i) The food balance sheet shows that the available food supply provides _____ calories per capita per day.
      (ii) So the available food supply equals _____ percent of calorie requirements.

Table 10–2

1995 National Food Balance Sheet for Sucrose

	Coconuts	Sugar
Sources (million kg)		
Production	_____	140
Imports	0	_____
Exports	150	0
Total domestic supply	500	170
Uses (million kg)		
Accumulation of stocks	_____	20
Waste	40	30
Processed as nonfood product	40	10
Food consumption	400	_____
Per capita kg/year consumed	400	100
Calories/kg	1,500	_____
Per capita calories/day	_____	962
Total per capita calories/day = _____		

Source: Derived from Timmer et al., *Food Policy Analysis.*

   c. Food supplies are adequate, on average. Sadly, though, the food supplies are not distributed equitably. Specifically, three quarters of the people are affluent landowners, but the other one quarter are landless workers living in poverty. All Sucrosians consume 100 kilograms per year of sugar, but coconut consumption varies with income.
      (i) The food balance sheet shows that national coconut consumption averages _____ kilograms per year per person. In fact, each landowner eats a gluttonous 450 kilograms per year. Given these

statistics, you can calculate that the landless workers (composing one quarter of the population) eat just _____ kilograms per year of coconuts per capita.

[Hint: $(3/4)(450) + (1/4)(X)$ = national average.]

(ii) Based on this information, fill in the first column of Table 10–3.

Table 10–3

Nutrition Analysis by Class, Sucrose, 1991

	Per capita kg/year consumed (1)	Calories/ kg (2)	Per capita calories/ day (3)
A. Landowners			
Coconuts	_____	_____	_____
Sugar	_____	_____	_____
B. Landless laborers			
Coconuts	_____	_____	_____
Sugar	_____	_____	_____

d. The rest of Table 10–3 can be completed step by step.
  (i) Fill in column 2 of Table 10–3, taking the data from Table 10–2 on the calorie value (per kilogram) of each type of food.
  (ii) Then calculate the average daily calorie supplies, and fill in column 3. Don't forget to convert from amounts *per year* to amounts *per day* (1/365 year).
  (iii) The total supply of calories per capita per day is

  _____ for the landowners,

  _____ for the landless laborers.

e. Although the overall daily supply of calories per capita exceeds 100 percent of the country's calorie requirement, has malnutrition been eliminated? Explain briefly, with reference to the data in Table 10–3.

f. The data on food supplies in Sucrose are quite reliable. So are most of the other figures in the food balance sheet. But the figure for waste is just a rough estimate, and the figure for food consumption by landless workers is a residual derived from the other statistics.
  (i) Suppose that the true amount of coconut waste is 80 million kilograms per year, not 40 million as shown in Table 10–2. Then

the actual supply of coconuts for food consumption per capita works out to _____ kilograms per year.

(ii) From this average for national coconut consumption and the fact that landowners consume 450 kilograms per capita per year, you can calculate that the true level of coconut consumption per capita for landless workers is _____ kilograms per year.

(iii) Therefore, the nutrition level for landless workers is just _____ calories per day, which is _____ percent of the daily requirement. (Remember to include the calorie value of their sugar consumption, and to convert annual into daily figures.)

No wonder the landless workers look so malnourished. The national averages, based on rough estimates for several important elements of the equation, do not provide very good information about nutrition status of the poor.

2. Table 10–4 provides data on per capita income (PPP) and six indicators of health and nutrition in the early 1990s for 23 low-income countries—all for data were available.

   a. (i) Plot in Figure 10–1 the 23 observations for per capita income (column 1) and life expectancy at birth (column 2). Then draw in an approximate best-fit line corresponding to the data. Label this line *LIFE*.

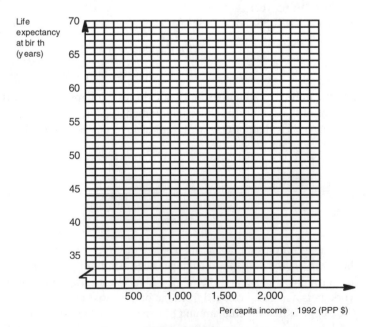

FIGURE 10–1

(ii) Comment on the relationship indicated by the data.

b. (i) Identify the country with the largest *favorable* deviation from the underlying average relationship.

(ii) Identify the countries with the largest *unfavorable* deviations (it's a tie between two countries, with a third close behind).

(iii) What factors might explain such deviations?

c. Differences in life expectancy ought to be related to various indicators of health and nutrition. To investigate the empirical links more closely, you now are asked to analyze the data in columns 2 to 7, without explicit guidance on how to test relationships. At a minimum, you can just "eyeball" the data to look for a relationship. Or you can draw graphs, as done above. To be more accurate, you might want to calculate correlation coefficients or run simple linear regressions using any computer spreadsheet program or statistical software.
(i) The book explains that improvements in life expectancy at birth come about largely through reductions in mortality among the very young. Examine the data in columns 2 and 3 of Table 10–4. Do the cross-section data for low-income countries reveal a strong correlation between life expectancy and infant mortality? Explain.

Table 10–4

Health and Nutrition Indicators, early 1990s

	Per capita income, 1992 (PPP$) (1)	Life expectancy at birth (years) (2)	Infant mortality rate (per 1,000) (3)	Low birth weight (% births) (4)	Access to health care (% population) (5)	Population per doctor (1,000s) (6)	Calorie supply per capita (% req'ts) (7)
Ethiopia	340	49	122	16	28	33.3	71
Mali	500	48	130	17	35	20.0	107
Mozambique	570	44	162	20	24	50.0	77
Tanzania	630	51	92	14	80	33.3	91
Guinea-Bissau	690	39	140	20	80	7.3	97
Madagascar	720	51	93	10	65	8.3	93
Burkina Faso	730	48	132	21	60	33.3	95
Malawi	730	44	134	20	80	50.0	87
Niger	740	46	123	16	30	33.3	98
Rwanda	770	46	117	17	80	50.0	80
Sierra Leone	770	43	143	17	37	14.3	86
Central African Republic	1,040	47	105	15	30	25.0	77
Togo	1,100	55	85	20	60	12.5	99
Bangladesh	1,230	55	91	50	60	6.7	94
Kenya	1,360	59	66	16	77	71.4	86
Mauritania	1,380	48	117	11	40	11.9	109
Nigeria	1,440	52	84	15	72	66.7	93
Ivory Coast	1,640	56	91	14	45	16.7	122
Senegal	1,750	49	68	11	40	20.0	95
Lesotho	1,770	60	46	11	80	18.6	93
Ghana	1,890	56	81	17	60	25.0	91
China	1,910	69	31	6	90	0.7	112
Honduras	1,930	66	49	9	66	3.1	91

Sources: World Development Report 1994 and UNDP, Human Development Report 1994.

(ii)   What explains the differences in infant mortality rates? One hypothesis is that infant mortality is directly related to the extent of prenatal malnutrition among mothers. A good indicator for this is provided in column 4: low-weight births as a percentage of total births. From the data in columns 3 and 4, do you find a positive association between infant mortality rates and the percentage of low-weight births? Explain.

(iii) A second hypothesis is that the infant mortality rate depends inversely on access to health care. Is there a strong positive association between the data in columns 3 and 5? Explain.

(iv)   Another test of the relationship between health care delivery and the infant mortality rate is to use the data in column 5 on population per doctor. It turns out that there is no hint of a correlation between these two variables. Why might this be so?

(v)   Finally, one might suppose that the infant mortality rate is inversely related to the overall adequacy of food supplies. You can test this using the data in column 6 on calorie supply per capita as a percentage of requirements. Here, too, the relationship turns out *not* to be statistically significant. What would account for the *absence* of a strong correlation between infant mortality rates and the supply of calories per capita?

3. This exercise examines some of the problems faced in evaluating the rate of return to an investment in health improvement. You may wish to refer to Chapters 5 or 9 to review discounting and rate-of-return calculations.

A mosquito-spraying project is planned for 1997 in the province of Hinterland. The project will cost F1,000,000 (F stands for francs). Health officials expect the spraying to reduce the incidence of malaria for two years. In economic terms, the benefits consist of

Increased production due to improved worker productivity plus an increase in the labor force due lower morbidity.

The direct value of better health itself.

Table 10–5 shows estimates of these benefits. The spraying costs incurred at the beginning of the project do not need to be discounted. The 1998 benefits have to be discounted one year, while 1999 benefits are discounted two years.

a. Economists at the Ministry of Finance argue that the direct health bene-fits (column 4) are far too subjective to be included in the analysis, so they limit their attention to the production benefits of reducing the incidence of malaria (column 5).

(i) If you ignore the direct health benefits shown in column 4, what is the net present value (NPV) of the project? Use a discount rate of 15 percent.

$$NPV = F\underline{\hspace{2cm}}.$$

(ii) What is the NPV using a discount rate of 10 percent?

$$NPV = F\underline{\hspace{2cm}}.$$

(iii) To the nearest percentage point, what is the internal rate of return on the project? Recall that the IRR is the discount rate for which NPV = 0.

$$IRR = \underline{\hspace{1.5cm}}\%.$$

(Hint: the preceding calculations guarantee that IRR lies between 10 and 15 percent.)

b. Health officials, however, consider that enhancing health of the population is a key policy goal in its own right. They insist on including direct health benefits in their appraisal of the project.

Table 10-5
Costs and Benefits of Health Project in Hinterland (francs)

Year	Cost (1)	Benefits				
		Productivity gains (2)	Output from increased labor force (3)	Value of health (4)	Production benefits = (2) + (3) (5)	Total economic benefits = (2) + (3) + (4) (6)
1997	1,000,000	0	0	0	0	0
1998	0	100,000	500,000	200,000	600,000	800,000
1999	0	100,000	500,000	200,000	600,000	800,000

    (i) Using column 6 as the measure of benefits, what is the NPV for the project using 15 percent as the discount rate?

$$NPV = F_____.$$

    (ii) What is the NPV using 10 percent as the discount rate?

$$NPV = F_____.$$

This time the IRR equals 38 percent. (You can check this if you want more practice with the calculation.)

c. Obviously, the return on this investment depends heavily on whether one includes an estimate of the direct health benefits and on how the estimate is made. But what about measurement of the production benefits? Is it likely that the figures shown in columns 2 and 3 of Table 10–5 are reasonably accurate? Explain.

4. Nutrition interventions are often appraised in terms of their cost effectiveness. This can be illustrated by the situation in the small African nation of Maskini, where people eat nothing but maize. Figure 10–2 shows the supply and demand curves in the maize market. The graph is more complicated than usual, so study it carefully. Line SAS, the supply curve, becomes horizontal to the right of point A because additional maize supplies are imported at a fixed world price of Sh15 per kilogram (Sh stands for shillings). Line DD is the demand curve; its strange shape is explained below. The free-market price is P^0 = Sh15 per kilogram. The minimum consumption level required for good health is 20 kilograms per person per month. At the free-market price this costs Sh300 per month.

a. Altogether, 200 people live in Maskini. Half are poor. They earn Sh150 per month and spend 100 percent of their income on maize. Line D_p shows demand for maize by the poor, at various prices.
    (i) At the equilibrium price of Sh15, the poor citizens of Maskini can afford to buy a total of _____ kilograms per month. (Remember: There are 100 poor citizens buying maize.)
    (ii) If the price were Sh10, the poor could afford to buy _____ kilograms per month.

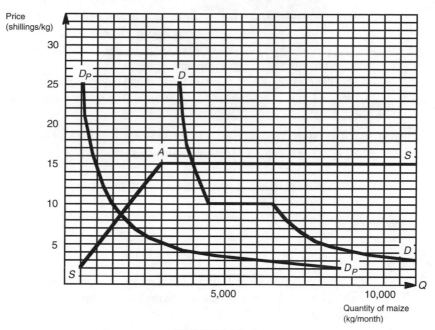

FIGURE 10–2

(iii) At a price of Sh5 they could afford to buy _____ kilograms per
month.

(iv) Given their income level, the poor can afford a nutritionally
adequate diet (20 kilograms per month per person) only if the price
is no higher than

$$P^* = \text{Sh}\underline{}.$$

b. The horizontal gap between lines D_p and DD reflects demand for maize
by the Maskini's 100 rich citizens. Their incomes are high enough so
they always eat their fill—30 kilograms per month—regardless of the
price. At the initial equilibrium price of Sh15,
(i) the rich people (all 100 together) buy _____ kilograms of maize.
(ii) the poor people buy _____ kilograms of maize.
(iii) total demand equals _____ kilograms of maize per month, of which
_____ kilograms are imported.

What about the kink in line DD? If the price of maize drops to 10
shillings or less, then the rich would buy an extra 2,000 kilograms
per month to feed to their chickens and mules.

c. Now you are in a position to consider two policies to ensure adequate
nutrition for the poor. Under Policy 1 the government assumes control
of maize marketing and sells at a price low enough so the poor can
afford a nutritious diet.
(i) As seen in part a, the poor can afford an nutritious diet only if the
price falls to $P^* = \text{Sh}\underline{}$ per kilogram.

(ii) Let the government sell maize at this price. Then the poor (collectively) would buy _____ kilograms, the rich would buy _____ kilograms (including "leakage" to feeding animals). Total demand would be _____ kilograms.

(iii) Label the corresponding point on the demand curve as point X.

(iv) Total government revenues ($P \times Q$) from selling maize would equal Sh_____.

d. (i) Looking at the supply curve, the government would have to pay Sh_____ per kilogram to procure a sufficient quantity of maize to satisfy this large market demand.

(ii) Label the point on the supply curve showing government maize procurement Y.

(iii) The total cost to the government of procuring maize is Sh_____.

(iv) Compare government revenues and costs. The bottom line is that under policy 1 the government would incur a net loss of Sh_____ per month.

Reality check 1. In addition to leakage of grain to feed animals, the low price also creates incentives for smuggling maize to neighboring countries where the price is not controlled, and for diverting of maize to the black market. The poor might find that the official shops have little to sell at the controlled price—as actually happened in countries like Tanzania, Zambia, and the former Soviet Union.

e. Policy 2 is to let the free market function and then give food coupons to the poor, entitling them to extra maize. The extra maize is imported at government expense.

(i) As calculated in part a, at the free-market price each poor person can afford to buy just _____ kilograms per month.

(ii) In order to raise their maize consumption to 20 kilograms per month, the government must provide each poor person with coupon entitlements worth an extra _____ kilograms per month.

(iii) To meet the extra demand created by distributing food coupons, the government must augment the market supply by importing _____ kilograms of maize per month. (Keep in mind that there are 100 poor people.)

(iv) This extra maize would cost the government Sh_____ per kilogram. (Hint: Examine the supply curve.)

(v) The bottom line is that policy 2 would cost the government a total of _____ shillings per month.

Reality check 2. Unfortunately, the coupons are likely to leak into the black market since they are as good as cash for purchasing maize. Even with policy 2, the poor might not wind up with nutritionally adequate diets. Also, it is far from a simple matter for bureaucrats to single out who is poor and who is not. So lots of extra coupons might be issued, and this would raise the cost of the program.

f. (i) To summarize, adequate nutrition for the poor can be provided at a cost to the government of

Sh_____ per month under policy 1,

Sh_____ per month under policy 2.

(ii) The required volume of maize imports would be

_____ kg per month under policy 1,

_____ kg per month under policy 2.

(iii) Which of the two policy options is more cost effective? What is the source of its advantage? Explain.

ANSWERS TO SELF-TEST

Completion

1. morbidity
2. WHO, World Health Organization
3. waterborne
4. barefoot
5. protein-calorie
6. Oral rehydration
7. maternal
8. increase
9. human
10. salt
11. subsidies
12. user fees

True-False

1.	T	7.	F
2.	T	8.	F
3.	F	9.	T
4.	F	10.	T
5.	T	11.	F
6.	F	12.	T

Multiple Choice

1.	b	7.	c
2.	a	8.	d
3.	b	9.	b
4.	d	10.	a
5.	a	11.	d
6.	a	12.	c

Part IV   Capital Resources

CHAPTER 11 | Capital and Saving

OVERVIEW

Capital accumulation no longer may be viewed as a panacea for underdevelopment, but saving and investment rates in excess of 15 percent of GDP still are considered essential for growth. Just as important as the level of investment is the quality or efficiency of projects as well as the soundness of the institutional and policy environment.

The data presented in the textbook shows that, for developing countries as a group (excluding India and China), the average investment rate rose from one sixth to one fourth of GDP during 1965–1998. In the same period, domestic saving rates (led by private savings) also rose proportionately to cover over 80 percent of the investment needs.

The resource gap was filled by foreign savings, which come in two major forms: official saving (foreign aid) and private foreign saving (taken up in Chapter 14). Official development assistance (ODA) from both multilateral and bilateral sources typically consists of those components of capital inflows to developing countries that cannot be generated by normal market incentives: long-term loans, grants, soft loans, technical assistance, and sale of surplus products payable in local currency. Over the past 50 years, some $1 trillion of financial assistance was provided to developing countries. Its level and effectiveness have, however, received much-needed scrutiny in the 1990s.

Foreign private savings come in four forms: direct investment, portfolio investment, commercial lending, and export credits. This has increased substantially in the past two decades, though concentrated heavily in a handful of middle-income or resource-rich countries.

The chapter also discusses various theories of saving behavior in developing countries, including absolute-income, relative-income, permanent-income, life-cycle, and class-savings hypotheses. The chapter concludes, however, that data and conceptual problems have left our understanding of the subject woefully inadequate.

MAIN LEARNING OBJECTIVES

After studying this chapter, you ought to understand and be able to explain

1. The empirical record of saving and investment in developing countries.

2. The relationship among tax revenues, public sector consumption expenditure, and government saving.

3. The observed patterns of household saving behavior and the theories of household saving.

4. The relative importance of foreign private saving.

5. The various ways foreign economic assistance is categorized and measured.

6. The institutional architecture of foreign aid, including the roles of multilateral and bilateral agencies.

7. The effectiveness of foreign aid, including its objectives (poverty alleviation, growth, sound policy, stabilization) and instruments (conditionality, fungibility, ownership).

ECONOMIC TOOLS AND TECHNIQUES

From what you have learned in this chapter, you should be able to

1. Apply the Harrod-Domar model to analyze the relationship between growth, investment rates, and ICORs, as in Table 11–2 in the textbook.

2. Calculate government savings from data on tax revenues and government expenditures.

3. Calculate the relative magnitudes of government, private, and foreign savings from data on the national income accounts and the balance of payments (you may want to reread the Principles of Macroeconomics, at the beginning of this *Study Guide*).

4. Explain the observed patterns of household saving behavior in terms of the various theories discussed in this chapter.

5. Evaluate the form and effectiveness of foreign aid as an approach for transferring money and ideas to the least-developed countries. For example, use the production possibilities frontier to illustrate the fungibility of project aid.

KEY TERMS AND CONCEPTS

bilateral aid
capital fundamentalism
capital-intensive investment
class theory
concessional terms
conditionality
corporate saving
foreign saving (official, private)
fungibility
government saving
incremental capital-output ratio
 (ICOR)
International Monetary Fund (IMF)
investment ratio (rate)
Keynesian absolute-income hypothesis
labor-intensive investment
life-cycle income hypothesis

Marshall Plan
multilateral aid
official development assistance (ODA)
permanent income
permanent-income hypothesis
precautionary motives
private domestic saving (household,
 corporate)
regional development bank
relative-income hypothesis
resource gap
tax ratio
technical assistance (cooperation)
transitory income
United Nations Development
 Programme (UNDP)
World Bank (IBRD)

SELF-TEST

Completion

1. To achieve sustained output growth of 5 percent per year with an ICOR
 equal to 4.0 requires an investment ratio of _____ percent.

2. The view that the development problem is essentially one of securing
 resources for investment is called *capital* _____.

3. The tax ratio is the ratio of _____ _____ to
 _____.

4. If a country's gross domestic saving is unchanged, its investment ratio still
 can rise if there is a net inflow of _____ savings.

5. Private domestic saving can be decomposed into two sources:
 _____ saving and _____ saving.

6. Policies that result in underpricing capital and overpricing labor seem to
 cause firms and governments to adjust by adopting more _____-
 intensive investments.

7. According to the Keynesian absolute-income hypothesis, household saving is a function of current _____ income.

8. According to the permanent-income hypothesis, people save a high proportion of _____ income.

9. Compared to urban households at comparable levels of income, rural households tend to save a _____ fraction of their income.

10. In the world's fastest-growing economies, the ratio of _____ to GDP is 30 percent or more.

11. Since 1965 the growth rate of private consumption has been _____ than the growth rate of GDP in developing countries, so the ratio of private consumption to GDP has _____.

12. Government budgetary saving is the excess of government revenues over government _____.

13. A loan from a rich government to a poor government is considered "foreign aid" if the grant equivalent of the concession is at least _____ percent.

14. The difference between domestic investment (I) and domestic saving (S) often is called the _____.

15. A _____ loan is one bearing lower interest rates and longer repayment periods than would be available on the commercial capital markets.

16. The _____ _____ _____ is the World Bank affiliate that channels contributions from the richer member countries to low-income developing countries on very soft terms.

17. Donors frequently extend foreign aid on the basis of _____ such as a requirement that the country's currency must be devalued.

18. Even project aid that is tied to investments is _____, because recipient governments can cut back their own funding of the investments to free up resources for any use the government wishes.

True-False

If false, you should be able to explain why.

_____ 1. In many low-income countries, the saving generated by government-owned enterprises represents a large part of government saving.

_____ 2. As per capita income rises, the share of investment financed out of foreign savings also rises.

_____ 3. Two countries with the same investment ratio and the same ICOR also must have the same rate of growth of per capita income.

_____ 4. For the group of low-income countries, excluding China and India, domestic saving rates were much lower in 1992 than in 1965.

_____ 5. *Capital flight* refers to the flow of international capital into those developing countries with policies that favor investment and growth.

_____ 6. If the government's marginal propensity to consume (MPC) out of tax revenues exceeds the private sector's MPC out of disposable income, then higher taxes will reduce total domestic savings.

_____ 7. Increased government budgetary savings have been a major source of the increase in total domestic savings in most developing countries.

_____ 8. Capital-intensive investments tend to have a higher ICOR than labor-intensive investments.

_____ 9. Countries A and B are similar in all respects except that income is more stable in A. The permanent-income hypothesis suggests that savings rates should be higher in country A.

_____ 10. In low-income countries, the primary source of domestic savings is corporate savings.

_____ 11. Negative saving rates are a logical impossibility.

_____ 12. High-income countries tend to have higher tax ratios than low-income countries.

_____ 13. Official development assistance (ODA) refers only to outright grants.

_____ 14. By 1991 the ratio of foreign savings to GDP no longer exceeded 5 percent in any developing country.

_____ 15. The net flow of official development assistance increased nearly sixfold in real terms from 1975 to 1992.

_____ 16. Most loans from the World Bank are nonconcessional flows consisting of funds borrowed by the World Bank at prevailing interest rates and then re-lent to developing countries at slightly higher rates.

_____ 17. During the 1990s, many donor countries incorporated environmental sustainability and democratization as aims of their foreign aid programs.

Multiple Choice

1. If a country with population growth of 2.4 percent per year seeks to increase real income per capita by 3 percent per year, then real GNP must grow by approximately
   a. 5.4 percent per year.
   b. 3 percent per year.
   c. 0.6 percent per year.
   d. 7.2 percent per year.

2. Table 11–1 in the text shows that low-income countries other than India and China had a resource gap in 1992 equal to 9 percent of GDP. This figure refers to the
   a. excess of government expenditures over government revenues.
   b. extent to which GDP fell short of the target.
   c. excess of domestic investment over domestic saving.
   d. extent to which domestic investment fell short of the target.

3. Which of the following items is not a government consumption expenditure?
   a. Government spending on military hardware.
   b. Government expenditure on an irrigation project.
   c. Payment of teachers' salaries.
   d. None of the above.

4. A few countries had negative domestic saving in 1992. This means that
   a. their GDPs were declining.
   b. their gross domestic investments were negative.
   c. their aggregate consumption expenditures exceeded GDP.
   d. all the above.

5. Economic theories of consumption seek to explain three patterns of household behavior. Which of the following is one of them?
   a. Within one country, higher-income households save a smaller fraction of their income than lower-income households.
   b. Within one country, household saving ratios tend to be relatively stable over time.
   c. Looking across countries, household saving ratios rise systematically with per capita income.
   d. All the above.

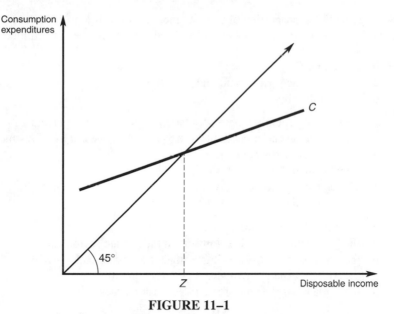

FIGURE 11–1

6. Figure 11–1 shows a Keynesian consumption function. When disposable income rises above level Z, then
   a. household saving becomes greater than consumption.
   b. household saving becomes positive.
   c. household consumption begins to exceed the subsistence level.
   d. total domestic saving becomes positive.

7. One model of household saving holds that workers save a lower fraction of their income than do those who derive their income primarily from property. This is the
   a. class-savings model.
   b. relative-income model.
   c. permanent-income model.
   d. Harrod-Domar model.

8. In the equation $S = a + b_1 Y_p + b_2 Y_t$, expressing the permanent-income hypothesis, the term Y_t stands for _____ and the coefficient b_2 is _____ the coefficient b_1.
   a. disposable income at time t, less than.
   b. disposable income at time t, greater than.
   c. transitory income, less than.
   d. transitory income, greater than.

9. The precautionary savings model argues that poor rural households
   a. lower their saving rates whenever their incomes exceed their previous peak levels.
   b. save to enjoy comfortable retirements.
   c. save to be able to survive if their incomes drop suddenly.
   d. save more when their incomes are more stable.

10. In general, the proportion of national income saved is a positive function of
    a. the fraction of households that are headed by adults beyond childbearing age.
    b. the tax ratio.
    c. the size of the government budget deficit.
    d. none of the above.

11. In a developing country where population is growing by 2 percent annually, per capita income can rise steadily at 2.5 percent per year if the investment is
    a. 10 percent and the ICOR is 4.
    b. 10 percent and the ICOR is 4.5.
    c. 17 percent and the ICOR is 3.8.
    d. 20 percent and the ICOR is 10.

12. Higher taxes lead to more savings if
    a. the government's MPC is lower than the private sector's MPC.
    b. the government's MPC is higher than the private sector's MPC.
    c. the MPC for the government is greater than 1.0.
    d. more than half the labor force lives in rural areas.

13. Which of the following is *not* defined as a form of foreign aid or official development assistance (ODA)?
    a. Multilateral aid.
    b. Food aid.
    c. Technical assistance.
    d. Loans on commercial terms from official agencies.

14. Four statements about foreign aid are listed below. Only one of them is factual. Which one is it?
    a. The ratio of aid received to GDP generally is higher for low-income countries than for middle-income countries.
    b. The most populous low-income countries receive disproportionately large inflows of foreign aid.
    c. Over the past three decades, the United States has provided an increasingly large share of total foreign aid.
    d. Most foreign assistance is in the form of food aid rather than project aid.

15. Which of the following multilateral institutions provides the largest amount of concessional assistance to developing countries?
    a. IMF   c. UNDP
    b. OPEC   d. IFC

16. Which of the following multilateral institutions provides support for private investment in developing countries through loans on commercial terms and equity investments?
    a. OECD   c. UNDP
    b. IFC   d. IDA

APPLICATIONS

Worked Example: Investment and Growth

Textbook Table 11–1 shows how economic growth is influenced by differences in the level of investment (I) and the ICOR. Here we look behind the scenes to see how the numbers were generated. Countries A and B start in 1995 with GDP = Y = 1,000 and I = 150. The example in the textbook assumes that the growth rate of investment $g(I)$ is constant. Two alternative values are explored for this variable. For present purposes, the "low" rate of $g(I)$ = 5.0 percent per annum is used. With this growth rate, investment expands from I = 150 in 1995 to

$$I = 150(1.05) = 157.5 \text{ in } 1996,$$
$$I = 150(1.05)^2 = 165.4 \text{ in } 1997,$$
$$I = 150(1.05)^3 = 173.6 \text{ in } 1998,$$

and so on. At this growth rate, investment in 2005 would be $I = 150(1.05)^{10}$ = 244.3.

The Harrod-Domar model from Chapter 3 can be written in the form $Y_{t+1} = Y_t + (I_t/\text{ICOR})$. So if we know the values of Y, I, and the ICOR for any one year, we can compute the value of GDP for the subsequent year and then iterate for each succeeding year. At the moment we know I for each year. Following the textbook, let ICOR = 4 for country A and ICOR = 3 for Country B. We know $Y(1995)$ for each country. So we can compute $Y(1996)$:

For A: $Y(1996) = 1,000 + (150/4) = 1,037.5.$
For B: $Y(1996) = 1,000 + (150/3) = 1,050.0.$

And knowing $Y(1996)$, we can calculate $Y(1997)$:

For A: $Y(1997) = 1,037.5 + (157.5/4) = 1,076.9$
For B: $Y(1997) = 1,050 + (157.5/3) = 1,102.5$

And so on, giving the values shown in the text table and beyond. For example, Table 11–1 below shows the results for country A out to 2005.

Table 11–1

GDP and Investment Projections to 2005, Country A

	2000	2001	2002	2003	2004	2005
Y_t	1,207.3	1,255.2	1,305.4	1,358.2	1,413.6	1,471.7
I	191.4	201.0	211.0	221.6	232.6	244.3
ICOR	4.0	4.0	4.0	4.0	4.0	4.0
Y_{t+1}	1,255.2	1,305.4	1,358.2	1,413.6	1,471.7	—

Over the decade, GDP increases by just under 50 percent in country A. Similar calculations for country B (see Exercise 1) show that with ICOR = 3 and identical investment levels, GDP would increase by more than 60 percent over the same time period.

Suppose the population in each country grows by 3 percent per year, or 34 percent for the decade $[(1.03)^{10} = 1.34]$. What is the increase in per capita income for the decade? In country A, GDP increases by a factor of 1.47, while population increases by a factor of 1.34. Hence, GDP/POP will increase by a factor of $1.47/1.34 = 1.10$, or 10 percent. In Exercise 1 you will compute the corresponding figure for country B and see that per capita income in B increases more than twice as much as in A. This difference is due wholly to the difference in ICOR values. If, realistically, investment also grows more quickly in B due to the higher level of income, then the disparity would be even more dramatic.

Exercises

1. Now it is your turn to investigate the relationship between investment and growth. Table 11–2 is set up for you to project country B's economic growth over the period 2000 to 2005. Country B's ICOR equals 3.0. The investment growth rate (5 percent per year) is identical to that of country A in the Worked Exercise. Country B's GDP for 2000 is taken from the example in the textbook.

   a. Complete Table 11–2 by finding GDP for the years 2000 to 2005.

Table 11–2

GDP and Investment Projections to 2005, Country B

	2000	2001	2002	2003	2004	2005
Y_t	1,276.3	_____	_____	_____	_____	_____
I	191.4	201.0	211.0	221.6	232.6	244.3
ICOR	3.0	3.0	3.0	3.0	3.0	3.0
===>Y_{t+1}	_____	_____	_____	_____	_____	

   b. (i) In 1995 country B had GDP = 1,000. Over the decade 1995 to 2005, GDP is projected to grow by a factor of _____.

      (ii) Suppose the population grows by 3 percent per annum. Then, the population will increase by a factor of _____ over the decade.

   (iii) Per capita income (GDP/POP) in country B will rise by _____ percent. Compare this to the rise in per capita income of 10 percent in country A. What explains the difference?

c. As the level of income in country B increases relative to the level of income in country A, one may assume that country B could afford more rapid investment growth as well. After 2000, let $g(I) = 10$ percent in country B. On the basis of this assumption, fill in the row in Table 11–3 showing the level of I for 2001 to 2004. Then complete the table by finding GDP for the years 2001 through 2005.

Table 11–3

GDP and Investment Projections to 2005, Country B

	2000	2001	2002	2003	2004	2005
Y_t	1,276.3	_____	_____	1,487.5	_____	_____
I	191.4	_____	_____	_____	_____	308.3
ICOR	3.0	3.0	3.0	3.0	3.0	3.0
===>Y_{t+1}	_____	_____	_____	_____	_____	

d. (i) Assuming $g(I) = 10$ percent per year after 2000, GDP in country B increases by a factor of _____ over the decade 1995 to 2005 (starting from GDP = 1,000 in 1995).

   (ii) Still assuming 3 percent per year population growth, per capita GDP will increase by _____ percent for the decade.

e. The textbook points out that a country with less-efficient investment would need a higher investment ratio in order to match the growth performance of a country where the ICOR is lower.

(i) Beginning in the year 2000 with $Y = 1,207.3$, what annual rate of GDP growth would country A require over the ensuing five years to match the 1995 level of GDP achieved by country B in Table 11–3?

$$g(Y) = \underline{\hspace{1cm}}\% \text{ per year.}$$

[Hint: The question implies a particular target level of GDP for 2005 and you know GDP for the year 2000; work backward from the target GDP to find $g(Y)$.]

(ii) With ICOR = 4, find the investment ratio that country A requires to achieve the growth rate that you just calculated. Remember that $s = I/Y$ in the Harrod-Domar model.

$$I/Y = \underline{\hspace{1cm}}\%$$

(iii) For comparison, you can see from Table 11–3 that country B achieves the same level of income in the year 2005 with an investment ratio (for that year) of

$$I/Y = \underline{\hspace{1cm}}\%.$$

2. This exercise investigates some saving, investment, and growth facts. Table 11–4 below provides data on the 1992 level of per capita income (in PPP$) and the 1980–1992 annual rate of growth of real GDP for 19 developing countries. You will find data on the domestic savings ratios and investment ratio for these countries in Table 11–3 of the textbook. (Only the countries with per capita income < $4,000 (PPP) are used here, to simplify the exercise.)

Table 11–4

Per Capita Income and GDP Growth Rates, Selected Countries

Country	Per capita income, 1992 (PPP$)	GDP growth 1980–1992 (% per annum)
Low-income countries		
Ethiopia	340	1.2
Mali	500	2.9
Tanzania	630	3.1
India	1,210	5.2
Bangladesh	1,230	4.2
Kenya	1,360	4.0
Nigeria	1,440	2.3
Senegal	1,750	3.0
Ghana	1,890	3.4
China	1,910	9.1
Honduras	1,930	2.8
Middle-income countries		
Pakistan	2,130	6.1
Bolivia	2,270	0.6
Cameroon	2,300	1.0
The Philippines	2,480	1.2
Sri Lanka	2,810	4.0
Indonesia	2,970	5.7
Peru	3,370	−0.6
Egypt	3,670	4.4

Source: World Development Report 1994.

a. In Figure 11–2 the horizontal axis measures per capita income (PCI) and the vertical axis measures the domestic saving rate (S/Y).

  (i) Plot the 19 points representing the country data on PCI and S/Y.

  (ii) According to the textbook, one "would ordinarily expect a lower ratio of saving in poor countries . . . simply because . . . there is less available for saving after subsistence needs are met." Is the expectation confirmed by your scatter plot of data for this sample of 19 countries? Explain.

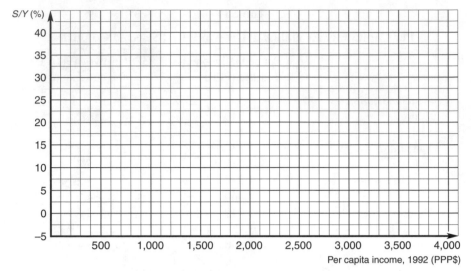

FIGURE 11–2

b. (i) Which two countries in the sample had the highest saving rate?

   (ii) Comment on their growth performance over the period 1980 to 1992?

c. (i) Which two countries had the highest investment ratios?

   (ii) Compare the investment ratios with the saving rates for these two countries. What accounts for the differences between I/Y and S/Y?

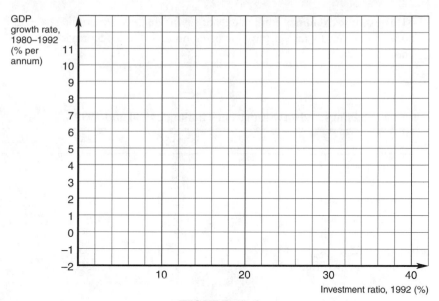

GDP growth rate, 1980–1992 (% per annum)

Investment ratio, 1992 (%)

FIGURE 11–3

d. In Figure 11–3 the horizontal axis measures the investment ratio and the vertical axis measures growth performance for the period 1980 to 1992.

(i) Plot the 19 points representing the country data on PCI and I/Y.

(ii) Draw in the best-fit line showing the relationship between these two variables. What do you observe? (Reality check: It is not strictly proper to compare 12 years of growth with the investment ratio for just 1 year; but for many countries the observed investment ratio is a reasonable proxy for the average over the past decade.)

(iii) Would the data point for a country with a high ICOR tend to be above or below the best-fit line in Figure 11–3? Explain.

3. This exercise examines components of saving and investment in Thailand, one of the world's fastest-growing economies. Table 11–5 provides the necessary data.

Table 11–5

Savings and Investment in Thailand, 1980 and 1990*

	1980	1990
Government budget		
Revenue	122.0	337.2
Current expenditure	120.5	206.2
Capital expenditure	42.1	49.6
Gross domestic product	829.3	1,790.1
Gross domestic saving	166.9	603.4
Gross domestic investment	219.1	738.2
Government Savings (S_g)	_____	_____
Private Savings (S_p)	_____	_____
Foreign savings (S_f)	_____	_____
Private-sector income (Y_{priv})	_____	_____

*Figures are in billions of baht, converted to constant 1987 prices using the GDP deflator. *Source*: World Bank, *World Tables 1994*.

  a. (i) Calculate government savings (S_g), which is defined as government revenue less current expenditure. Fill in the first blank line of Table 11–5.

       (ii) Calculate private savings (S_p), which is the difference between gross domestic savings and government savings. Fill in the second blank line of Table 11–5.

      (iii) Calculate foreign savings (S_f), which is the difference between gross domestic investment and gross domestic savings. Fill in the third blank line of Table 11–5. (The negative of S_f is called the *resource gap*.)

      (iv) Finally, calculate private sector income (Y_{priv}) as the difference between GDP and tax payments to the government. Fill in the fourth blank line of Table 11–5.

b. The marginal propensity to *consume* is defined as MPC = (change in consumption)/(change in income). In a similar manner the marginal propensity to *save* is defined as MPS = (change in savings)/(change in income). Since the change in income must equal the change in savings *plus* the change in consumption expenditure, the two marginal propensities are related by the formula MPS = 1 – MPC.
   (i) For the period 1980 to 1990, the marginal propensity to save was

$$MPS_{gov} = \underline{\hspace{1cm}} \text{ for the government sector,}$$

$$MPS_{priv} = \underline{\hspace{1cm}} \text{ for the domestic private sector,}$$

   (ii) Given these figures for the MPS, a transfer of 10 billion baht from the private sector to the government sector would cause gross domestic savings to _____ by _____ billion baht. (Hint: The transfer of income will cause private-sector savings to fall and public-sector savings to rise.)

c. Define the tax ratio as the ratio of government revenue to GDP.
   (i) Thailand's tax ratio went from _____ percent in 1980 to _____ percent in 1990.
   (ii) The textbook says that the government's MPC in most developing countries is so high (and the MPS so low) that a rise in the tax ratio reduces gross domestic savings. (This is the Please effect.) Is that what happened in Thailand?

d. (i) In 1980, government capital expenditure exceeded government savings. How can the government capital outlays be larger than the amount of government savings out of revenue?

   (ii) In 1990 the situation was reversed: Government savings exceeded government capital expenditure. What happens to government savings that is not channeled to government capital expenditure?

4. This exercise deals with some of the models of household saving behavior discussed in the textbook.

   a. According to the Keynesian absolute-income hypothesis, savings is a simple function of disposable income. Let the savings function for the economy be

   $$S = -100 + 0.5Y^d.$$

   (i) Calculate savings (S) and the savings ratio (S/Y^d) for the following levels of disposable income:

	S	S/Y^d
$Y^d = 200$	_____	_____%
300	_____	_____%
400	_____	_____%

   (ii) Is this simple savings function consistent with the observed tendency of S/Y to be roughly constant over time within a particular country? Explain.

   b. According to the permanent-income hypothesis, current consumption depends primarily on permanent income, whereas a large fraction of transitory income is saved. To illustrate this hypothesis, let the savings function be

   $$S = 0.167Y_p + 0.5Y_t,$$

   where Y_t is the transitory component of current disposable income and Y_p is permanent income. In this case one sixth of permanent income is saved and five sixths spent, whereas half of transitory income is saved. Over time, the transitory component averages out to zero.

   (i) Suppose that households perceive that their permanent income is Y_p = 300. Calculate S and S/Y^d for the following levels of disposable income:

	S	S/Y^d
$Y^d = 200$	_____	_____%
300	_____	_____%
400	_____	_____%

   The savings behavior should look familiar.

   (ii) In the long run, households may adjust their perception of permanent income as they see actual income rise. As an example, suppose that households adjust their concept of permanent income to Y_p = 400. With this adjustment, we find that S = _____ when actual disposable income is Y^d = 400, and S/Y^d = _____ percent.

(iii) Review the last two parts of the exercise. In the short run (when Y_p is fixed at 300), we get $S/Y^d =$ _____ when Y^d equals 300 and $S/Y^d -$ _____ when Y^d rises to 400. In the long run (after Y_p adjusts), then $S/Y^d =$ _____ when Y^d equals 400.

c. (i) Is the permanent-income model consistent with the observed tendency of S/Y to be roughly constant over time? Explain.

(ii) Is this model consistent with the fact that higher-income households tend to save a larger fraction of their income? Explain. (Hint: At any given time, the group of high-income households includes many with positive transitory incomes; the group of low-income households includes many with negative transitory incomes.)

(iii) Consider a country like Uganda, where the main product (coffee) is an export crop with a highly variable price in the world market. If household behavior conforms to the permanent-income hypothesis, how would the savings rate vary over time as coffee prices rise and fall? (Hint: What happens to transitory income as a percentage of total income?)

5. This exercise analyzes the economic impact of foreign aid.

a. Begin with the simple Harrod-Domar growth equation $g = s/k$. This is a reasonable starting point if we assume that more investment is always undertaken in association with more employment and other complementary factors of production. The Republic of Xanadu has a domestic savings ratio of $s = 20$ percent and an ICOR of $k = 5$.

(i) If Xanadu relied only on domestic savings, what growth rate would be achieved, according to the Harrod-Domar model?

$$g = \text{_____}\% \text{ per annum.}$$

(ii) Now suppose that Xanadu receives foreign aid equal to 20 percent of GDP. If the domestic savings rate and the ICOR remain as before, then the ratio of total savings to GDP will rise to

$$s = \text{_____} \%.$$

According to the Harrod-Domar model, Xanadu would then achieve a growth rate of

$$g = \text{_____} \% \text{ per annum.}$$

b. But will total savings increase by the full amount of the aid? Figure 11–4 shows Xanadu's production possibilities frontier (PPF). It assumes that total GDP = $100, and the composition of GDP may consist of any combination of investment goods (I) plus consumption goods (C) summing to $100. The figure also contains representative indifference curves. The initial optimum point along the PPF is at point X, where $C = \$80$ and $I = \$20$ (so $s = 20$ percent).

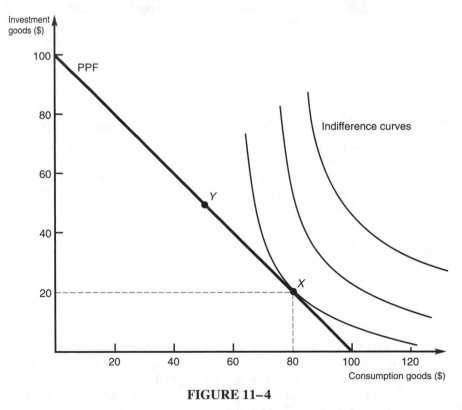

FIGURE 11–4

(i) Consider now the impact of foreign aid in the form of $20 worth of investment goods (= 20 percent of GDP). Identify the point in Figure 11–4 that would be attained if I increased by the full $20 of aid, as assumed in the simple Harrod-Domar model. Label this point X'.

(ii) Suppose that instead of starting at point X, Xanadu had originally been at point Y, where $C = \$50$ and $I = \$50$. Now the $20 in aid will allow investment to rise to $70. Label this new point Y'.

(iii) In general, $20 in foreign aid will permit Xanadu to invest $20 more than before, for *any* initial level of consumption. We thus generate a *consumption possibilities frontier*, which will be $20 above the PPF. Draw this line and label it AA; note that it goes through points X' and Y'.

(iv) Given the indifference curves in Figure 11–4, find Xanadu's optimal point along line AA. Label it point E.

(v) At point E, Xanadu will have

$$C = \$\underline{\hspace{1cm}},$$

$$I = \$\underline{\hspace{1cm}}.$$

c. Therefore, following receipt of the aid, total savings (and investment) in Xanadu will not increase by the full $20.

(i) Total savings (domestic plus foreign) would now equal $\underline{\hspace{1cm}}$, an increase of $\underline{\hspace{1cm}}$.

(ii) The aid causes the ratio of total savings to GDP (still $100) to increase to $s = \underline{\hspace{1cm}}$ percent, but *domestic* savings fall to $\underline{\hspace{1cm}}$ percent of GDP.

(Notice that investment exceeds domestic savings by $20, the amount of foreign savings.)

(iii) Applying the Harrod-Domar equation, the rate of growth therefore increases to

$$g = \underline{\hspace{1cm}}\% \text{ per annum.}$$

The foreign aid is *fungible*; even if all of it is destined for investment, it frees a country to use resources, which were originally intended for investment, for consumption. This substitution effect reduces the impact of the foreign aid on growth.

d. Aid may also affect Xanadu's ICOR. For example, suppose that the policy advice accompanying the aid enables Xanadu to reduce its ICOR to $k = 4$.

(i) Then, using the value for s found in part c, the country would achieve a growth rate of

$$g = \underline{\hspace{1cm}}\% \text{ per annum.}$$

(ii) Is it possible for aid to cause Xanadu's ICOR to rise rather than fall? Explain briefly.

e. The foreign aid supplements Xanadu's domestic savings rate, albeit with some substitution effects. In terms of the Harrod-Domar model, how would the impact of foreign direct investment and commercial borrowing differ from the impact of aid?

(i) In the year received?

(ii) In future years?

6. The text makes a number of statements about empirical patterns of foreign aid and direct investment flows. This exercise lets you check out the facts.

a. The countries listed in textbook Table 11–7 may be divided into very large countries (population above 60 million) and others. The very large ones are India, Bangladesh, China, Pakistan, Nigeria, the Philippines, Indonesia, Brazil, and Mexico.

(i) In Figure 11–5, plot the foreign aid ratio (that is, net official development assistance as a percentage of GNP) against per capita income for the nine very large countries. Draw the best-fit line through these data points. Label the line *BIG*.

(ii) Plot the foreign aid ratio against per capita income for the remaining countries, using a different symbol to distinguish these observations from those plotted earlier. Draw the best-fit line through these 13 data points. Label it *NOTSOBIG*.

(iii) The text asserts that very large countries receive proportionately less aid than smaller ones and that, as per capita income rises, countries receive proportionately less aid. Are these two assertions borne out by the data you plotted in Figure 11–5? Explain.

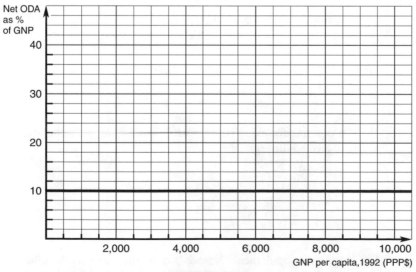

FIGURE 11–5

Table 11–6

Foreign Direct Investment, Selected Countries, 1992

	Per capita income, 1992 (PPP$)	Foreign direct investment ($ million)	Per capita FDI ($)
Very large countries			
India	1,210	151	0.17
Bangladesh	1,230	4	0.03
China	1,910	11,156	9.60
Pakistan	2,130	275	2.31
Nigeria	2,160	897	8.80
The Philippines	2,440	228	3.55
Indonesia	2,970	1,774	9.63
Brazil	5,260	1,454	9.45
Mexico	7,490	5,366	63.13
Other countries			
Ethiopia	340	6	0.11
Mali	500	−8	−0.89
Tanzania	630	0	0.00
Kenya	1,360	6	0.23
Senegal	1,750	0	0.00
Ghana	1,890	23	1.46
Sri Lanka	1,970	123	7.07
Bolivia	2,270	93	12.40
Guatemala	3,370	94	9.69
Egypt	3,670	459	8.39
Colombia	5,760	790	23.65
Malaysia	8,050	4,118	221.40
South Korea	8,950	−497	−73.00

Sources: World Development Report 1994 and World Bank, World Tables 1994.

b. Table 11–6 contains information on net foreign direct investment (FDI) in 1992 for the same countries. Most FDI is directed toward other wealthy countries and a handful of the more successful developing countries (see Chapter 14 for a detailed discussion).

(i) Are these figures consistent with this generalization? Does there appear to be a positive correlation between FDI and per capita income? Explain.

(ii) China stands out as getting a large inflow of FDI despite a low level of per capita income. What does this observation suggest about a possible link between net FDI and population size? From the data provided, does this link appear generally to hold? Explain.

(iii) Korea stands out as not getting a large inflow of FDI despite quite a high level of per capita income. In fact, the FDI figure for Korea is *negative*. What exactly does this mean?

c. The text explains that many developing countries underwent large macro-economic adjustments when net resource flows moved adversely after the debt crisis. Let's see how foreign savings flows changed between 1980 and 1990 for three African countries with above-average debt burdens. Table 11–7 (which follows the logical structure of textbook Table 11–4, with a bit of reformatting) presents data on foreign savings flows for Kenya, Senegal, and Zambia.

(i) The *net resource transfer* represents financing to support the excess of imports over exports of goods and nonfactor services. The 1980 figure for Kenya, $839.1 million, is provided on line 2. Fill in the remaining entries on this line.

(ii) The *net resource flow* represents financing to support the excess of imports over exports inclusive of payments for factor services. The 1980 figure for net resource flows to Kenya, $1,033.4 million, is shown on line 4. Fill in the remaining entries on this line.

(iii) The net resource flow is commonly used as a measure of foreign savings. For these three countries, was there a large decline in the net inflow of foreign savings between 1980 and 1990? Explain.

(iv) To put this in perspective, one can restate the net resource flows on a per capita basis. The 1980 per capita figure for Kenya, $61.9, is shown on line 6. Fill in the remaining entries on this line.

(v) In per capita terms, did these countries suffer a large decline in the net inflow of foreign savings between 1980 and 1990? Explain.

Table 11-7
Foreign Saving and Balance of Payments for Three African Countries
(millions of U.S.$)

	Kenya 1980	Kenya 1990	Senegal 1980	Senegal 1990	Zambia 1980	Zambia 1990
1 Trade in goods and nonfactor services						
a Exports	2,007.3	1,910.7	808.8	1,474.7	1,609.0	1,361.0
b Imports	(2,846.4)	(2,562.3)	(1,214.7)	(1,749.1)	(1,765.0)	(1,897.0)
2 *Net resource transfer* ($ millions)	839.1	—	—	—	—	—
3 Income payments						
a Earned	53.9	23.9	23.7	22.8	16.0	2.0
b Paid	(248.2)	(334.3)	(122.3)	(258.6)	(221.0)	(439.0)
4 *Net resource flow* ($ millions)	1,033.4	—	—	—	—	—
5 Population (millions)	16.7	24.9	5.7	7.3	5.6	8.1
6 *Net resource flow per capita* ($)	61.9	—	—	—	—	—

Source: IMF, *International Financial Statistics Yearbook 1994.*

(vi) A more meaningful evaluation would take into account the decline in the value of the dollar between 1980 and 1990. During this period the U.S. price level rose by 58.5 percent. You can multiply the 1980 figures by 1.585 to get a constant-price comparison with the figures for 1990. How does this affect your assessment of the change in net resource flows per capita for each country?

d. Several other points can be drawn from Table 11–7.

(i) What percentage of the 1990 net resource flow for each country was needed to cover net income payments, as indicated by the algebraic sum of lines 3a and 3b? It is useful to know that this net outflow of income payments consists largely of interest payments on foreign debt.

(ii) One often hears about the huge burden of debt service borne by poor African countries. Did Kenya, Senegal, and Zambia bear large debt-service burdens in 1980? In 1990?

(iii) Each of these countries benefited from a large net inflow of foreign savings—enough to meet debt-service payments and still have finance to cover an excess of imports over export earnings. What is the most likely source of the foreign savings: foreign aid, direct foreign investment, or foreign commercial borrowing? Explain.

(iv) Finally, what can you infer about the gap between domestic savings and investment in these three countries in 1980? In 1990?

Obviously one cannot generalize about all of Africa from three examples, but at least one can learn how to analyze the foreign savings flows.

7. The text presents useful calculations about the effect of foreign aid on economic growth, based on the assumption that aid augments investment in the recipient country. The calculations make use of the neoclassical sources-of-growth model from Chapter 2. The exact relationship is from equation 2–18 in the text:

$$g_y = a + w_K g_K + w_L g_L + w_T g_T$$

where K is the stock of capital, L is the size of the labor force, T is the stock of natural resources including arable land, a is the residual capturing productivity gains, g_i are growth rates, and w_i are weights.

a. Assume that $w_K = 0.3$, $w_L = 0.6$, $w_T = 0.1$, and $a = 2$ percent.
   (i) Complete the table below, with g_K, g_L, and g_T taking the values as shown.

g_K (%)	g_L (%)	g_T (%)	therefore	g_Y
10	2	1		_____
10	3	1		_____
11	2	1		_____
11	3	1		_____

   (ii) As you can see, an increase of 1 percentage point in the growth of the capital stock causes GDP growth to rise by _____ percentage points, other things being equal. If this additional capital is supplied by foreign aid, then we have a measure of the effect of foreign aid on growth.

b. You can measure the potential contribution of foreign aid to economic growth, assuming that aid leads to additional investment. There are two steps to the analysis:

   1. Calculate the potential impact of the available aid on the growth rate of the capital stock, using the formula $dg_K = (S_f/Y)(Y/K)$. Take care to note that the term Y/K is the reciprocal of the capital-output ratio Y/K.
   2. Calculate the impact on GDP growth, using the formula $dg_Y = w_K dg_K$.

   (i) Use the illustrative data shown below for these calculations; then fill in the blanks in the last two columns. Since the foreign saving ratio is expressed in percentage units, the answers will be derived as percentage point changes in the growth rates.

S_f/Y (%)	K/Y	w_K	therefore	dg_K	dg_Y
4	4	0.3		_____	_____
4	3	0.3		_____	_____
4	4	0.4		_____	_____
5	4	0.3		_____	_____

(ii) Interpret in plain English the meaning of the numbers that you get for dg_Y.

(iii) Why might the numbers you computed above for dg_Y *understate* the contribution of aid to growth?

(iv) Why might the numbers *overstate* the contribution of aid to growth?

ANSWERS TO SELF-TEST

Completion

1. 20
2. *fundamentalism*
3. tax collections, GNP (GDP)
4. foreign
5. household, corporate
6. capital
7. disposable
8. transitory
9. larger
10. investment
11. slower, fallen
12. consumption
13. 25
14. *resource balance*
15. soft or concessional
16. International Development Association (IDA)
17. conditionality
18. fungible

True-False

1.	F	10.	F
2.	F	11.	F
3.	F	12.	T
4.	T	13.	F
5.	F	14.	F
6.	T	15.	F
7.	F	16.	T
8.	T	17.	T
9.	F		

Multiple Choice

1.	a	9.	c
2.	c	10.	a
3.	b	11.	c
4.	c	12.	a
5.	b	13.	d
6.	b	14.	a
7.	a	15.	c
8.	d	16.	b

CHAPTER 12 | Fiscal Policy

OVERVIEW

The need for governments to provide public goods explains why a high proportion of government spending goes for services such as education, health, law and order, roads and parks, and the military. Concerns about income redistribution are reflected in subsidies (especially for food) and transfer payments. There is a tendency for government spending as a share of GNP to rise with per capita income; this is called *Wagner's law*. In poor countries, most types of government expenditure are chronically starved for funds. The best prospects for cost cutting usually involve military expenditures and subsidies for inefficient state-owned enterprises.

The main source of funds to pay for public services is taxation. The structure and level of taxation affects national saving and investment, the distribution of income, and economic efficiency. Most governments spend more than they raise from taxes and finance the difference by borrowing.

Governments seeking to boost revenues often resort to raising tax rates. Frequently, though, higher tax rates fail to boost revenue because they induce more avoidance (legal), evasion (illegal), and smuggling. Improving tax administration is harder to achieve but offers greater scope for boosting revenues. Over the past decade several developing countries have adopted wide-ranging tax reforms. The reforms typically include widening the tax base by including more goods or persons in the tax net, while paring deductions, credits, and tax preferences. Broadening the tax base permits governments to lower tax rates and improve tax administration. Many developing countries have also adopted the value-added tax (VAT), which is a robust form of sales tax.

The effect of taxes on private saving is often ambiguous. One clear point is that taxes used to finance state-administered pension plans will lower private saving if the revenue is paid directly to retirees (pay as you go) rather than being invested (prudential fund). Also, high corporate income taxes tend to deter investors who can find ways to move their capital abroad.

As a device for improving equity, the personal income tax is effective (even without highly progressive tax rates) because the tax falls almost exclusively on the top 20 percent of the income distribution in most developing countries. Luxury taxes also help. But high-yielding excise taxes on tobacco and cigarettes tend to be regressive; that is, they take a higher percentage of income from the poor than from the rich. The record of redistribution effects is more encouraging on the expenditure side of the budget. Public services like primary education, public investments like irrigation, and some types of subsidy can provide disproportionate benefits to the poor.

Virtually all taxes create an excess burden, which is the loss in welfare due to the tax, in excess of revenue collected. An optimal tax structure minimizes such welfare losses. This is theoretically attractive as a basis for taxation, but impractical to administer. Therefore, the guiding principle favored by the authors is tax neutrality, whereby taxes are designed to have a minimum impact on relative prices and the structure of private incentives. In general, tax neutrality entails uniform tax rates applied to a broad tax base.

MAIN LEARNING OBJECTIVES

After studying this chapter, you ought to understand and be able to explain

1. Why government expenditures are needed even in a market economy.

2. The main categories of government spending in developing countries.

3. Why there often is little scope for augmenting government saving through cuts in recurrent expenditure.

4. The main types of taxation used in developing countries.

5. The prospects for boosting government saving by increasing tax rates, introducing new types of tax, improving tax administration, and fundamental tax reform.

6. How the level and structure of taxation may affect private saving and investment.

7. Why governments have little success in redistributing incomes through the tax system.

8. How government expenditures can be used to improve equity.

9. How various taxes create efficiency losses and why neutrality is a favored principal of taxation in developing countries.

ECONOMIC TOOLS AND TECHNIQUES

From what you have learned in this chapter, you should be able to

1. Explain how an attempt to increase revenues by raising tax rates—for example, import taxes—may fail to achieve the intended result, while breeding unintended inefficiencies such as accidental protection for domestic suppliers.

2. Explain the incidence of a corporate-profit tax in the short run and long run.

3. Distinguish between effective tax rates and statutory tax rates.

4. Explain how a social security system that is financed by payroll taxes will have different effects on domestic saving depending on whether the system operates on a pay-as-you-go basis, or as a provident fund.

5. Analyze the excess burden of a commodity tax and the Ramsey rule, and show why a neutral tax is not an efficient tax.

KEY TERMS AND CONCEPTS

consumption-based taxes, income-based taxes

current expenditure versus capital expenditure

effective tax rate

fiscal policy

excess burden of taxation

import duty, export tax

neutral taxation, efficient taxation

personal and corporate income tax

progressive versus regressive taxes and expenditures

public goods

Ramsey rule

sales tax, excise tax, value-added tax (VAT)

state-owned enterprises

taxable capacity, tax ratio

tax evasion versus tax avoidance

tax haven

tax holiday

tax incidence

tax rate, tax base, tax administration

transfers to substantial governments

Wagner's law

SELF-TEST

Completion

1. The set of policy instruments relating to the level and structure of government revenues and expenditures is called _____ *policy*.

2. The goal of _____ in taxation is best achieved by applying uniform tax rates to each broad tax base (for example, income or sales).

3. The amount of income tax *actually* collected as a proportion of income is called the _____ tax rate.

4. The term _____ *goods* refers to goods or services that are characterized by nonrival consumption and nonexcludability.

5. A _____ tax is one that collects a higher proportion of income from richer persons and a lower proportion from poorer persons.

6. Taxes levied on specific goods such as tobacco or fuel are called _____ taxes.

7. The _____ tax is a modern form of sales tax that has been widely adopted in tax reform programs, partly because of its reputation as a "money machine."

8. Tax avoidance involves taking advantage of legal arrangements to reduce tax payments, whereas tax _____ involves illegal maneuvers to reduce tax payments.

9. _____-based taxes are more likely than income-based taxes to favor growth of private savings.

10. An _____ tax system is one that imposes the minimum amount of excess burden for raising a required amount of revenue.

11. One common type of investment incentive is a tax _____, with which approved investments are exempted from paying income tax for a specified number of years.

12. *Tax* _____ refers to the ultimate distributional impact of a tax: who finally bears the burden, as distinct from who pays the bill initially.

True-False

If false, you should be able to explain why.

_____ 1. Import duties account for more than 50 percent of total tax revenues in many low-income countries.

_____ 2. In most developing countries, personal income-tax collections are derived primarily from the wealthiest 20 percent of the population.

_____ 3. Deficits of state-owned enterprises averaged 4 percent of GDP across all developing countries in the mid-1970s, and the losses worsened in the early 1980s.

_____ 4. In most developing countries there is substantial potential for increasing tax revenues by improving tax administration, but these improvements are not easy to achieve.

_____ 5. Public-sector capital stock deteriorates quickly in many developing countries due to underfinancing of the maintenance costs.

_____ 6. Sales taxes are imposed on all goods except those specifically exempted, while excise taxes are imposed only on specifically enumerated items.

_____ 7. By the mid-1980s, the top marginal income tax rate in most developing countries was above 100 percent.

_____ 8. In most low-income countries the cost of subsidies and other transfer payments represents more than 20 percent of total government expenditures.

_____ 9. In most developing countries the personal income tax provides less than 20 percent of total tax revenue.

_____ 10. Corporate profit taxes are progressive, both in theory and in practice.

_____ 11. Taxes on alcohol generally are progressive.

_____ 12. In theory, higher tax rates can reduce tax revenues, but in the context of most developing countries, higher tax rates almost always increase tax revenues.

Multiple Choice

1. Taxable capacity is positively related to a country's
   a. per capita income.
   b. fuel and mineral production.
   c. openness (that is, share of foreign trade in GDP).
   d. all the above.

2. If the price and income elasticities of demand for alcohol are low, then an increase in the excise tax rate on alcohol will
   a. be regressive.
   b. cause tax revenues to decline.
   c. cause a large excess burden.
   d. all the above.

3. Wagner's Law states that the _____ size of the public sector tends to _____ as per capita income increases.
   a. relative, increase   c. relative, decrease
   b. absolute, increase   d. absolute, decrease

4. A provident fund is a fund for
   a. stabilizing foreign exchange reserves.
   b. cushioning the government budget from cyclical declines in tax revenue.
   c. financing social security programs.
   d. financing disaster and famine relief programs.

5. The term *tax haven* refers to
   a. a country with low consumption taxes.
   b. a high-priority industry that is granted a tax holiday.
   c. an industry such as minerals or fuels that provides a major source of tax revenue.
   d. a country that attracts large capital inflows by imposing very low tax rates on capital income.

6. Studies of irrigation projects in southeast Asia concluded that
   a. the benefits accrued primarily to wealthy large farmers.
   b. large farmers gained at the expense of small farmers.
   c. small farmers and landless laborers experienced significant gains in income.
   d. small farmers benefitted, but earnings for landless laborers declined.

7. The case study of comprehensive tax reform in Colombia shows that
   a. powerful economic interests were able to get many of the reforms watered down or repealed.
   b. the reforms initially caused revenues to rise twice as fast as GDP.
   c. the reforms initially shifted as much as 1.5 percent of GDP away from the top 20 percent of the income earners.
   d. all the above.

8. Which of the following is budgeted as a capital expenditure rather than a recurrent expenditure?
   a. Teachers' salaries.
   b. Road maintenance costs.
   c. An irrigation project.
   d. Military equipment.

9. Relative to the industrial nations, developing countries raise a _____ share of tax revenue from taxes on trade and a _____ share from social security taxes.
   a. higher, lower
   b. higher, higher
   c. lower, lower
   d. lower, higher

10. The cost of salaries for civil servants in most developing countries
    a. could easily be cut by one fourth because government offices are heavily overstaffed
    b. could easily be cut by one fourth because pay scales are unrealistically high.
    c. cannot easily be cut because pay scales are already far too low to attract qualified and motivated workers.
    d. cannot easily be cut because the number of civil servants is far too low to handle the essential functions of government.

11. The excess burden of a tax is the
    a. cost of collection as a percentage of the amount of tax collected.
    b. drop in private consumption due to imposition of the tax.
    c. loss of government revenue as consumers reduce their consumption of taxed goods.
    d. loss in private welfare due to the tax, net of the amount of revenue collected by the government.

12. The incidence problem with regard to the corporation income tax (CIT) refers to the fact that
    a. CIT rates are often higher for large companies than for small companies.
    b. tax holidays reduce the amount of tax that can be collected.
    c. the ultimate impact of the tax may fall on persons other than those who are liable for the tax payment.
    d. developing countries tend to set CIT rates close to those in the United States, because capital is a mobile factor of production.

APPLICATIONS

Worked Example: Tax Rates and Tax Revenues

Teenagers in Buibui fall in love with a cartoon about a superhero named Spidercomrade. As a result, Spidercomrade T-shirts become the country's major import. These T-shirts are imported at $5 = Sh50 each (Sh stands for shillings).

The demand curve for T-shirts is curve DD in Figure 12–1. This curve is drawn so that the demand is highly price elastic. Initially the T-shirts are imported duty free, so the domestic price equals the world price, $P_0 = $ Sh50. At this price $Q_0 = $ 1,000 T-shirts are bought (per day). The government then decides to levy an import duty of $t = $ Sh20 per T-shirt. As a result, the domestic price jumps to $P_1 = $ Sh70 = world price + tariff. Figure 12–1 shows that the quantity demanded consequently drops to $Q_1 = 364$. The government collects tariff revenue equal to $R_1 = $ Sh7280 (=364 shirts $\times$ Sh20 per shirt).

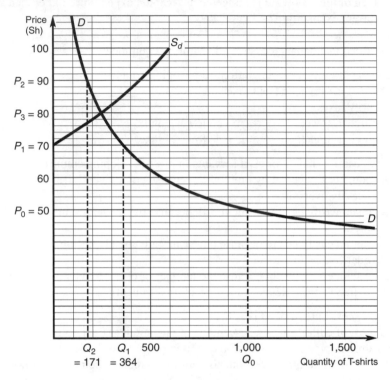

FIGURE 12–1

In an effort to collect even more revenue, the government doubles the tariff to $t = $ Sh40. With the new tariff, the domestic price rises to $P_2 = $ Sh90. The demand curve shows that consumers will buy only $Q_2 = 171$ at this price. So government revenue from the duty is $R_2 = $ Sh6840 (= 171×40). Officials at the tax department are chagrined to find that revenues dropped as a result of the higher duty.

They are even more chagrined to find that a new domestic industry soon sprouts in response to the high, duty-ridden price of imported T-shirts. Local entrepreneurs begin to import unfinished T-shirts at $10 each. (Since these are raw materials for domestic industry, no tariff is charged). Then they silk screen the Spidercomrade logo and sell their product for $P_3 = $ Sh80. In Figure 12–1, the curve S_d shows the domestic supply curve for T-shirts. You can see that domestic production becomes profitable only when the price of imported shirts rises above Sh70. Because of the domestic supply response to so-called accidental protection, imports of Spidercomrade T-shirts fall to zero. So does the revenue from import duties. The increased tax *rates* led to a precipitous drop in tax *revenues*.

(A subsequent effort to introduce a tariff on unfinished T-shirts failed in the face of intense opposition from the new domestic T-shirt industry.)

Had the tariff remained Sh20 per shirt, tax revenue would have grown over time as the demand curve shifted outward. With rising income and population, the tax *base* would grow and generate additional tax *revenues*. If the demand for Spidercomrade T-shirts—and later, Batcomrade T-shirts—is income elastic, then revenues will expand faster than GDP, and this will lead to a rising tax ratio. Together with prudent controls on the growth of public consumption expenditure, this income-elastic revenue source can facilitate public-sector investment and contribute to macroeconomic stability.

Exercises

1. This exercise gives you a turn to investigate the relationship between tax rates and tax revenues in Buibui, as discussed in the Worked Example.

   a. Some of the price-quantity combinations from the demand curve *DD* in Figure 12–1 are listed in Table 12–1. The three completed rows (for prices of Sh50, Sh70, and Sh90) were discussed in the Worked Example.
      (i) Given the world price of Sh50 per Spidercomrade T-shirt, the domestic price depends on the tariff rate (so many shillings per shirt). Fill in column 3 of Table 12–1 with the tariff rate corresponding to each price.

Table 12–1

Tariff Revenues in Buibui

Price (Sh) (1)	Quantity (2)	Tariff (Sh per T-shirt) (3)	Tariff revenue* (SH) (4)
50	1,000	0	0
55	751	_____	_____
60	579	_____	_____
65	455	_____	_____
70	364	20	7,280
75	296	_____	_____
80	244	_____	_____
85	204	_____	_____
90	171	40	6,840

*Ignoring domestic supply response.

      (ii) Then fill in column 4 of Table 12–1 with the amount of revenue the government would collect with each tariff rate. For the moment suppose that there is no supply response. (Hint: Revenue = $t \times Q$.)

b. (i) From among the avrious tariff rates shown in Table 12–1, government tariff revenues will be maximized when the tariff is

$$t^* = \text{Sh} \underline{\hspace{2cm}} \text{ per T-shirt}$$

and the domestic price is

$$P^* = \text{Sh} \underline{\hspace{2cm}} \text{ per T-shirt.}$$

(ii) Briefly explaing why tax collections would decline if the tariff rate were increased beyond t^*.

c. Now let's stop ignoring the domestic supply response.
   (i) Look at the domestic supply curve S_d in Figure 12–1. What quantity of Spidercomrade T-shirts will be produced domestically when the tariff rate is t^* and the price is P^* (from part b above)?

$$Q_s = \underline{\hspace{2cm}} \text{ T-shirts.}$$

   (ii) Given the quantity demanded and the quantity supplied domestically at price P^*, what quantity will be imported at this price?

$$Q_m = \underline{\hspace{2cm}} \text{ T-shirts.}$$

   (iii) So what will be the actual amount of government tariff revenue when the tariff level is t^*?

$$\text{Revenue} = \text{Sh} \underline{\hspace{2cm}}.$$

(iv) Briefly explain why government revenues from a tariff of t^* fall so far short of the amount you calculated when completing Table 12–1.

(v) Taking into account the domestic supply response, the government would maximize revenues with a tariff rate of

$$t^* = \text{Sh} \underline{\hspace{2cm}} \text{ per T-shirt.}$$

(Note: Limit your attention to those tariff rates shown in Table 12–1.)

d. Suppose that the government had adopted an excise tax on Spidercomrade T-shirts, instead of an import duty. The excise tax is levied on domestically produced units as well as imports.

(i) With the excise tax, what revenue would hte government collect with a tax of Sh25 per shirt?

$$\text{Revenue} = \text{Sh} \underline{\hspace{2cm}}.$$

(ii) What revenue would the government collect with a tax on Sh40 per shirt?

$$\text{Revenue} = \text{Sh} \underline{\hspace{2cm}}.$$

e. Now pull together some conclusions about tax policy.

(i) Comparing your calculations in parts c and d, which tax—the excise tax or the import duty—is more effective in raising revenue? Why?

    (ii) Which tax is superior in terms of tax neutrality? Explain.

    (iii) With the excise tax instead of the import duty, will a tax rate above Sh20 per shirt still induce domestic production in place of imports? Explain.

    (iv) Which tax is superior in terms of resource allocation efficiency? Explain. (To answer this, you might find it useful to know that the production of logo T-shirts is a very low priority in the development plan for Buibui.)

    (v) Which tax is likely to have lower tax administration costs? Explain.

2. This exercise examines some data facts relating to Wagner's law of expanding state activity, and then explores the determinants of taxable capacity.

   a. Table 12–1 in the textbook presents data on central government expenditures as a share of GNP for the four standard income groups (defined in terms of PPP $ for 1992). Combine those group averages with the following per capita income figures (which are simply midpoints for the four income ranges):

	Per capita income, 1992 (PPP$)
Low-income countries	1,000
Lower-middle-income countries	3,500
Upper-middle-income countries	7,500
High-income countries	15,000

(i) Plot the four points for these income groups on Figure 12–2 and connect the points. Label this line *G/Y*.

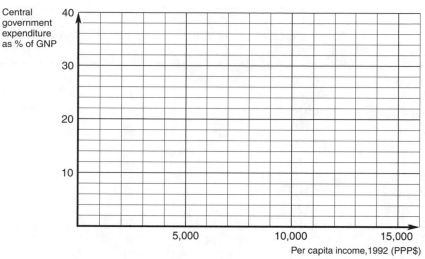

Central government expenditure as % of GNP

Per capita income,1992 (PPP$)

FIGURE 12–2

(ii) Does the graph suggest that Wagner's law (which was formulated a century ago) is a reasonable description of the relationship between the size of government and per capita income in 1992?

(iii) Refer again to textbook Table 12–1 to find group average data on housing, social security, and welfare expenditures as a share of GNP. Plot this information on Figure 12–2 and connect the points. Label this line *WELFARE/Y*.

(iv) What does the graph tell you about how spending on social services varies with per capita income, on average? What is the reason for the relationship you observe?

b. The relative size of government can also be measured in terms of the *tax ratio*, which is the ratio of tax revenues to GNP. Columns 1 and 2 in Table 12–2 provide data on per capita income and the tax ratio for twenty countries that are selected to span the full range of income from $1,000 to $15,000 in 1992 dollars (PPP).

Table 12–2

Government Spending and Tax Ratios for Selected Countries, 1992

Country	(1) GNP per capita, 1992 (PPP$)	(2) T/GNP[*] (%)	(3) X/GDP[†] (%)	(4) FMM/X[†] (%)
Nepal	1,100	9.6	19	0
Kenya	1,360	26.2	27	16
Zimbabwe	1,970	30.6	32	17
The Philippines	2,480	17.4	29	8
Indonesia	2,970	19.7	29	38
Paraguay	3,510	12.3	22	1
Jordan	4,220	30.0	43	34
Ecuador	4,380	18.0	31	45
Tunisia	5,130	29.5	38	16
Costa Rica	5,550	22.9	39	1
Thailand	5,890	18.1	36	2
Uruguay	7,450	29.7	21	1
Malaysia	8,050	30.1	78	17
Korea	8,950	18.2	29	3
Portugal	10,120	37.9	25	5
Mauritius	11,390	24.4	64	2
Ireland	12,070	42.9	64	2
Spain	13,170	30.7	18	5
New Zealand	14,400	35.4	31	7
Israel	14,600	37.7	29	2

[*]T = central government revenue.
[†]X = exports of goods and nonfactor services.
[†]FMM = exports of fuels, minerals, and metals.

Sources: *World Development Report 1994*, Tables 30, 11, 9, and 15, supplemented by data from IMF, *International Financial Services Yearbook 1994*.

    (i) In Figure 12–3 plot the tax-ratio data for these 20 countries as a function of per capita income. Draw an approximate best-fit line representing the average relationship between these two variables. Label the line *TR* for tax ratio.

    (ii) Does the line *TR* provide support for Wagner's Law? Explain.

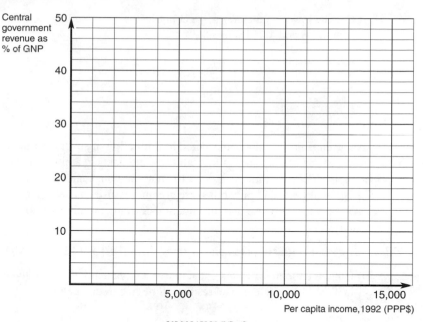

FIGURE 12–3

c. The *TR* line is sometimes interpreted as a measure of *taxable capacity* because it shows how much revenue (as a share of GNP) can be expected, on average, for any given level of per capita income.

   (i) The point corresponding to Zimbabwe is far above the *TR* line; therefore, the actual tax ratio is quite high relative to the average for Zimbabwe's level of income. Identify this point on the graph and label it as *ZIM*.

   (ii) What factors might explain Zimbabwe's high tax ratio? (Hint: Refer to the data in Table 12–2 for ideas. Keep in mind that trade is easy to tax, especially trade in bulk raw materials.)

   (iii) For which three countries do you find the data plot is farthest *below* line *TR*? Label each of these three points with the first three letters of the respective country's name.

    (iv) Can the low tax ratios for these countries be explained by the data in columns 3 and 4 of Table 12–2?

d. Taxable capacity usually is measured as a function of several variables, not just per capita income. In fact, all three elements examined above— per capita GNP, the ratio of exports to GDP, and the share of exports consisting of fuels and minerals—are commonly used as determinants of tax capacity. Suppose that the equation defining an index of tax capacity (TC) is

$$TC = 12.13 + 0.0014(\text{GNP per capita}) + 0.0817(X/GDP) + 0.12 * (FMM/X).$$

    (i) Compute the index of tax capacity for Kenya using the data given in Table 12–2. (Note: The result will be in percentage units.)

    (ii) Is Kenya's actual tax ratio higher or lower than the index of taxable capacity? Should this be interpreted as a good thing? Explain.

e. (i) Now compute the tax capacity index for Korea. Compare the result with the actual tax ratio.

    (ii) In 1992 Korea's central government ran a deficit of 1 percent of GNP. In view of your answer to question (i), could Korea have easily erased this deficit by raising taxes? Explain.

(iii) If Korea were to increase the actual tax ratio to the estimated tax level of its tax capacity, would gross domestic saving necessarily increase? Explain briefly.

3. The text notes that the value-added tax (VAT) has become very popular in developing countries over the past decade and has steadily replaced other forms of sales tax. This question explores the essential mechanics of a VAT; in the process the reasons for its popularity will become clearer.

   To set up the problem, suppose that there are just four firms in an economy, as follows:

Firm 1. Cotton farmer, who sells $100 worth of cotton to Firm 2.

Firm 2. Textile factory, which buys the cotton from the farmer, spins and weaves it into cloth, and sells it for $300 to Firm 3.

Firm 3. Garment factory, which buys the cloth from the textile maker, and makes shirts which it sells for $700 to Firm 4.

Firm 4. Retailer, who buys shirts from the garment factory and sells them to you and me for $1,500.

a. (i) A traditional retail sales tax would just tax the final output. Suppose the tax is 10 percent. How much tax will be collected?

   (ii) Retailers can be difficult to tax, especially when they are very small businesses, as in most developing countries. How much revenue would the sales tax yield if it were levied at the manufacturer level (meaning that firm 3's sales constitute the tax base)?

b. (i) Value added is the value of sales minus the value of physical inputs. Assume that the cotton farmer buys no inputs. Then,

   Value added by firm 1 is _____.

   Value added by firm 2 is _____.

   Value added by firm 3 is _____.

   Value added by firm 4 is _____$800_____.

   Total value added is _____.

   Note that total value added is the same as the value of final sales, so taxing value added should yield just as much as taxing the value of final sales.

(ii) Under the most common form of VAT, a firm pays tax on the value of its sales and then deducts a credit for the VAT paid on its inputs. For example, if the VAT rate is 10 percent, firm 3 has to pay VAT of 10 percent × $700 = $70. But if the supplier charged VAT on the sale of the cloth (10 percent × $300 = $30) and provides proper documentation to firm 3, then firm 3 gets a $30 credit to deduct from its tax obligation. Net, firm 3 only has to pay $40 in tax. Thus, with a 10 percent VAT,

Firm 1 has to pay _____ in VAT (net).

Firm 2 has to pay _____ in VAT (net).

Firm 3 has to pay __$40_ in VAT (net).

Firm 4 has to pay _____ in VAT (net).

Total VAT paid is _____, which is _____ percent of the total value added as tabulated in part (i).

(Note: If firm 3 lacked documentation that firm 2 paid VAT on the cloth, firm 3 could not qualify for the credit. So firm 3 has an incentive to ensure that VAT paid on purchased inputs is duly recorded. This is the so-called self-enforcing feature of the VAT.)

c. Until recently the VAT in Indonesia exempted retailers. If the VAT here did the same, how much VAT would each firm pay and how much VAT would be collected overall?

d. Return to the case where retailers are included in the tax base. Some countries exempt farmers from paying VAT on their sales. In our example, how much VAT would be collected in toto if farmers were exempted from VAT? (Be careful. Firm 2 no longer will be paying just $20 in VAT. Do you see why?)

e. Most countries do not wish to penalize exports by taxing them. So they *zero rate* exports. This means that exporting firms do not have to pay VAT on goods that are exported, yet they still get full credit for VAT paid on inputs. Exporters even may qualify for a refund from the government. Suppose that half the output of shirts is exported by the garment maker, firm 3. Will firm 3 be liable to pay VAT or will it qualify for a refund? How much?

In summary, VAT is favored over other forms of sales tax for several reasons. It makes it easy to remove tax from exports. It can collect substantial revenue even if retailers, or small firms in general, are excluded. It has certain self-policing properties that leave a paper trail, which can be helpful when tax inspectors conduct audits.

4. In this exercise we analyze the incidence of excise taxes.

   a. Figure 12–4 shows the supply and demand for turbans in Hatistan. Near to the equilibrium, demand is inelastic, whereas supply is quite elastic. The initial equilibrium market price is $P_0 = $ Rs10 (10 rupees). The equilibrium quantity is Q_0. Now let the government impose an excise tax of Rs5 per turban.

      (i) One way to analyze this is to shift the supply curve upward to reflect the tax. For example, output Q_0 would now be supplied at a market price of Rs10 *plus* the tax, or Rs15. Each point on the

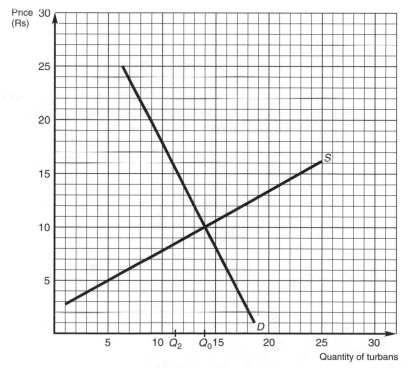

FIGURE 12–4

supply curve similarly shifts upward by the amount of the tax. Carefully draw in the new market supply curve; label it $S'S'$.

(ii) The new equilibrium price in the turban market will be

$P_1 = $ Rs _____ (to the nearest integer).

(iii) Why does the equilibrium price rise by less than the amount of the tax?

b. (i) At the new equilibrium price the turban sellers receive a net revenue of Rs _____ per hat, after taking out the Rs5 that goes to the government.

(ii) Compared with the pretax market equilibrium, consumers now pay Rs _____ per hat more than before, while sellers receive (net) Rs _____ per hat less than before. (Hint: These two answers sum to Rs5, the amount collected by the government on each hat.)

(iii) In this simple example, the incidence of the tax is

Consumers bear _____ percent of the tax burden.

Sellers bear _____ percent of the tax burden.

c. Figure 12–5 shows the supply and demand for mangoes in Hatistan. Note that the demand curve for mangoes has the same form as in Figure 12–4, but now supply is quite inelastic. The initial equilibrium market price is $P_0 = $ Rs10 (10 rupees) per bag. The equilibrium quantity is Q_0. Now suppose that the government imposes an excise tax of Rs5 per bag of mangoes.

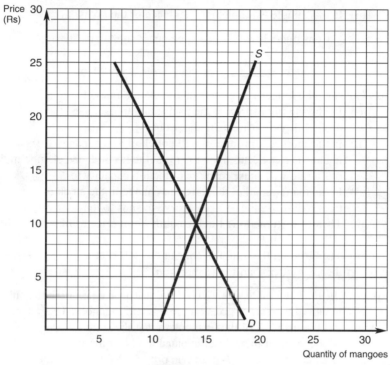

FIGURE 12–5

(i) Carefully draw in th new market supply curve; label it $S'S'$.

(ii) The new equilibrium price in the mango market will be

$P_1 = $ Rs _____ per bag.

d. (i) At the new equilibrium price, the mango sellers receive a net revenue of Rs _____ per bag, after taking out the Rs5 that goes to the government.

(ii) Compared with the pretax market equilibrium, consumers are now paying Rs _____ per bag more than before, while sellers are receiving (net) Rs _____ per bag less than before.

(iii) In this simple example, the incidence of the tax is

Consumers bear _____ percent of the tax burden.

Sellers bear _____ percent of the tax burden.

e. Consider the longer-run effects on the mango market.
   (i) Following imposition of the excise tax on mangoes, the profitability of growing mangoes has _____.
   (ii) In the short run, producers will not chop down mango trees and put in banana trees. But in the long run, the tax-induced change in the profit rate will cause mango production capacity to _____.
   (iii) In the mango market the long-run change in the stock of mango trees will cause the _____ curve to shift to the _____.
   (iv) Therefore, in the long run the equilibrium price of mangoes will be _____ than P_1.
   (v) Therefore, in the long run consumers will bear a _____ share of the tax burden than in the short run.

2. *More difficult.* The graphs from Exercise 4 are used again here to study the excess burden of the excise taxes on turbans and mangoes. This exercise generalizes Figure 12–2 of the textbook in that the supply curves are not horizontal. Because of this a brief explanation is required.

Suppose that, in Figure 12–4, turban production were to increase from Q_2 to $Q_2 + 1$. The extra unit of turban production is of benefit to society. Its value is measured by the height of the demand curve; at Q_2 the marginal social benefit is Rs15. But resources are needed to produce the extra turban. The opportunity cost of these resources is measured by the height of the (pretax) supply curve, which is Rs9 at Q_2. The net benefit to society of producing this extra turban is therefore Rs6. In general, the vertical gap between the two curves at any value of Q shows the gain in social welfare achieved from having the marginal unit of output produced. Hence, the area enclosed by the supply and demand curves above any *interval* on the horizontal axis gives the total welfare gain that accrues when the corresponding units output are produced—or the total welfare loss when these units of output are foregone.

a. In Figure 12–4 darkly shade the triangle corresponding to the welfare loss caused by the drop in turban production when the excise tax is imposed.

b. In Figure 12–5 darkly shade the triangle corresponding to the welfare loss caused by the (short-run) drop in mango production when the excise tax is imposed.

c. Review the textbook's Figure 12–2 so you understand that the rectangle represents the amount of tax revenue collected by the government. The same idea may be applied to Figures 12–4 and 12–5, in which you have already marked two prices (from Exercise 4): the price paid by buyers and the price, net of tax, received by suppliers.

   (i) Lightly shade the area between these two prices, starting at the vertical axis and extending out to the market equilibrium quantity (posttax). This shaded area is the total tax revenue.

   (ii) The lightly shaded area represent a loss of welfare to consumers and producers. But it is not included in measuring the excess burden of the tax. As defined in text, the excess burden is given by the heavily shaded triangle alone. Why?

d. In Figures 12–4 and 12–5, equal tax rates are imposed on turbans and mangoes, but the market responses are different.

   (i) Is the excess burden of the tax in the market for mangoes greater than, equal to, or less than the excess burden in the market for turbans? Prove it. (Hint: The proof uses the formula for the area of a triangle: $\frac{1}{2}$ base × height.)

   (ii) The tax rates and the demand elasticities are the same in Figures 12–4 and 12–5, but the supply elasticities are different. Formulate a simple rule linking differences in the supply elasticity to the size of the excess burden from the tax.

ANSWERS TO SELF-TEST

Completion

1. *fiscal*
2. neutrality
3. effective
4. *public*
5. progressive
6. excise
7. value-added
8. evasion
9. Consumption
10. efficient
11. holiday
12. *incidence*

True-False

1.	F	7.	F
2.	T	8.	F
3.	T	9.	T
4.	T	10.	F
5.	T	11.	F
6.	T	12.	F

Multiple Choice

1.	d	7.	d
2.	a	8.	c
3.	a	9.	a
4.	c	10.	c
5.	d	11.	d
6.	c	12.	c

CHAPTER 13 | Financial Policy

OVERVIEW

Financial policy encompasses a broad range of measures relating to the development and management of the financial system. In any modern economy the financial system serves four essential functions. It supplies liquid assets—money—that are used as the medium of exchange for payments of all kinds. It plays the lead role in mobilizing private domestic savings and allocating savings efficiently to productive investment. In the process, financial intermediaries and markets encourage saving and investment by transforming and distributing risks. Finally, the financial system provides government with instruments to manage macroeconomic stabilization policy and influence the pattern of investments.

Perhaps the most obvious problem of financial policy is maintaining control of inflation. In extreme cases of hyperinflation, the effect is devastating to the economy. Some countries have managed to sustain satisfactory growth with moderate inflation, but even then the adverse effects far outweigh any alleged benefits of using inflation as a source of forced savings or tolerating inflation so the economy can keep running at a high pitch.

The textbook explains that maintaining a realistically positive real interest rate is the hallmark of deep financial strategies. This often necessitates decontrol of interest rates and discipline on the part of the monetary authorities. What undergirds an orderly financial liberalization is an appropriate regulatory framework that balances the need for insurance against ever-present panics with the goal of building a diversified and competitive financial system.

The chapter ends with a discussion of monetary policy and price stability. The operation of monetary policy depends on the exchange-rate regime. To maintain a pegged exchange rate, central banks must buy and sell foreign currencies to offset imbalances in supply and demand; this greatly constrains the management of the money supply. Central banks have more control over the determinants of money supply growth with a floating exchange-rate system. In any case, excessive expansion of domestic credit will trigger inflation. High inflation usually can be traced to the rapid expansion of credit to the government to cover fiscal deficits. Thus, poor fiscal policy also constrains effective monetary management. To the extent that the central bank has discretion, it operates monetary policy through open-market operations, changes in reserve requirements, direct credit ceilings, management of interest rates, and moral suasion.

MAIN LEARNING OBJECTIVES

After studying this chapter, you ought to understand and be able to explain

1. The functions and characteristics of the financial systems in developing countries.

2. The definition of money and liquid assets.

3. The diversity of inflation experience in developing countries and the pros and cons of using inflation as a device to mobilize forced savings.

4. How inflation affects real interest rates and how real interest rates, in turn, affect savings and the demand for liquid assets.

5. The characteristics, causes, and consequences of deep finance versus shallow finance.

6. The character of informal credit markets in developing countries.

7. How management of monetary policy depends on the exchange-rate regime.

8. The causes and consequences of excessive money supply growth.

9. The main tools of monetary policy in developing countries.

10. The causes and consequences of financial panics.

ECONOMIC TOOLS AND TECHNIQUES

From what you have learned in this chapter, you should be able to

1. Calculate the implicit inflation tax rate on money balances.

2. Calculate the real interest rate (with and without taxes).

3. Analyze the relationship between the real interest rate and the demand for liquid assets.

4. Explain how changes in international reserves under a fixed exchange-rate system limit the ability of the central bank to control the money supply.

5. Show how government budget deficits relate to domestic credit creation, expansion of the money supply, and inflation.

KEY TERMS AND CONCEPTS

central bank, commercial banks
credit ceilings
chronic, acute, and runaway (hyper-)
    inflation
demand deposits, time deposits
domestic credit
financial intermediation
financial panics
financial policy
financial system
fixed (pegged) versus flexible
    (floating) exchange rate
forced savings
inflation tax
informal credit market

interest elasticity of savings
international reserves
liquid financial assets
managed float, crawling peg,
    adjustable peg
monetary policy
money supply, narrow money (M1),
    broad money (M2)
moral hazard
nominal and real interest rate
open-market operations, reserve
    requirements, rediscount rate,
    and moral suasion
shallow finance, deep finance

SELF-TEST

Completion

1. The process of gathering savings from multitudes of savers and channeling
    the funds to investors is done by _____ _____ such
    as commercial banks, pension funds, and insurance companies.

2. Both time deposits and demand deposits are types of _____
    financial assets.

3. The textbook uses the term *acute inflation* to describe inflation in excess of
    _____ percent for more than three years.

4. Inflation acts as a tax on holdings of _____ balances.

5. _____ money (M1) consists of _____ in circulation
    outside banks plus demand deposits.

6. When real interest rates on deposits become _____, savers
    increase their holdings of liquid financial assets.

7. _____-finance policies impair the growth of the financial system.

8. The essence of a policy of financial deepening is the avoidance of sharply negative _____ _____ _____.

9. As the formal financial system expands and develops, the _____ credit market tends to shrink in size and coverage.

10. Large budget deficits triggered Peru's _____ inflation in the late 1980s, which wrought economic and social havoc.

11. Changes in the money supply can be explained in terms of two components: the expansion of _____ _____ and changes in international reserves.

12. Under a _____ exchange-rate system, a central bank has very limited control over the international component of changes in the money supply.

True-False

If false, you should be able to explain why.

_____ 1. A commercial bank located in the capital city is referred to as a central bank.

_____ 2. The ratio of liquid financial assets to GDP often is used as a measure of the extent of financial intermediation in developing countries.

_____ 3. Most low-income countries suffered from chronic inflation, as defined in the text, during the entire period from 1970 to 1990.

_____ 4. If the nominal interest rate is held constant, then the real interest rate will drop as the inflation rate rises.

_____ 5. If the income elasticity of demand for liquid assets is above unity, then price stability is not necessarily threatened when M2 grows a bit more quickly than income.

_____ 6. Inflation reduces the riskiness of undertaking large-scale investments since it enables corporations to raise prices.

_____ 7. Shallow finance tends to lower the efficiency of investment and increase the capital-output ratio for the economy.

_____ 8. Markets for stocks and bonds evolve most rapidly in countries where the commercial banking system is poorly developed due to shallow financial policies.

_____ 9. A well-functioning financial system furnishes a means for diversifying risks among large numbers of savers and investors.

_____ 10. In developing countries, as in developed countries, open-market operations are the primary tool of monetary policy.

_____ 11. In most developing countries, government budget deficits are financed primarily by borrowing from the central bank, which increases the money supply.

_____ 12. Empirical evidence indicates that the demand for liquid financial assets in developing countries is strongly related to the level of nominal interest rates.

Multiple Choice

1. Which of the following financial assets is included in the broad money supply (M2), but not in the narrow money supply (M1)?
   a. Checking deposits.
   b. Time deposits.
   c. Both a and b.
   d. Neither a nor b. In developing countries, M1 and M2 are identical.

2. Which of the following statements about inflation in developing countries has proven generally to be valid?
   a. Double-digit inflation is incompatible with even moderate growth of per capita income.
   b. Efficiency losses from the inflation tax are small relative to the efficiency losses from conventional types of tax.
   c. The government's marginal propensity to invest out of inflation taxes is unity or greater.
   d. None of the above.

3. In low-income countries the ratio of broad money to GDP is in the range of
   a. 1 to 10 percent.   c. 50 to 100 percent.
   b. 10 to 50 percent.   d. 100 to 300 percent.

4. The financial system provides four basic services essential for the smooth functioning of an economy. Which of the following is *not* one of the four?
   a. Supplying a medium of exchange (money).
   b. Mobilizing savings and channeling them to investors.
   c. Providing a set of instruments for stabilization policy.
   d. Reducing inequalities in the distribution of income.

5. Shallow finance is characterized by
   a. slow growth or even declines in the ratio of liquid assets to GDP.
   b. negative real interest rates.
   c. pervasive nonprice rationing of credit.
   d. all the above.

6. In Peru from 1974 to 1982 nominal interest rates rose from 5 to 55 percent but real interest rates fell from −19 to −43 percent. From these facts one can infer that
   a. inflation increased sharply.
   b. there was rapid financial deepening.
   c. the banking system was a monopoly.
   d. the country had a floating exchange rate.

7. If authorities intervene in the foreign exchange market at their discretion, without committing to defend a particular exchange rate, the exchange-rate regime is called
   a. a managed float.
   b. a crawling peg.
   c. an adjustable peg.
   d. all the above, as they are synonymous.

8. In the equation $L/P = d + d_1Y + d_2q + d_3r$,
   a. the coefficient d_1 is negative.
   b. the coefficient d_2 is negative.
   c. the coefficient d_3 is negative.
   d. none of the coefficients is negative.

9. Which of the following tools of monetary control is widely used in developing countries but not in developed countries?
   a. Changes in reserve requirements.
   b. Credit ceilings imposed by the central bank.
   c. Changes in the rediscount rate.
   d. Moral suasion.

10. In developing countries, negative real interest rates generally are
    a. an objective of monetary policy.
    b. encouraged to induce savers to invest directly rather than hold liquid financial assets.
    c. a result of inflexible interest rate controls during periods of rising inflation.
    d. a major instrument for combating inflation.

11. In developing countries, the term *curb market* refers to
    a. financial markets with credit ceilings that force banks to curb their lending.
    b. financial markets that operate with interest rate controls.
    c. informal lenders who operate outside the regulated, institutional financial system.
    d. illegal lending activities, usually operated by organized criminal groups.

12. The case study on small-scale savings and credit institutions shows that the BRI's rural banking system in Indonesia
    a. has an on-time repayment rate of 97 percent.
    b. has attracted sufficient savings deposits to more than finance its loan program.
    c. is a major profit center for the bank.
    d. has all the above characteristics.

APPLICATIONS

Worked Example: Inflation and Real Returns on Financial Assets

In an inflationary environment, nominal interest rates overstate the real cost of borrowing and the real return on lending or holding financial assets. Suppose that the (nominal) interest rate on a one-year loan is 15 percent (so $i = 0.15$). A bank that lends $1,000 at this interest rate will be repaid an amount of $1,000 $(1 + i)$ = $1,150 one year later. If the *expected* inflation rate over the next year is 10 percent (so $p = 0.10$), then the expected real value of this repayment is $1,150/(1 + p)$ = $1,045.45. The lender expects a *real* return—after adjusting for inflation—of $45.45 on the $1,000 loan. This represents a real interest rate of just over 4.54 percent. Algebraically, $1,045.45 = $1,000$(1 + r)$, so $r = 0.0454 = 4.54$ percent.

Suppose, however, that the *actual* inflation rate is 25 percent ($p = 0.25$). Then the $1,150 repayment of principal plus interest has an inflation-adjusted value of $1,150/(1 + p)$ = $920. The lender earns a *real* return of –$80 on the $1,000 loan, so the real interest rate is –8 percent. Formally, $920 = $1,000$(1 + r)$, so $r = -0.08 = -8$ percent. In this case, borrowing is an obvious bargain, but saving is a losing proposition. If savers foresee that inflation will exceed the nominal interest rate, then savings will be diverted to physical assets like jewelry and gold, which offer a hedge against inflation, or other financial assets held abroad (capital flight). Financial intermediation is repressed. This is an example of shallow financial policy.

In these numerical examples, the real interest rate is found by applying equation 13–4 from the textbook:

$$r = (1 + i)/(1 + p) - 1.$$

A simpler and more familiar relationship is given by equation 13–4 of the text: $r = i - p$. This is actually an approximation, not an exact formula. The approximation is satisfactory when p is fairly small, but less accurate for larger values. In the examples above, with 10 percent inflation the approximation gives a real interest rate of $15 - 10 = 5$ percent, compared to the true value 4.54 percent. With 25 percent inflation the approximation gives a real interest rate of $15 - 25 = -10$ percent, compared to the true value of –8 percent. If the inflation rate were 100 percent (as in Zambia in 1991), then the approximation gives a result that is *double* the true value of –42.5 percent—which is bad enough!

It is worse still if interest earnings are subject to income tax. In this case the interest reward accruing to savers is diminished by the tax obligation. Instead of i, one would insert $i(1 - t)$ into the formulas. Suppose that the tax rate is 30 percent, so $t = 0.30$. With an interest rate of 15 percent, the after-tax nominal return is $i(1 - t) = 0.105 = 10.5$ percent. If the inflation rate is 25 percent, then the real interest rate is not -8 percent but

$$r = [1 + i(1 - t)]/(1 + p) - 1 = -0.116 = -11.6\%.$$

Money is a special case. Narrow-money balances are held in the form of cash and demand deposits, which earn zero interest in most countries. So $i = 0$ in the formula (and income taxes are irrelevant here). With 10 percent inflation, the real return on money balances is $r = 1.00/(1 + p) - 1 = -0.09$, or -9 percent. With 25 percent inflation, the real return is -20 percent. The decline in the purchasing power of money constitutes a genuine loss of command over real resources for money holders. The resources can be utilized by the government, which prints money to make its various payments. So this is an *inflation tax*. If the inflation tax is too onerous, due to runaway inflation, then the private sector will shun holding domestic money balances. Monetization, with all of its attendant efficiency advantages, suffers.

Exercises

1. It is your turn to calculate the real interest rate and the inflation tax.

   a. Table 13–1 shows the nominal interest rates and inflation rates for five countries in mid-1995. The inflation rate is based on price data for the latest 12 months. Assume that savers used these inflation figures as the basis for formulating their expectations of the inflation rate for the near future.

Table 13–1

Real versus Nominal Interest Rates, 1995
(% per annum)

Country	Nominal interest rate (1)	Inflation rate (2)	Real interest rate (3)	Approximate real interest rate (4)	Inflation tax rate (5)
Malaysia	5.9	3.8	_____	_____	_____
S. Korea	14.7	5.1	_____	_____	_____
Turkey	75.6	82.4	_____	_____	_____
Venezuela	17.5	71.2	_____	_____	_____
Russia	242.4	205.2	_____	_____	_____

Source: "Emerging Market Indicators," *Economist*, July 1, 1995.

   (i) Calculate the expected real interest rate in each of the five countries and put your answer in column 3.
   (ii) For comparison, also calculate the approximation to the real interest rate, using the simple formula $r = i - p$; put your answer in column 4. Before going on, notice the pattern of differences between the figures in columns 3 and 4.
   (iii) Finally, calculate the inflation-tax rate on money balances; put your answer in column 5. (Hint: If you earn a real return on money balances of $-X$ percent, your money holdings are subject to a tax of X percent.)

b. Who benefits when the inflation rate exceeds the nominal interest rate on a financial asset: borrowers (issuers of financial assets) or lenders (holders of the financial assets)? Briefly explain.

c. Consider how taxes affect the interest rate analysis. In Zambia in mid-1992, the controlled interest rate on bank deposits was 48 percent and the inflation rate was 112 percent.
   (i) The real interest rate on bank *deposits* was _____ percent.

   (ii) Interest earned on bank deposits was subject to 10 percent income tax. Hence, the 48 percent interest rate produced a nominal *after-tax* yield for depositors of _____ percent. (For help, see the Worked Example.)

   (iii) The *real after-tax* interest rate on deposits was _____ percent.

   (iv) How did this affect the supply of deposit funds to the banking system?

d. Continuing the example of Zambia, while the inflation rate was 112 percent the controlled interest rate on bank loans was 68 percent.
   (i) The real interest rate on bank *loans* was _____ percent.

(ii) Most borrowers getting bank loans were corporations facing a 35 percent tax on income. Since interest costs are deducted from the amount of income subject to tax, 35 percent of the interest cost is effectively offset by a smaller tax bill. Therefore, the 68 percent loan rate represented a net-of-tax nominal interest rate of _____ percent.

(iii) The corresponding *real after-tax* interest rate on bank loans was _____ percent.

(iv) How did this affect the demand for loan funds from the banking system?

e. Think about your answers concerning the supply of deposit funds and the demand for loan funds in Zambia in 1992.
   (i) How did the interest rate controls affect the overall balance between supply and demand for finance?

   (ii) What does this imply about the way the banks allocate credit?

   (iii) What does this imply about the market for informal finance in Zambia?

2. This exercise analyzes the efficiency gains from financial intermediation and the efficiency costs of shallow finance. Each family in Kapital saves $100 per year. Initially there are no banks or other financial intermediaries, so household savings are either invested in hens (productive capital) or jewelry (unproductive assets). The inflation rate is zero, and we will ignore tax considerations. Hens cost $1 each; the rate of return on marginal additions to the flock varies inversely with the number of birds. The rate of return on jewelry is zero.

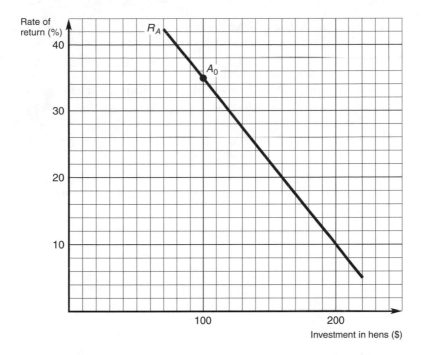

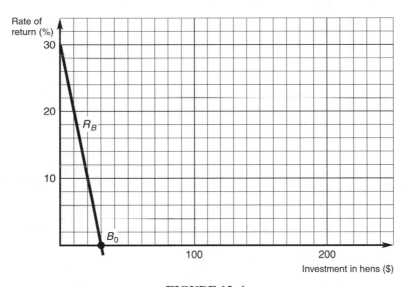

FIGURE 13–1

a. The top panel of Figure 13–1 refers to family A. The bottom panel refers to family B. Line R_A shows the relationship between the investment in hens and the rate of return earned on the marginal hen, for family A. Line R_B shows the corresponding relationship for family B. The rate of return on jewelry is always zero.

    (i) Members of family A are outstanding hen farmers. They invest all $100 of their savings and earn a rate of return on the marginal hen of _____ percent (see point A_0). Only a lack of funds prevents them from investing in even more hens.

    (ii) Members of family B are terrible hen farmers. If they have more than _____ hens, the marginal rate of return becomes negative (see point B_0).

    (iii) Family B invests only $_____ in productive assets (hens); the remaining $_____ of their savings go for jewelry.

b. In aggregate, the two families save $200. But the savings are not being allocated to investment as efficiently as possible. Explain why.

c. Banks now appear. In addition to hens and jewelry, families can hold their savings in the form of deposits that pay 10 percent interest. Also, loans are now available at an interest rate of 15 percent.

    (i) Curve R_B shows that family B earns a rate of return that exceeds the deposit rate (10 percent) when they invest up to $_____ of their savings in hens.

    (ii) Now that interest-bearing bank deposits are available, how will Family B allocate its savings to earn the highest rate of return? Explain.

    (iii) So banks receive deposit funds of $_____ from family B.

    (iv) Examine curve R_A. Why would family A decide *not* to hold any of its $100 in savings in bank deposits?

    (v) Family A wants to obtain a bank loan at 15 percent interest to purchase hens, in addition to the hens that they can buy with their $100 of self-finance. Explain why.

(vi) How much do they want to borrow? (Hint: Borrowing is profitable as long as the marginal rate of return on hens exceeds 15 percent.)

d. In aggregate the two families still save $200. In what respect has the appearance of banks enhanced efficiency in the allocation of the savings?

e. Suppose *nominal* interest rates on loans and deposits remain unchanged, but the inflation rate rises to 100 percent per year.
   (i) How will this inflation affect the willingness of family B to hold savings in the form of bank deposits?

   (ii) Would it be profitable for someone to seek a bank loan to use for purchasing jewelry, which is completely unproductive? Explain.

   (iii) In general, how does inflation affect the efficiency of savings allocations? Be sure to take into account the productivity of the various investments financed by bank loans, as well as the volume of intermediation.

3. This exercise explores the relationship between money supply growth and inflation.

   a. (i) In Harganya the 1996 level of GDP is $Y = \$1,000$. The money supply is $M = \$300$, so the ratio of money to GDP is $M/Y = $ _____.

(ii) Real GDP is expected to grow by 6 percent during the following year. On the basis of past experience, the income elasticity of the demand for money is $E = 1.5$. So if real GDP grows by $g_Y = 6$ percent, the money supply can expand by $g_M = $ _____ percent without causing inflationary pressure. (Hint: $g_Y \times E$. Do you see why?)

(iii) As GDP grows 6 percent, from $1,000 to $1,060, an increase in the money supply to $_____ would maintain price stability.

(iv) The money supply can grow more rapidly than GDP without stimulating inflation because E (the income elasticity of demand for money) exceeds unity. Why is the value of E in low-income countries likely to exceed unity?

b. Suppose that the government of Harganya is content to hold the inflation rate to 10 percent.
   (i) Simplifying a bit, assume that prices rise by 1 percent for every 1 percent that g_M exceeds the noninflationary value found above. Then 10 percent inflation is compatible with $g_M = $ _____ percent.
   (ii) So the policy makers can permit M to increase from $300 to $_____ without the inflation rate exceeding 10 percent.
   (iii) If the money supply were to grow by $g_M = 25$ percent, then inflation would spurt to a rate of _____ percent.

4. The example from Exercise 3 continues here, with a focus on the relationships between government deficits, the growth of the money supply, and the availability of private credit. Expansion of the money supply is equal to the net inflow of international reserves (since this creates new deposits in local banks) plus the expansion of domestic credit to either the government or the private sector. Repeating equation 13–9 from the textbook,

$$\Delta M = \Delta DC + \Delta IR.$$

a. Recall the 1996 conditions in Harganya: $Y = $1,000$, $M = 300, and $E = 1.5$.
   (i) In Exercise 3 you calculated that a 10 percent inflation rate would result if the money supply increased to $M = $_____. Call this the money supply *target*.
   (ii) The government expects that the change in international reserves will be zero. In this case the money supply target can be achieved by permitting domestic credit to expand by $\Delta DC = $_____.
   (iii) This amount of domestic credit creation may consist of the government borrowing $50 and the private-sector borrowing $_____.
   (iv) Or it may consist of the government borrowing $20 and the private-sector borrowing $_____.
   (v) Or any other combination of government plus private-sector borrowing from the banking system adding up to $_____.

b. Government revenues in Harganya are expected to fall short of expenditures by an amount equal to 5 percent of GDP during 1996.
   (i) In absolute terms this means that the budget deficit is projected to be $BD = \$$_____.
   (ii) This deficit is financed by borrowing from the central bank, that is, by domestic credit creation of an amount equal to BD. Given the credit creation needed to finance the government deficit, the money supply target can be achieved if credit expansion to the private sector is limited to $_____.
   (iii) Outstanding bank credit to the private sector previously totaled $250. Now it can increase to no more than $_____.
   (iv) In percentage terms, credit to the private sector can expand by only _____ percent.
   (v) With an inflation rate of 10 percent, this means that *real* bank credit to the private sector will _____ by _____ percent.
   (vi) Is this consistent with the projected 6 percent rate of growth of real GDP? Explain briefly.

c. (i) To avoid a real decline, credit to the private sector must expand in nominal value by no less than _____ percent, to $_____.
   (ii) If this increase in nominal credit to the private sector were allowed, then the money supply target can be achieved only by holding the government budget deficit to no more than $_____, or _____ percent of GDP.

d. The government astonishes everyone by cutting the deficit enough to achieve the warranted value of ΔDC without squeezing the real volume of credit that is available to the private sector. Unhappily, an unexpected inflow of international reserves occurs, with the result that $\Delta IR = \$24$. (Recall that the government anticipated $\Delta IR = \$0$.) How will this unexpected event affect ΔM? How will it affect the rate of inflation? Give specific numerical answers.

5. The textbook says that interest rates have little effect on saving-consumption decisions in developing countries, although there is a clear link between real interest rates and the extent to which savings are held in the form of liquid financial assets. Let's look at some empirical evidence.

Table 13–2

1992 Financial Statistics, Selected Countries

Country	(1) Deposit interest rates (avg % p.a.)	(2) Inflation (% p.a.)	(3) Real deposit interest rate (avg % p.a.)	(4) Gross domestic savings (% GDP)	(5) Government savings* (% GDP)	(6) Private-sector savings (% GDP)
Nepal	8.5	20.4	–9.9	12	5.4	
Kenya	13.7	25.1	–9.1	15	3.1	
Zimbabwe	3.8	34.6	–22.9	10	0.7	
The Philippines	14.3	7.8	6.0	18	1.6	
Indonesia	20.4	6.2	13.4	37	9.2	
Paraguay	20.1	14.7	4.7	13	4.6	
Jordan	3.3	5.3	–1.9	–18	4.9	
Ecuador	47.4	50.3	–1.9	25	4.5	
Tunisia	7.4	5.8	1.5	21	2.8	
Costa Rica	15.8	18.6	–2.4	23	1.2	
Thailand	12.3	4.1	7.9	35	8.0	
Uruguay	54.5	62.3	–4.8	13	0.0	
Malaysia	7.2	4.4	2.7	35	5.6	
Korea	10.0	6.3	3.5	36	2.9	

*Latest year, generally 1991.

Sources: UNDP, *Human Development Report 1994*, Table 27; *World Development Report 1994*, Table 12; and World Bank, *World Tables 1994*, country tables.

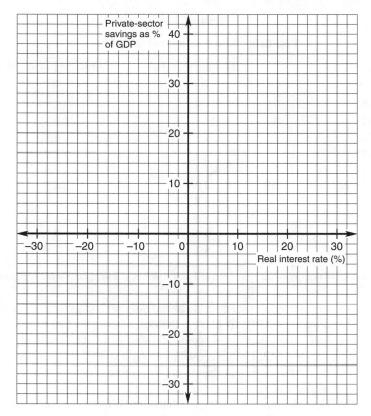

FIGURE 13-2

a. Chapter 11 showed that GDS $= S_g + S_p$, where GDS is gross domestic savings, S_g is government savings, and S_p is private savings. Table 13–2 provides data on GDS and S_g as percentages of GDP, along with data on real interest rates (r), for 14 developing countries. This sample has been selected to cover a wide range of per capita incomes.

   (i) From the data on GDS/Y and S_g/Y in columns 4 and 5, calculate S_p as a percentage of GDP and fill in the blanks in column 6.

 (ii) In Figure 13–2, plot the 14 points representing the values for r and S_d for each country.

(iii) Does the graph reveal a significant relationship between real interest rates and savings rates for this sample of countries? Explain briefly.

(iv) You probably noticed that the private savings rate in Jordan is *negative* 23 percent of GDP and gross domestic savings also is negative. What does this mean? How is it possible?

Table 13–3

Financial Data for Indonesia, 1970–1979

Year	Real interest rate (%)	Growth rate of M2/Y (%)
1970	13.8	15.1
1971	20.4	29.3
1972	−6.3	18.8
1973	−9.4	−3.9
1974	−2.3	−6.8
1975	4.0	14.7
1976	8.8	8.9
1977	5.4	−3.5
1978	7.5	3.7
1979	−5.7	−1.8

Source: Calculated from data reported in Bank Indonesia annual and weekly reports.

    b. Table 13–3 shows data on real interest rates (r) and growth of the ratio of broad money to GNP $g(M2/Y)$ in Indonesia during the first decade following Indonesia's successful stabilization program. The textbook explains that the ratio $M2/Y$ often is used as an indicator of financial deepening.

      (i) In Figure 13–3, plot the ten points representing the values of r and $g(M2/Y)$.

     (ii) Does the graph reveal a significant relationship between the real interest rate and financial deepening in Indonesia during this period? Explain briefly.

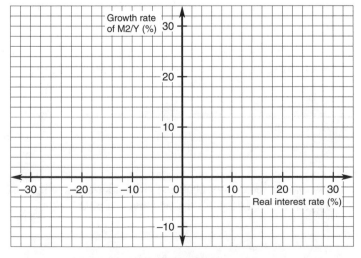

FIGURE 13–3

6. This exercise shows how changes in international reserves lead to changes in the money supply under a fixed exchange rate system. Consider Sombrero, a country where the peso is the domestic currency. For simplicity, assume that the dollar is the only foreign exchange unit. The government is committed to maintaining a fixed exchange rate of 20 pesos per dollar. Think of this as the price of the dollar in terms of the Sombrero peso.

   a. Sombrero's international transactions generate a supply of dollars (for example, from exports) that exceeds the demand for dollars (for example, for imports) by $100 million.
      (i) With supply in excess of demand, free market forces would cause the price of the dollar to _____.
      (ii) The government can prevent this change in the exchange rate by eliminating the excess supply of dollars. This can be accomplished by purchasing $_____ million in the foreign exchange market, to add to Sombrero's stock of international reserves.
      (iii) The government pays for the dollars with _____.
      (iv) As a result of the government's action to maintain the fixed exchange rate, the supply of domestic money in circulation increases by _____ million pesos.

   b. Suppose instead that international transactions create a demand for dollars that exceeds the supply of dollars by $50 million.
      (i) With demand in excess of supply, free-market forces would cause the price of the dollar to _____.
      (ii) The government can prevent this change in the exchange rate by _____ $50 million in the foreign exchange market.
      (iii) As a result of the government's action to maintain the fixed exchange rate, Sombrero's stock of international reserves will _____ by $50 million.
      (iv) And the supply of domestic money in circulation will _____ by _____ million pesos.

   c. Finally, suppose that the foreign exchange market is in equilibrium at the exchange rate of 50 pesos per dollar. But domestic inflation is zero, while the foreign inflation rate averages 15 percent.
      (i) As prices in foreign markets rise, dollar earnings from Sombrero's exports will _____.
      (ii) Because foreign goods become increasingly expensive, the people of Sombrero will _____ their purchases of imports.
      (iii) Consequently, in Sombrero's foreign exchange market the supply of dollars increasingly will _____ the demand for dollars.
      (iv) To prevent market forces from causing a change in the exchange rate, the government of Sombrero must _____ dollars in the foreign exchange market.
      (v) This government action will cause Sombrero's stock of international reserves to _____.
      (vi) And it will cause the domestic money supply to _____.
      (vii) This change in the domestic money supply will tend to cause Sombrero's inflation rate to _____.

You can see that the central bank can maintain a fixed exchange rate only if it cedes control of the money supply and allows domestic prices to be influenced by foreign inflation.

ANSWERS TO SELF-TEST

Completion

1. financial intermediaries
2. liquid
3. 50
4. money
5. Narrow, currency
6. positive
7. Shallow
8. real interest rates
9. informal
10. runaway (or hyper-)
11. domestic credit
12. fixed (or pegged)

True-False

1.	F	7.	T
2.	T	8.	F
3.	F	9.	T
4.	T	10.	F
5.	T	11.	T
6.	F	12.	F

Multiple Choice

1.	b	7.	a
2.	d	8.	b
3.	b	9.	b
4.	d	10.	c
5.	d	11.	c
6.	a	12.	d

CHAPTER 14

Private Foreign Capital, Debt, and
Financial Crises

OVERVIEW

Private foreign capital historically has played an important role in financing
infrastructure (railroads) and extractive activities (mining) in late-comers from
Brazil to the United States. At its peak in 1997, private capital flows accounted
for nearly 90 percent of total capital flows to developing countries. Foreign
private capital flows come in two forms: equity (foreign direct investment and
portfolio investment) and debt (commercial bank debt and trade credits). Table
14–1 in the textbook provides the relevant data for the 1990s.

Foreign direct investment (FDI) to developing countries, which accounts for
half of the flows, comes primarily from nonfinancial multinational corporations
(MNCs). Developing countries account for some 40 percent of FDI today,
although half of it is concentrated in just three countries (China, Brazil, and
Mexico). FDI has numerous potential benefits, including long-term commitment,
jobs, transfer of know-how, and access to world markets. However, these benefits
can be fully realized only if the host country is sufficiently attractive (in terms of
good infrastructure, a competitive and sensibly regulated domestic market, a
productive workforce, political stability) and it has farsighted policy makers
capable of striking mutually beneficial bargains.

Another source of investable funds is foreign borrowing from various sources:
official (bilateral and multilateral, as discussed in Chapter 11), commercial bank
loans, trade credits, and bonds. Commercial lending boomed in the 1970s while
bonds acquired prominence in the 1990s. Foreign debt can be beneficial if it
supports productive investments with high rates of return. Many developing
countries, however, incurred unsustainable debts, which became especially
evident after the 1982 Mexican default. In the absence of sufficient resource
flows to cover their debt-service payments, debtor countries were compelled to
implement painful adjustment programs along with debt relief arrangements.

Just as the debt crisis subsided everywhere but in sub-Saharan Africa, a
number of emerging markets (Mexico, Argentina, Brazil, Russia, and East Asia)
were hit, especially beginning in 1994, by severe financial crisis. The chapter
discusses the genesis of the crises (domestic economic weaknesses and the volatility
of short-term capital flows) as well as ways of stopping creditor panics, which often
are self-fulfilling. It ends with a discussion of the lessons from this experience,
including the need for a gradualist approach to capital-account liberalization, better
management of short-term flows, more flexible exchange rates, domestic banking
reform, and a possible revamping of the current international financial architecture.

273

MAIN LEARNING OBJECTIVES

After studying this chapter, you ought to understand and be able to explain

1. The patterns of foreign investment (direct and portfolio) and loans to developing countries.

2. The investment packages that MNCs provide to developing countries.

3. The kinds of policies that should be pursued by developing countries to make the most of foreign capital.

4. The external and internal factors that precipitated the external debt crisis of the 1970s and 1980s.

5. The lessons from the manner in which the debt crisis was handled.

6. The external and internal factors that precipitated the financial crises in emerging markets and transition economies in the 1990s.

7. The lessons of experience from the emerging market financial crises.

ECONOMIC TOOLS AND TECHNIQUES

From what you have learned in this chapter, you should be able to

1. Analyze the adverse effects for the host country of granting monopoly privileges and tax holidays to multinationals in order to attract their investments.

2. Compare the advantages and disadvantages of FDI and non-FDI capital flows from the standpoint of long-term economic growth.

3. Apply the equations for determining the sustainable debt ratios, in terms of the foreign exchange gap and the investment-saving gap.

4. Identify the relationships among the balance of payments, exchange rates, and bank balance sheets of developing countries whose capital markets are liberalized.

KEY TERMS AND CONCEPTS

Baker Plan	insolvency
banking crisis	international financial architecture
Brady Plan	investment package
buybacks	investment-savings gap
commercial bank loans	Mexican peso crisis
currency crisis	multinational corporations (MNCs)
debt-equity swaps	offshore borrowing
debt overhang	portfolio equity
debt-service ratio	rational panics
debt standstill (rollover)	self-fulfilling panics
foreign direct investment (FDI)	self-insurance
foreign exchange gap	sovereign debt
HIPCs	stabilization and structural
illiquid	adjustment programs
income tax incentives	sustainable debt

SELF-TEST

Completion

1. Foreign saving is the difference between gross domestic investment and gross domestic _____.

2. The purchase of host country bonds or stocks by foreigners, without managerial control, is called _____ *investment.*

3. The acronym MNC stands for _____ _____.

4. Of the three major forms of foreign investment (FDI, equity, bonds), _____ clearly is a source of future external indebtedness for the host country.

5. _____ holidays are the most widely used inducements offered to multinationals to invest in developing countries.

6. A country's debt service burden consists of obligations to repay loan principal plus _____.

7. Countries can _____ their foreign debt by reaching an agreement with the creditor banks to postpone repayment of principal to a later date.

8. When debt is owed or guaranteed by a country's government, it is called _____ *debt.*

9. Creditor panic is considered _____ when some creditors believe that other creditors will pull out of a borrower country even when the latter is solvent.

10. The experience of South Korea following the 1997–1998 crisis shows that _____ can be an effective instrument for ending a currency crisis.

True-False

If false, you should be able to explain why.

_____ 1. There are very few developing countries where multinational corporations employ more than 1 percent of the labor force.

_____ 2. In theory, foreign direct investment produces a technology transfer for the host country, but in practice the developing countries obtain virtually no technology benefits from dealing with MNCs.

_____ 3. Most industrial countries provide foreign aid amounting to at least 1.5 percent of their GNP.

_____ 4. A country cannot benefit from external debt unless the funds are used to finance projects with rates of return higher than the interest rate on the debt.

_____ 5. *Fortune* magazine's list of the world's 500 largest companies includes enterprises originating from 15 developing countries.

_____ 6. The debt crisis in the early 1980s resulted from a combination of external shocks and policy mismanagement on the part of the developing countries.

_____ 7. Many of the developing countries hardest hit by the debt crisis in the 1980s suffered a decline in per capita income, a reduction in the ratio of investment to GDP, and rising inflation.

_____ 8. Of the 50 foreign investment projects that Dennis Encarnation and Louis Wells studied in a large Asian country, all the projects oriented toward domestic markets had rates of return above 10 percent, while most export-oriented projects were socially unprofitable.

_____ 9. The experiences of Mexico, Thailand, Indonesia, and Korea in the 1990s suggest that fixed exchange rates are an effective tool for stopping the spread of financial panics.

_____ 10. Rapid financial liberalization of the type recommended by the IMF renders emerging economies highly prone to crisis caused by the volatility of short-term capital flows.

Multiple Choice

1. Four statements about multinational corporations (MNCs) are listed below. Only one of them is factual. Which one is it?
   a. The vast majority of all cross-border investments made by MNCs go to developing countries offering large tax breaks.
   b. Most MNC investments in the developing countries go for manufacturing activities that take advantage of cheap labor.
   c. MNCs adopt production methods that are far more capital-intensive than those of domestic firms in the same industry.
   d. In recent years, developing countries have made progress in capturing more benefits by "unbundling" the MNC investment packages.

2. In addition to capital, the package provided by multinational investments typically includes all the following *except*
   a. low-cost labor supplies.
   c. managerial resources.
   b. technology.
   d. access to world markets.

3. Foreign direct investment, portfolio investment, commercial bank lending, and export credits are all forms of
   a. foreign exchange constraints.
   c. foreign private savings.
   b. foreign aid.
   d. fungibility.

4. The standard definition of the debt-service ratio is the ratio of _____ to _____.
   a. interest on foreign debt, GDP
   b. interest plus repayments of principal, GDP
   c. interest on foreign debt, exports of goods and service
   d. interest plus repayments of principal, exports of goods and services

5. Which of the following was a significant factor contributing to the international debt crisis in the early 1980s?
   a. A sharp increase in real interest rates.
   b. A decline in export earnings due to the deep recession in the industrial economies.
   c. A large accumulation of debt during the preceding years.
   d. All the above.

6. Some countries such as South Korea and Indonesia avoided a debt crisis because they
   a. did not have large foreign debts in the first place.
   b. adopted successful adjustment policies to cope with the external shocks.
   c. allowed domestic income to decline enough to meet their debt obligations.
   d. received massive amounts of foreign aid that allowed them to pay their debt service.

7. Which of the following measures was *not* part of the solution to Mexico's debt crisis in the 1980s?
   a. Loans from the IMF and the World Bank tied to conditionality requiring appropriate policy changes.
   b. An agreement allowing Mexico to buy back its debt on the secondary market at a large discount.
   c. Unilateral cancellation of 70 percent of the commercial debt.
   d. A severe economic contraction.

8. History shows that the use of significant amounts of foreign savings by developing countries
   a. almost inevitably brings more costs than benefits.
   b. is a very recent phenomenon.
   c. is essential for development.
   d. is helpful, but not essential, for development.

APPLICATIONS

Worked Example: Anatomy of a Debt Crisis

Indonesia and Nigeria are large tropical countries blessed with oil wealth. Both are members of OPEC. Both were torn by civil war in the 1960s. Until 1980 both had similar levels of per capita income. Yet by 1989 Indonesia's GDP per capita was nearly double Nigeria's, in terms of constant-dollar PPP measures. (See line 2 of Table 14–1.) During the 1980s per capita GDP *fell* by 4.5 percent per year in Nigeria while it *rose* by 4.0 percent per year in Indonesia (from line 2). Between 1980 and 1989 Nigeria's foreign debt grew from 9 to 119 percent of GDP, compared to an increase from 28 to 59 percent in Indonesia. Nigeria has a severe debt problem and had to arrange to reschedule its payments. Indonesia avoided this.

What explains Nigeria's poor performance?

External factors bear part of the blame for Nigeria's problems. The country's terms of trade (that is, the price of exports relative to the price of imports) more than halved between 1980 and 1989 (see line 8), due to the dramatic fall in oil prices in 1986. Indonesia suffered less of a decline in terms of trade, but only because its exports were less concentrated on oil (see line 9). Both economies faced the same world recession in the early 1980s, and Indonesia suffered a larger rise in the interest rate on its external debt (line 7). So one cannot very well explain the *differences* in performance by external factors.

Internal factors provide the best explanation. Nigeria's macroeconomic policies were inappropriate in many ways, quite in contrast to Indonesia's. Throughout the 1980s Nigeria maintained an overvalued exchange rate that penalized export performance (line 18). Government policy also inhibited any diversification of exports (line 9); this left the country vulnerable to the collapse of oil prices. Nigeria's policies failed to achieve much development in manufacturing (line 10) and prevented agricultural growth from even keeping pace with population growth (lines 19 and 16), unlike the situation in Indonesia.

Nigeria ran astonishingly large government deficits throughout the period, in contrast to Indonesia's more manageable deficits of just over 2 percent of GDP (line 11). Nigeria and Indonesia entered the 1980s with comparable investment and savings rates, but Nigeria's domestic performance got worse while Indonesia's got better. Moreover, investment efficiency in Nigeria was so poor that GDP actually fell, despite much capital formation; in Indonesia the excellent ICOR value for the 1970s was not sustained into the 1980s, but the ICOR did not become particularly high. In part this was due to Nigeria's shallow financial policies (evident from line 12), which reduced the effectiveness of the financial system in mobilizing savings and channeling them to productive investments.

In short, Nigeria borrowed heavily, but failed to grow because of inappropriate macroeconomic policies. The country ended the 1980s with $33 billion in foreign debt and little to show for it. Indonesia had a larger debt in absolute terms, $53 billion, but the resources were used to support a decade of robust economic growth, despite tumultuous world market conditions. Exercise 1 examines some of these themes in more detail.

Table 14–1

Economic Indicators for Nigeria and Indonesia

	Nigeria		Indonesia	
A. Level variables for the year	1980	1989	1980	1989
1 Population (millions)	71	94	148	175
2 GDP per capita (1985 PPP$)	1,438	952	1,281	1,826
3 External debt/GNP (%)	9.0	119.0	28.0	59.0
4 External debt/exports (%)	32.0	390.0	94.0	211.0
5 Debt service/exports (%)	4.0	21.0	14.0	35.0
6 Debt interest/exports (%)	3.0	16.0	7.0	15.0
7 Average interest rate on debt (%)	6.0	7.1	2.6	6.1
8 Terms of trade	100	46	100	68
9 Fuels/exports (%)	93.2	95.6	71.9	40.2
10 Manufacturing value-added/GDP (%)	7.8	10.0	13.0	17.0
11 Government deficit/GDP (%)	18.1	10.5	2.2	2.1
12 M3/GDP (%)	22.0	18.0	13.0	30.0
13 Gross investment/GDP (%)	23.3	13.0	24.3	35.0
14 Domestic savings/GDP (%)	33.9	21.0	37.1	37.0
15 Foreign savings/GDP (%)	10.6	–8.0	12.8	–2.0
B. Intertemporal variables for the period	1965–1980	1980–1989	1965–1980	1980–1989
16 Population growth (% p.a.)	2.2	3.1	3.8	1.9
17 GDP growth (% p.a.)	12.1	–1.5	12.8	5.2
18 Growth of exports (% p.a.)	11.1	–2.3	9.6	2.4
19 Growth agricultural output (% p.a.)	1.7	1.3	4.3	3.2
20 Growth of energy production (% p.a.)	17.3	0.3	9.9	0.7
21 ICOR	5.1	neg. denom.	2.6	5.5

Sources: Population and GDP data from *Penn World Tables database*, version 5.6; other figures from *World Development Report 1991* and World Bank, *World Tables 1994*.

Exercises

1. In this exercise, we will explore the ways in which Nigeria differed from Indonesia in the 1980s. The goal is to clarify why Nigeria faced a debt problem and declining GDP, while Indonesia did not.

   a. Consider first the extent of the debt burden.
      (i) Explain how Indonesia's accumulation of foreign debt differed from that of Nigeria during the 1980s.

(ii) Between 1980 and 1989 the ratio of debt to GNP exactly doubled in Indonesia (line 3) but the debt-service ratio (line 6) more than doubled. What explains this discrepancy? (Hint: Recall that the debt-service ratio equals principal plus interest payments divided by exports.)

(iii) *Harder.* Between 1980 and 1989 the ratio of debt to GDP rose more than tenfold in Nigeria, but the debt-service ratio rose just fivefold. How can you explain this discrepancy?

(iv) Which country had a more onerous debt burden at the beginning of the decade? Explain.

b. The performance difference between the two countries is most prominent in the growth of GDP per capita.
  (i) Between 1980 and 1989 Nigeria's GDP per capita (line 2) declined by a total of _____ percent while Indonesia's rose by a total of _____ percent.

  (ii) The growth of GDP per capita in Nigeria was _____ percent per year; the corresponding figure for Indonesia was _____ percent per year. [Hint: Value for year t = (value for year 0)$(1 + g)^t$.]

c. Some, although not all, of Nigeria's difficulties may be explained by adverse external factors.
  (i) Why did Nigeria's terms of trade fall more sharply than those of Indonesia? (Hint: World oil prices collapsed in 1986.)

(ii) Indonesia paid an average interest rate of just 2.6 percent on its foreign debt in 1980. This was well below the market interest rate. What is the explanation for this? And why did the interest rate paid by Indonesia rise so much during the decade?

(iii) Interest rates in the world financial markets were substantially lower in 1989 than in 1980, yet the average interest rate on Nigeria's debt rose over this period. How can one explain this disparity?

(iv) There was a major world recession in 1982. What trace of this, if any, can be discerned from the information presented in Table 14–1?

d. Internal causes go far toward explaining Nigeria's poor performance.
   (i) Compare the experience of Nigeria and Indonesia in terms of mobilizing domestic savings; cite at least two pieces of evidence from Table 14–1.

   (ii) Which country did a better job of promoting nonfuel exports during the 1980s? Explain.

    (iii) On the basis of agricultural performance statistics, which country would you expect to have reduced its need for food imports during the 1980s? Which would have increased its need for food imports? Explain.

    (iv) Nigeria's investment was less efficient than Indonesia's. What evidence of this do you see in Table 14–1? How might this be related to financial market policies? To government budget policies? Explain.

    (v) Can any of the difference in per capita income growth be explained by population growth rates? Explain.

    (vi) Between 1970 and 1989 Nigeria's pubic foreign debt rose by $31 billion; Indonesia's debt rose more, by $38 billion. Yet by 1989 Indonesia had *lower* debt-to-GDP and debt-to-export ratios than did Nigeria. Why?

e. You now have enough information to evaluate the two countries' debt strategies.
    (i) Considering the facts shown in Table 14–1, do you think that Indonesia would have been wiser to avoid foreign borrowing altogether? Explain your position.

    (ii) Considering the facts shown in Table 14–1, do you think that Nigeria would have been wiser to avoid foreign borrowing altogether? Explain your position.

(iii) What are the main adjustments that would have been required for either country to have avoided foreign borrowing altogether?

2. This exercise gives you practice working with the equations on debt dynamics. To avoid errors and confusion, all the data given in percentages should be *converted to decimal units* before being plugged into the equations. As an example, use 0.12 instead of 12 percent even if the data set is expressed in the latter format.

a. The basic equation showing how the amount of foreign debt changes over time is $dD/dt = iD + M - E$. That is, the change in foreign debt equals the amount of interest payments on existing debt (iD) plus the financing needed to cover the trade deficit ($M - E$). We may divide both sides of this equation by D and reorganize the terms to obtain an expression for the proportionate growth rate of the foreign debt, G_d, as follows:

$$G_d = \frac{dD/dt}{D} = i + \left(\frac{M-E}{E} \bigg/ \frac{D}{E}\right).$$
[14–1]

The growth rate of foreign debt equals the interest rate plus the size of the trade deficit (relative to total exports) divided by the debt-to-export ratio. Given values for the right-side variables, we may calculate the proportionate change in the foreign debt consistent with the *foreign exchange constraint*.

(i) Table 14–2 presents pertinent data for four highly indebted countries at the end of the 1980s. Complete the blanks in the right-hand column.

Table 14–2

Debt Service in Four Countries

Country	Imports/GDP (%)	Exports/GDP (%)	Debt/exports	Interest rate on debt (%)	G_d (%)
India	11	8	2.6	6.4	20.8
Jamaica	51	47	1.9	7.9	_____
Madagascar	22	17	7.8	0.7	_____
Zambia	32	28	4.5	9.1	_____

(ii) To cover its debt-service payments plus its foreign exchange gap, India would have to permit its foreign debt to rise by almost 21 percent per year (in nominal dollar terms). If GDP were growing by 7 percent per year (also in nominal terms, converted to dollars), what would happen to the ratio of debt to GDP?

(iii) This situation cannot be sustained for long without accumulating an unbearable debt burden. With reference to equation 14–1, what kinds of adjustments were required for India to reduce G_d to more a manageable level?

b. Equation 14–3 in the text shows that debt dynamics can also be stated in terms of the savings-investment gap: $dD/dt = iD + I - S_d = iD + vY - sY = iD + (v - s)Y$. This says that the change in foreign debt equals the amount of interest payments on existing debt (iD) plus the excess of investment over domestic savings, which must be financed by a net inflow of foreign savings (that is, an increase in liabilities to foreigners). Here again, we may divide both sides of this equation by D and then reorganize the terms to obtain an expression for the proportionate growth rate of the foreign debt:

$$G_d = \frac{dD/dt}{D} = i + \frac{I - S_d}{Y} \bigg/ \frac{D}{Y}.$$ [14–2]

In words, foreign debt grows at a rate equal to the interest rate plus the size of the savings-investment gap (relative to GDP) divided by the debt-to-GDP ratio. Given the values for all the right-side variables, we may calculate the proportionate change in the foreign debt consistent with the *savings-investment gap*.

(i) Complete the blanks in Table 14–3,which presents pertinent data for the same four countries in 1989. You will need to use some data from the previous table.

Table 14–3

Debt Service in Four Countries

Country	Investment/GDP (%)	S_d/GDP (%)	Debt/GNP	Interest rate on debt (%)	G_d (%)
India	24	21	0.24	6.4	18.9
Jamaica	29	26	1.34	7.9	_____
Madagascar	13	8	1.54	0.7	_____
Zambia	9	5	1.59	9.1	_____

(ii) With reference to equation 14–2, what kinds of adjustments would be required for India to reduce G_d to more manageable levels?

c. The textbook also shows that the equation for debt equations can be solved to obtain the long-run debt ratio implied by the prevailing dynamics. Using the foreign exchange gap form of the relationship, the long-run debt ratio is

$$\frac{D}{E} = \frac{(M - E)/E}{g_e - i} \qquad [14\text{--}3]$$

where g_e is the growth rate of exports. This is the *steady-state* solution to equation 14–1; it gives the long-run debt-to-export ratio that would be sustained given the values of $(M - E)/E$, i, and g_e.

(i) This formula can be turned around to answer the question, What export growth rate is needed to prevent the D/E from rising? For this purpose, you plug in the prevailing value of D/E and solve for g_e. Using the data from Table 14–2, the answer to this question is

$$g_e = \underline{20.8 \text{ percent}} \text{ for India.}$$

$$g_e = \underline{} \text{ for Jamaica.}$$

$$g_e = \underline{} \text{ for Madagascar.}$$

$$g_e = \underline{} \text{ for Zambia.}$$

(ii) Are these values of g_e plausible as sustainable characteristics in the long run? (Keep in mind that exports are measured here in nominal dollars.)

d. The same analysis can be cast in terms of the savings-investment gap. In this case, the long-run debt ratio is

$$D/Y = (v - s)/(g_y - i) \qquad [14\text{--}4]$$

where v is the share of investment in GDP, s is the share of domestic savings, and g_y is the growth rate of GDP. This is the *steady-state*

286 / CHAPTER 14

solution to equation 14–2; it gives the long-run debt-to-income ratio that would be sustained, given the values of $(v - s)$, i, and g_y.

(i) This formula can be turned around to answer the question, What GDP growth rate is needed to prevent D/Y from rising? For this purpose, you plug in the prevailing value of D/Y and solve for g_y. Using the data from Table 14–3, the answer to this question is

$$g_y = \underline{18.9 \text{ percent}} \text{ for India.}$$

$$g_y = \underline{\hspace{2cm}} \text{ for Jamaica.}$$

$$g_y = \underline{\hspace{2cm}} \text{ for Madagascar.}$$

$$g_y = \underline{\hspace{2cm}} \text{ for Zambia.}$$

(ii) Are these values of g_y plausible as sustainable characteristics in the long run? (Keep in mind that exports are measured here in nominal dollars.)

e. What do you conclude about the need for an adjustment program in these countries?

3. In this exercise, we explore the financial crisis (currency and/or banking crises) in emerging markets. As the discussion in Chapter 14 of the textbook notes, emerging markets undergoing full liberalization of their capital markets tend to be prone to financial crises. Although the process is not well understood, there are two major contending explanations. What may be called the *fundamentals view* attributes the financial crises primarily to excessively foreign credit-driven investment, large budget deficits, and uncompetitive firms or banks. The *expectations view*, on the other hand, argues that excessively large and short-term foreign credits make even otherwise sound economies vulnerable to speculative attacks or self-fulfilling creditor panics. This is all the more likely in situations where the loans are advanced to banks willing to engage in risky investments and in countries with pegged exchange rates.

Table 14−4 provides additional data to what is contained in Table 14−9 in the textbook for a number of emerging markets. The macroeconomic data focus on financial systems, exchange rate regimes, foreign debt, and government finances prior to or soon after the crises.

a. List the countries with the following characteristics:
   (i) Countries whose inflation rates exceed 20 percent.

   (ii) Countries whose budget deficits exceed 3 percent of GDP.

   (iii) Countries whose CA/GDP exceeds 5 percent.

   (iv) Countries whose currency does not float freely.

   (v) Countries whose loan-LIBOR interest-rate spreads are in double digits.

   (vi) Countries whose share of short-term debt in total debt exceeds 20 percent.

Table 14–4
Some Financial Characteristics of Emerging Markets, 1997 (percent)

Country	ER type	O/P	Inflation rate	BC/Y	LR/BA	L–LIBOR	IRCRG	IC	ST/T	BD/Y	FBD/Y	CA/GDP	SMC/Y
Argentina	P	100	12.2	27.2	2.6	3.5	74.5	S	14.6	-2.0	2.8	-3.0	18.2
Brazil	MF	100	475.7	43.1	11.0	—	65.3	S	18.6	-6.1	—	-4.0	31.3
Chile	MF	90	10.2	64.7	2.8	9.9	74.8	M	31.6	2.3	—	-5.0	93.5
India	IF	90	8.6	49.7	10.9	8.1	64.8	M	5.3	-5.2	0.2	-1.0	33.7
Indonesia	IF	90	8.6	58.0	3.9	16.1	41.0	M	26.4	1.2	-0.5	-2.0	13.5
Ireland	MF	100	1.8	44.6	2.8	0.8	88.3	—	—	-0.14	—	2.0	32.2
South Korea	IF	100	5.3	86.1	1.9	6.1	70.0	L	37.5	0.1	-0.1	-1.0	—
Malaysia	P	—	4.5	165.1	11.3	3.8	67.8	M	31.6	2.0	-0.9	-4.0	95.1
Mexico	IF	1.0	19.3	30.0	49.4	18.8	67.5	L	19.0	-0.2	-0.2	-1.0	12.4
Poland	MF	100	29.5	36.9	8.0	19.2	82.0	L	9.6	-2.2	-0.2	-4.0	8.9
Russia	MF	—	298.8	25.9	13.3	26.3	49.0	L	4.9	-4.5	1.5	0.0	28.7
Thailand	MF	100	4.8	140.4	6.1	7.9	69.3	M	37.3	2.4	0.1	-1.0	15.3
Turkey	MF	100	79.3	34.1	10.3	—	52.3	M	24.8	-8.4	-0.9	-1.0	32.2

Exchange rates: P = pegged, MF = managed float, IF = independent float, O/P = ratio of official rate to parallel market rate. Inflation rate is average annual growth of the implicit GDP deflator for 1990–1997.

Financial depth: BC/Y = domestic credit provided by domestic banking sector as a percent of GDP (Y), LR/BA = ratio of bank liquid reserves to bank assets, L – LIBOR = lending rate minus LIBOR rate (in percentage points), ICRG = international country risk guide rating for portfolio investment (lowest risk = 100), SMC/Y = stock market capitalization as a percent of GDP.

External debt: IC = indebtedness classification (S = severe, M = moderate, and L = low), ST/T = short-term debt as a percent of total debt, CA/GDP = current-account deficit as a percent of GDP.

Government finances: BD/Y = overall budget deficit (including grants) as a percent of GDP, FBD/Y = financing of budget deficit from abroad (by nonresidents) as a percent of GDP.

Source: World Bank, World Development Indicators 1999.

(vii) Countries whose ICRG risk level for portfolio investment falls below 70 percent.

(viii) Countries whose ratio of bank liquid reserves to bank assets are in double digits.

(ix) Countries whose stock market capitalization falls below 50 percent of GDP.

b. The fundamentals view emphasizes structural and policy distortions which are captured mainly by the first five characteristics:

(i) Which countries show up in at least three of the listings in part a, (i)–(v)?

(ii) Which of these countries experienced a financial crisis in the 1990s?

c. The expectations view of financial crises suggests that panics resulting from imperfect information can lead to a financial collapse even when the economic fundamentals are sound. Combining the data in Table 14–9 (from the textbook) and Table 14–4:

(i) Which countries show up in at least three of the listings in part a, (vi)–(ix)?

(ii) Which of these countries experienced a financial crisis in the 1990s?

d. Which of the countries that did not appear in your answers for part b, (ii) and part c, (ii) nonetheless experienced financial crises in the 1990s?

e. Only a handful of the emerging economies continue to maintain pegged exchange rates or imposed restrictions on short-term capital flows following the 1997 Asian crisis. Name those countries.

f. Looking at your answers for parts b–e, what can you say about a possible reconciliation of the two views as suggested in the following remark regarding the 1997–1998 East Asian crisis:

> Fixed exchange rate regimes, capital inflows . . . led to real appreciation, an investment boom in wrong sectors, an asset price bubble and large current account deficits that led to the accumulation of a large stock of short-term foreign liabilities . . . The exchange rate crisis that followed made things only worse as the currency depreciation increased the real burden of the foreign-currency denominated debt. Weak and not very credible governments that were not committed to structural reform exacerbated the policy uncertainty and the financial panic that followed.[*]

[*]*From* Nuriel Roubini, "An Introduction to Open Economy Macroeconomics, Currency Crises and the Asian Crisis," Part 5, online manuscript, Stern Business School, NYU, 1999, available at www.stern.nyu.edu/globalmacro/.

ANSWERS TO SELF-TEST

Completion

1. savings
2. *portfolio*
3. multinational corporation
4. bonds
5. Tax
6. interest
7. reschedule
8. *sovereign*
9. self-fulfilling
10. standstill on debt payment

True-False

1.	T	6.	T
2.	F	7.	T
3.	F	8.	F
4.	T	9.	F
5.	T	10.	T

Multiple Choice

1.	d	5.	d
2.	a	6.	b
3.	c	7.	c
4.	d	8.	d

Part V   Production and Trade

CHAPTER 15 | Agriculture

OVERVIEW

While most topics covered in earlier chapters relate in some way to agriculture, Chapter 15 focuses directly on the problems of this sector. The chapter opens with a review of the multifaceted role of agriculture in economic development. Among other things, healthy agricultural development reduces poverty, releases labor to other productive sectors, and earns foreign exchange. Agriculture also supplies food and generates incomes to support the demand for other sectors' goods and services. In turn, agricultural development depends on social and economic conditions. Property rights and land tenure relations, for example, have a major bearing on incentives, efficiency, and equity. Yet land reform is a highly charged political issue, which has produced mixed results depending on how it has been carried out.

Traditional agriculture made use of an efficient set of techniques that evolved slowly as a result of long-term trial and error. Modern agricultural technologies are based on scientific research. Most innovations fall into two categories: mechanization to substitute for labor and Green Revolution advances in biological techniques that can boost yields dramatically. Unlike manufacturing technology, agricultural techniques must be carefully adapted to local conditions because the weather, soil quality, and economic circumstances differ greatly from place to place. No single technology is efficient in all countries.

Property rights and technology are two basic determinants of agricultural productivity. A third is capital to invest in rural infrastructure, such as roads and irrigation facilities. Some countries have had success in implementing labor-intensive public works projects to develop the infrastructure, but projects of this sort are difficult to carry out efficiently. Other institutional developments that facilitate agriculture include rural savings and credit institutions, extension services, and of course, the development of markets.

While the issues mentioned above have long-run effects, pricing policy can have an immediate and profound impact on agriculture, either positive or negative. Pricing policies affect farm production, rural incomes, the urban cost of living, and in many countries, the government budget. These policies are complicated by inevitable conflicts between the interests of farmers and the interests of urban consumers. Many developing countries resolve these conflicts by introducing subsidies or market interventions (such as overvalued exchange rates). But these interventions often turn out to inhibit agricultural development and destabilize macroeconomic balances.

MAIN LEARNING OBJECTIVES

After studying this chapter, you ought to understand and be able to explain

1. Agriculture's fundamental role in economic development.

2. The issues in the debate about food self-sufficiency and food security.

3. The various forms of land tenure in developing countries and the effect of property rights on incentives in agriculture.

4. The political and economic issues relating to land reform programs.

5. The characteristics of traditional and modern agricultural technologies, including the modern mechanical and biological packages.

6. The importance of road and irrigation systems, credit institutions, extension services, and market networks and the problems generally faced in developing this rural infrastructure.

7. How pricing policies affect agricultural output, farmers' incomes, the urban cost of living, and the government budget.

ECONOMIC TOOLS AND TECHNIQUES

From what you have learned in this chapter, you should be able to

1. Use isoquants and isocost lines to illustrate the characteristics of agricultural technologies and the efficient choice of technology.

2. Apply the profit maximization rule—increase output to the point where marginal cost equals marginal revenue—to demonstrate how relative prices for farm inputs and outputs influence farm production decisions.

3. Analyze the effect of subsidies and overvalued exchange rates on the balance between supply and demand for food.

KEY TERMS AND CONCEPTS

CIMMYT, IRRI
economies of scale
extension services
famines
food self-sufficiency
free-rider problem
land reform
land tenure
mechanical package, biological
   package, Green Revolution
moneylenders, rural credit institutions

overvalued exchange rate
plantation agriculture, latifundia,
   tenancy, sharecropping, communal
   farming, collectivized agriculture
property rights
rural infrastructure, rural public works
rural traders
traditional agriculture, slash and burn,
   fallow
work points

SELF-TEST

Completion

1. Economies of _____ are at the heart of farm specialization.

2. Communal farming, family farming, and latifundia are alternative forms of land _____ arrangements.

3. The form of tenancy in which the land owner receives a given share of the farmer's harvest is called _____.

4. Land _____ programs sometimes involve laws limiting the crop share that a _____ can demand as rent or laws requiring long-term contracts for tenant farmers.

5. According to the text, the greatest barrier to farm specialization in many developing countries is the high level of _____ costs.

6. The mechanical package of agricultural technology involves the introduction of machinery primarily as a substitute for _____.

7. _____ services provide the key link between agricultural research centers and the farmers who ultimately must adopt what the researchers develop.

8. In traditional agriculture small farmers have access to only two sources of credit—the family and the local _____.

9. The form of government policy that has a rapid and profound effect on agricultural production and consumption is intervention to influence

   _____.

10. An overvalued exchange rate tends to _____ food imports and to _____ food production.

11. Communes in _____ tried to overcome the free-rider problem by awarding points on the basis of the amount of work done by each member.

12. The most important price relationship affecting agricultural production is that between farm outputs and purchased inputs, especially chemical

    _____.

True-False

If false, you should be able to explain why.

_____ 1. A critical world food crisis is imminent due to the limited supply of productive land and biological limits on potential food production.

_____ 2. In low-income countries, poor families spend more than 50 percent of their budgets on food, so an increase in food prices causes a sharp drop in their real incomes.

_____ 3. Depending on conditions, the impact of land reform on productivity can be positive or negative.

_____ 4. In Japan, labor productivity in agriculture is only a fraction of that in the United States, but land productivity is several times higher.

_____ 5. Slash-and-burn cultivation methods are most common in agricultural regions that are densely populated.

_____ 6. In countries like India, where labor costs are extremely low, it is never efficient to substitute machines for labor in agriculture.

_____ 7. In practice, farmers have not benefited much from having government marketing boards replace private middle traders in marketing operations.

_____ 8. The dominant form of land tenure in Asia and in Africa is the family farm.

_____ 9. Uneducated peasant farmers generally do not change production decisions in response to changes in the relative price of various farm products.

_____ 10. Many developing countries have adopted food pricing policies that reduce farm income and farm output.

_____ 11. The acronym CIMMYT refers to the name (in Spanish) of a successful agricultural research center in Mexico.

_____ 12. The main characteristic of plantation agriculture is the use of slave labor on large private estates.

Multiple Choice

1. As defined in the text, collective agriculture is distinguished from communal farming in that under collective agriculture
   a. land is jointly owned by many families.
   b. workers share in the output on the basis of the amount of labor they contribute.
   c. land is divided into family plots for cultivation.
   d. none of the above; the two terms are synonymous.

2. Land reform has the greatest positive impact on productivity in cases in which
   a. the government maintains an overvalued exchange rate.
   b. the previous system was one of small farms, insecure tenure, and absentee landlords.
   c. former landowners are fully compensated for their land.
   d. private ownership is replaced by collective farming.

3. In which of the following countries was land reform used to consolidate support for a revolution and eliminate the economic base of the landlord class?
   a. China   c. India
   b. Mexico   d. All the above

4. Empirical evidence confirms the general validity of which of the following statements about peasant farmers?
   a. They use available resources efficiently.
   b. They respond to changing price incentives.
   c. Neither a nor b.
   d. Both a and b.

5. Between 1980 and 1991 food production failed to keep pace with population in
   a. Africa.   c. Latin America and Africa.
   b. the Far East and Africa.   d. Latin America, Asia, and Africa.

6. According to the text, what has been the main difficulty in mobilizing off-season labor for rural public works projects?
   a. Peasant farmers are too tradition bound to care about development.
   b. There is a lack of direct connection between work and benefits.
   c. Rural workers can earn more money in other jobs.
   d. Governments have neglected rural conditions.

7. The Green Revolution has three key components: the introduction of _____, the application of chemical fertilizers, and adequate and timely supplies of _____.
   a. tractors, credit   c. plantations, labor
   b. roads, advice   d. improved plant varieties, water

8. An income-maximizing farmer continues to add fertilizer as long as extra units of fertilizer
   a. increase output.
   b. increase the value of output.
   c. increase the value of output more than the cost of production.
   d. receive a subsidy from the government.

9. After decades of experimenting with various land tenure arrangements, China introduced reforms in 1981 that
   a. made large collective farms highly efficient.
   b. fully compensated the original landlords for property confiscated during the Communist revolution.
   c. eliminated the need for extension services.
   d. returned Chinese agriculture to a system based on family farming.

10. A common result of government food subsidies for urban consumers is a food
    a. shortage that leads to rationing or a rise in food imports.
    b. shortage that leads to collectivization of farms.
    c. surplus that leads to high storage costs or exports.
    d. surplus that weakens the grip of absentee landlords.

11. In low-income countries, the agricultural sector employs _____ percent
    of the labor force, compared to about _____ percent in the United States.
    a. more than 70, 3   c. 30 to 50, 15
    b. more than 90, 10   d. 50 to 70, 1

12. The text's discussion of food self-sufficiency reveals that
    a. world supplies of food for export have diminished steadily in recent decades.
    b. food self-sufficiency often is justifiable on grounds of national defense.
    c. the planet is not anywhere near its biological capacity for food production
       using today's technology.
    d. all the above.

APPLICATIONS

Worked Example: Farm Production Decisions

Standard microeconomic tools provide insight into farm production decisions and the effects of price changes. Consider a representative farmer in Basmati who owns 1 hectare (about $2\frac{1}{2}$ acres) of land for growing rice. The first three columns of Table 15–1 show for various amounts of chemical fertilizer (F), the required labor input (L), and the corresponding quantity of rice output (Q). Figure 15–1 portrays this technical relationship as a rice-fertilizer production function. The graph clearly shows diminishing returns to successive increments of F input.

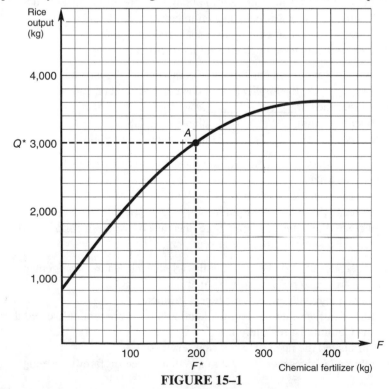

FIGURE 15–1

Table 15-1
Parameters for Rice Farming in Basmati*

Chemical fertilizer (F) (kg) (1)	Labor (L) (2)	Rice output (Q) (kg) (3)	Production cost (C) (Rs) (4)	Value of output (V) (Rs) (5)	Net income (Y) (Rs) (6)	Incremental cost (ΔC) (Rs) (7)	Incremental output value (ΔV) (Rs) (8)
0	4	800	800	800	0		
						350	700
50	5	1,500	1,150	1,500	350		
						350	600
100	6	2,100	1,500	2,100	600		
						350	500
150	7	2,600	1,850	2,600	750		
						350	400
200	8	3,000	2,200	3,000	800		
						350	300
250	9	3,300	2,550	3,300	750		
						350	200
300	10	3,500	2,900	3,500	600		
						350	100
350	11	3,600	3,250	3,600	350		
						150	0
400	11	3,600	3,400	3,600	200		

*Assumes P_R = Rs1, P_L = Rs200, and P_F = Rs3.

Technically, the seed variety being used can yield as much as 3,600 kilograms of rice per hectare. But the actual yield achieved by the farmer is an economic decision that depends on prices as well as technical conditions. Suppose that the price of fertilizer is $P_F = 3$ rupees per kilogram, the price of rice is $P_R = 1$ rupee per kilogram, and the price of labor is $P_L = 200$ rupees per worker. At these prices, the cost of production (C), the value of output (V), and the farmer's net income (Y) can be calculated for each level of fertilizer usage. The results are shown in columns 4, 5, and 6 of Table 15–1. As can be seen, the maximum income level of $Y^* = 800$ rupees is achieved when $F^* = 200$ kilograms of fertilizer are used; it yields $Q^* = 3,000$ kilograms of rice. The farmer will choose to operate at point A in Figure 15–1, even though higher yields are feasible.

Has the extension worker failed to convince the farmer to use the "best" cultivation method? No. Agronomists must recognize that farmers will add fertilizer only up to the point where the extra costs are offset by the extra value of rice output. Columns 7 and 8 of Table 15–1 show the incremental cost (ΔV) for each successive 50 kilogram dose of fertilizer. These data clarify the basis for the farmer's decision. Beyond $F^* = 200$ kilogram, incremental costs exceed the value of the extra rice output.

This analysis can be restated in the familiar framework of marginal cost (MC) and marginal revenue (MR), defined with respect to Q. The marginal revenue for successive units of rice output is simply $P_R = 1$ rupee per kilogram. The marginal cost for successive units of output can be calculated as follows. The 700 kilograms of extra rice produced when F goes from 0 to 50 are obtained at an incremental cost of 350 rupees. So for this range of rice output, $MC = 350/700 = 0.50$ rupees per kilogram. Similarly, when F increases from 50 to 100, Q increases by 600 kilograms (from 1,500 to 2,100 kilograms) while costs rise by 350 rupees. So $MC = 350/600 = 0.58$ rupees per kilogram. Proceeding in this way, one obtains the MC curve shown in Figure 15–2, along with the MR curve.

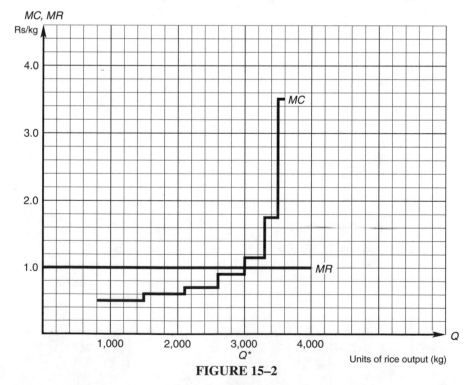

FIGURE 15–2

The level of output that maximizes net income is $Q^* = 3,000$ kilogram, as before. This, of course, is the point where $MC = MR$.

Two concluding remarks: First, if all rice output were marketed, the MC curve would represent the supply curve for the representative farmer in Basmati. You can see that Q increases as a function of P_R. Aggregation across farmers would generate a standard market supply curve. Second, the effect of prices on the quantity supplied is even more pronounced if one considers that the acreage devoted to rice and the share of rice output that gets marketed will both be positive functions of the market price.

Exercises

1. Now, it is your turn to analyze farm production decisions and price effects. This exercise builds upon the Worked Example, so be sure you have read it carefully.

   a. Let's redo the Worked Example using a rice price of $P_R = 2$ rupees per kilogram, while keeping the price of fertilizer at $P_F = 3$ rupees per kilogram and the price of labor at $P_L = 200$ rupees per worker.

      (i) Table 15–2 has a format similar to that of Table 15–1. The numbers in the first three columns, which summarize the production technology, are identical. Fill in all of the blanks in Table 15–2. Some of the numbers are provided to help you with your calculations. Keep in mind that ΔC and ΔV refer, respectively, to the increase in production cost and the increase in output value per incremental 50 kilogram dose of fertilizer.

      (ii) When P_R changes from 1 rupee to 2 rupees, would any shifts occur in the curves shown in Figures 15–1 and 15–2? Explain.

      (iii) With $P_R = 2$ rupees per kilogram, the income-maximizing farmer in Basmati would choose to produce an output of

      $$Q' = \underline{\hspace{1cm}} \text{ kg of rice,}$$

      using $F' = \underline{\hspace{1cm}}$ kg of fertilizer.

      The farmer's net income in this case would be

      $$Y' = \text{Rs}\underline{\hspace{1cm}}.$$

      (Note: By drawing the new MR line in Figure 15–2 you can confirm your result, using the $MC = MR$ rule.)

Table 15–2
Parameters for Rice Farming in Basmati*

Chemical fertilizer (F) (kg) (1)	Labor (L) (2)	Rice output (Q) (kg) (3)	Production cost (C) (Rs) (4)	Value of output (V) (Rs) (5)	Net income (Y) (Rs) (6)	Incremental cost (ΔC) (Rs) (7)	Incremental output value (ΔV) (Rs) (8)
0	4	800	—	1,600	—	—	—
50	5	1,500	—	—	1,850	—	—
100	6	2,100	—	—	—	—	—
150	7	2,600	—	—	—	—	800
200	8	3,000	2,200	—	—	—	—
250	9	3,300	—	—	4,050	350	—
300	10	3,500	—	—	—	—	—
350	11	3,600	—	—	—	—	—
400	11	3,600	—	—	—	—	—

*Assumes P_R = Rs2, P_L = Rs200, and P_F = Rs3.

b. To see the effects of increasing the price of rice from 1 rupee to 2 rupees, compare the outcome in part a with the outcome in the Worked Example.

   (i) As a result of the higher price of rice, the income-maximizing farmer in Basmati increases output by _____ kilograms, or _____ percent.

   (ii) After adjusting to the high price, the farmer's net income will increase by _____ rupees, or _____ percent.

   (iii) Suppose that the average farmer markets rice output only in excess of 1,500 kilograms—the amount needed for family consumption. Then, the increase in P_R to 2 rupees would expand the quantity of rice supplied by the average farmer to the market from _____ to _____ kilograms, an increase of _____ percent.

   (iv) Think about the rural labor market. Will the increase in the price of rice affect the demand curve for farm labor? What about the labor supply curve? What does this imply about the average wage for farm workers? Explain.

   (v) How will the farmer's outcome be affected by these changes in the rural labor market?

c. Return now to the original rice price of $P_R = 1$ rupee but now suppose that the price of fertilizer is cut in half, to $P_F = 1.5$ rupees.

   (i) Table 15–3 is similar to Table 15–1, but for simplicity columns 7 and 8 have been omitted. The numbers in the first three columns of Table 15–3 are identical to those in Table 15–1. Given the new price of subsidized fertilizer, fill in the blanks in Table 15–3.

   (ii) With $P_F = 1.5$ rupees, the income-maximizing farmer in Basmati would choose to produce an output of

$$Q'' = \text{_____} \text{ kg of rice,}$$

using $F'' = \text{_____}$ kg of fertilizer.

The farmer's net income in this case would be

$$Y'' = \text{Rs_____}.$$

   (iii) Explain how the effects of this fertilizer subsidy would alter Figures 15–1 and 15–2.

Table 15–3
Parameters for Rice Farming in Basmati*

F (kg) (1)	L (2)	Q (kg) (3)	C (Rs) (4)	V (Rs) (5)	Y (Rs) (6)
0	4	800	800	800	____
50	5	1,500	____	____	425
100	6	2,100	____	____	____
150	7	2,600	1,625	____	____
200	8	3,000	____	____	____
250	9	3,300	____	____	____
300	10	3,500	____	____	1,050
350	11	3,600	____	____	____
400	11	3,600	____	____	____

*Assumes P_R = Rs1, P_L = Rs200, and P_F = Rs1.5.

Before proceeding, think about the important insights that one gains from applying basic microeconomics tools to a farm enterprise—insights about price effects on food supplies and rural incomes.

2. Now let's introduce a technical innovation, along with risk considerations.

   a. The Basmati Agricultural Research Farm (never referred to by acronym) develops a new variety of rice seed that is far more responsive to fertilizer. Specifically, for each level of fertilizer use in Table 15–1, the new seed variety doubles output. The new technology also doubles the required labor input for each level of fertilizer use.
      (i) On the basis of this technological information about the new biological package, fill in the blanks in columns 2 and 3 of Table 15–4.
      (ii) Assuming that prices initially are the same as in the Worked Exercise (so P_R = Rs1, P_F = Rs3, and P_L = Rs200), fill in the blanks in columns 4, 5, and 6 of Table 15–4.
      (iii) Using this new variety of rice seed, the income-maximizing farmer in Basmati would choose to produce an output of

      $$Q^* = \underline{\hspace{2cm}} \text{ kg of rice,}$$

      using $\quad F^* = \underline{\hspace{2cm}}$ kg of fertilizer.

      The farmer's net income (if all the output were marketed) would be

      $$Y^* = \text{Rs}\underline{\hspace{2cm}}.$$

Table 15–4
Parameters for Farming New Variety of Rice Seeds in Basmati*

F (kg) (1)	L (2)	Q (kg) (3)	C (Rs) (4)	V (Rs) (5)	Y (Rs) (6)
0	___	___	___	___	___
50	___	___	___	___	___
100	___	___	___	___	___
150	___	___	3,250	___	___
200	16	6,000	___	___	___
250	___	___	___	___	2,250
300	___	___	___	___	___
350	___	___	___	___	___
400	___	___	___	___	___

*Assumes $P_R = $ Rs1, $P_L = $ Rs200, $P_F = $ Rs3, but with the high-yielding rice variety.

b. Unhappily, this is not the whole story. In normal years farmers can expect to realize the outcome Q^* and Y^* as just calculated. But the new rice variety is highly susceptible to a periodic plant disease. When this plant disease strikes, farmers using new seeds lose 2,000 rupees because income from the poor crop does not cover the cost of fertilizer, planting, and weeding.

   (i) The plant disease strikes one year out of four, on average. A farmer's *expected* income with the new variety of rice is $Y_e = $ _____ rupees. (Hint: Expected income, here, equals average income over the four-year cycle.)

   (ii) Your calculations should show that expected income from using the new seed variety (Y_e) still exceeds the income generated with traditional seeds (which is 800 rupees, from the Worked Example), despite the plant disease problem. Considering risk as well as income, should one expect poor peasant farmers to adopt eagerly the new variety of rice? Explain.

c. Agronomists then develop an even better seed that is not susceptible to plant disease. Even so, problems with the rural infrastructure may block successful introduction of the new variety of rice.

  (i) How can problems with rural credit block the successful introduction of the new variety of rice?

  (ii) How can problems with rural roads block the successful introduction of the new variety of rice?

  (iii) How can problems with rural extension services block the successful introduction of the new variety of rice?

3. This exercise investigates one more variation on the Worked Example: the effect of land tenure arrangements. You will need to refer repeatedly to the data in columns 1 through 6 of Table 15–1 for background information.

  a. The income figures in column 6 of Table 15–1 implicitly assume that rice farmers are independent proprietors. Suppose, instead, that the farmers are *sharecroppers* who must pay 25 percent of their gross harvest as rent to the landlords, while bearing the full burden of paying input costs.

  (i) For each level of output shown in Table 15–5, calculate the net income retained by the sharecrop farmer after paying the landlord. Place your answers in the column labeled *Sharecrop farmer*. [Hint: $Y = V(0.75) - C.$]

  (ii) What amounts of F and Q will be chosen by the sharecropper to maximize net income (after share payments to the landlord)?

$$F = \underline{\hspace{1cm}} \text{ kg of fertilizer.}$$

$$Q = \underline{\hspace{1cm}} \text{ kg of rice.}$$

Table 15–5

Alternative Land Tenure Arrangements

| Rice output (Q) (kg) | Net income (Rs) retained by | |
	Sharecrop farmer	Tenant farmer
800	_____	_____
1,500	–25	_____
2,100	_____	_____
2,600	_____	350
3,000	_____	_____
3,300	_____	_____
3,500	_____	_____
3,600	_____	_____

(iii) You should have found that the sharecropper chooses less F and less Q than the independent proprietor. With reference to marginal revenue and marginal cost as shown in Figure 15–2, why does this difference occur?

(iv) Whose production decision is more efficient—the sharecropper or the independent proprietor? Briefly explain.

b. Instead of paying the landlord a fixed share of the crop, suppose that the farmer is a *tenant* who pays the landlord a *fixed sum* of 400 rupees.
   (i) Calculate the net income retained by the tenant farmer for each output level shown in Table 15–5. Place your answers in the column labeled *Tenant farmer*. [Hint: $Y = V - (C + 400)$.]

(ii) What amounts of F and Q will be chosen by the tenant farmer to maximize net income (after rent payments to the landlord)?

$$F = \underline{\hspace{1cm}} \text{ kg of fertilizer.}$$

$$Q = \underline{\hspace{1cm}} \text{ kg of rice.}$$

(iii) You should have found that the tenant chooses the same levels of F and Q as the independent proprietor. Use the analysis of marginal cost and marginal revenue conditions summarized in Figure 15–2 to explain why these two different land tenure arrangements lead to the same outcome.

c. Think again about the logic underlying Figure 15–2. What would be the effect on the *sharecropper's* production decision if the landlord paid 25 percent of the input costs, as well as receiving 25 percent of the gross crop?

4. This exercise uses supply-and-demand analysis to study the effects of food price controls and subsidies. Curves D_r and S_r in Figure 15–3 are the *retail* market demand and supply curves for grain in the Republic of Nafaka. Curve S_f shows the *farm-gate* supply curve. As discussed in the text, marketing costs account for the vertical gap between S_f and S_r.

In the absence of government intervention, curves D_r and S_r establish the equilibrium price in the retail market at $P_0 = $ N\$1.00 per kilogram of grain. (N\$ stands for the Nafaka dollar, which is worth U.S.\$0.50.) The equilibrium quantity is $Q_0 = 200$ million kilograms of grain. Curve S_f shows that the price paid to farmers for supplying quantity Q_0 is $P_1 = $ N\$0.60 per kilogram. So the marketing cost of moving food from the farm gate to the retail consumer is $C_0 = $ N\$0.40 per kilogram of grain.

a. Now the government of Nafaka imposes price controls: Grain must be sold in the retail market for $P^* = $ N\$0.80 per kilogram.

(i) From curve D_r you can see that the retail quantity demanded at price P^* is

$$Q_1 = \underline{\hspace{1cm}} \text{ million kg of grain.}$$

(ii) The traders still incur marketing costs of $C_0 = $ N\$0.40. After these costs are deducted from the retail price, farmers receive

$$P_2 = \text{N\$}\underline{\hspace{1cm}} \text{ per kg of grain.}$$

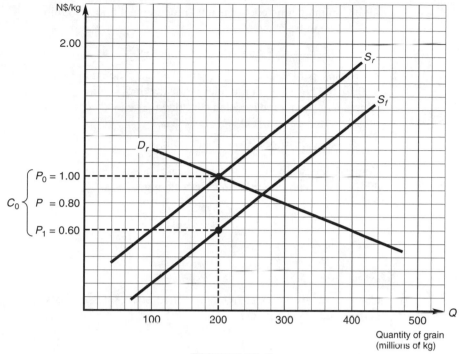

FIGURE 15–3

   (iii) At this price, farmers are willing to supply to the market only

$$Q_2 = \text{_____} \text{ million kg of grain.}$$

   (iv) Consequently, a shortage (excess demand) emerges in the retail market of

$$Q_1 - Q_2 = \text{_____} \text{ million kg of grain.}$$

b. With the price control in effect, the government has three options for handling the excess demand. First, the government can simply live with the shortage. Second, it can import grain to satisfy the excess demand.
   (i) To satisfy the excess demand created by the price controls, the government has to import $Q_m = \text{_____}$ million kilograms of grain. If the world price of grain is U.S.\$0.50 = N\$1 per kilogram, these imports entail a foreign exchange cost of U.S.\$_____ million.
   (ii) In domestic-currency terms, the government would be buying imported grain for N\$1.00 per kilogram and selling it to consumers for $P^* = $ N\$0.80. So the government would be providing a subsidy to consumers of $S_0 = $ N\$_____ per kilogram of imported grain. Altogether this subsidy would cost the government

$$Q_m \times S_0 = \text{N\$_____} \text{ million.}$$

c. Alternatively, the government can eliminate the shortage by raising farm prices enough to induce domestic grain production that will match demand at Q_1.
   (i) Curve S_f shows that domestic farmers will increase output to Q_1 only if they are paid

$$P_3 = \text{N\$_____} \text{ per kg.}$$

Adding in marketing costs, the total procurement price of grain would have to be

$$P_4 = P_3 + C_0 = N\$ \underline{\qquad} \text{ per kg.}$$

(ii) If it pays P_4 per kilogram of grain and then sells the grain for $P^* =$ N\$0.80, the government provides a subsidy of $S_1 = N\$ \underline{\qquad}$ per kilogram of grain produced and consumed. The total cost of the subsidy to the government is

$$Q_1 \times S_1 = N\$ \underline{\qquad} \text{ million.}$$

(iii) Compare the two policies—boosting farm prices versus covering the shortage with imports—in terms of budget costs.

(iv) Compare the two policies in terms of their effect on incentives for agricultural development in Nafaka.

5. This exercise uses isoquant analysis to examine how factor productivity in agriculture can depend on factor endowments. North Nasi and South Nasi are identical in terms of land fertility and farmers' capabilities. They have the same agricultural technology, as depicted in Figure 15–4. Isoquant QQ shows the alternative combinations of land (D) and labor (L) that can be used to produce 10 tons of rice. For simplicity, we ignore other inputs, such as capital and fertilizer.

a. In other ways, the two countries do differ. In North Nasi, the currency is the dollar, whereas South Nasi uses pesos. (You need not know the exchange rate.) Also, in North Nasi land is plentiful relative to the population. The annual rental cost of land is $200 per hectare, while the wage is $300 per year. South Nasi, in contrast, is heavily populated. There, the annual land rent is P1,800 per hectare, while wages are P300 per year.

(i) The optimal factor proportions for a farmer in North Nasi can be determined by finding the point on QQ that lies on the lowest possible isocost line. For a cost of $C = \$1,200$, a farmer in North Nasi can afford \underline{\qquad} hectares of land with zero labor, \underline{\qquad} workers with zero land, or any other combination of L and D costing a total of $1,200.

(ii) In Figure 15–4, draw the $C = \$1,200$ isocost line faced by a farmer in North Nasi.

(iii) You should find that the line is tangent to isoquant QQ. Label the point of tangency point N^*.

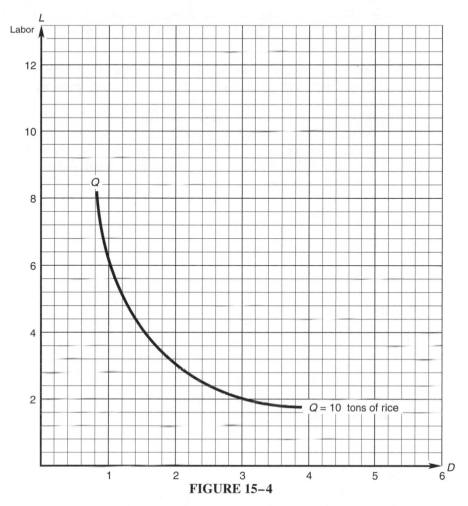

FIGURE 15–4

   (iv) For a farmer in North Nasi, the optimal technique for producing 10
tons of rice involves the use of $D =$ _____ hectares of land, and
$L =$ _____ workers.
   (v) For farmers operating efficiently in North Nasi, *land* productivity is
_____ tons of rice per hectare; *labor* productivity is _____ tons
of rice per worker.

b. Now consider the optimal factor proportions for a farmer in South Nasi,
where the wage is P300 and the land rent is P1,800 per hectare.
   (i) In Figure 15–4, construct a few representative isocost lines for a
farmer in South Nasi. (Hint: Try cost levels of P1,800 and P3,600.)
   (ii) Find the point on isoquant QQ that is tangent to an isocost line for
farmers in South Nasi. Label the point of tangency point S^*.
   (iii) For a farmer in South Nasi, the optimal technique for producing 10
tons of rice involves the use of

$$D = \text{_____ hectares of land}$$

$$L = \text{_____ workers.}$$

(Hint: The answer involves only integers.)

    (iv) For farmers operating efficiently in South Nasi, land productivity is _____ tons of rice per hectare and labor productivity is _____ tons of rice per worker.

  c. Farmers in each country are adapting optimally to their respective factor costs. Yet factor proportions and factor productivity levels are very different.

    (i) Output per hectare of *land* is much higher in _____ Nasi.

    (ii) Output per *worker* is much higher in _____ Nasi.

    (iii) What can one conclude from these differences in factor productivity about the relative efficiency of rice production in North and South Nasi? Briefly explain.

ANSWERS TO SELF-TEST

Completion

1. scale
2. tenure
3. *sharecropping*
4. reform, landlord
5. transportation
6. labor
7. Extension
8. moneylender
9. prices
10. increase, reduce
11. China
12. fertilizer

True-False

1.	F	7.	T
2.	T	8.	T
3.	T	9.	F
4.	T	10.	T
5.	F	11.	T
6.	F	12.	F

Multiple Choice

1.	b	7.	d
2.	b	8.	c
3.	a	9.	d
4.	d	10.	a
5.	a	11.	a
6.	b	12.	c

CHAPTER 16 | Primary Exports

OVERVIEW

Chapter 16 deals with countries whose comparative advantage lies in primary products. The chapter opens with an exposition of the static theory of comparative advantage. This time-honored theory establishes that every country can gain from trade, that the potential gains tend to be greatest for smaller countries, and that the best trade prospects lie in exporting commodities that use the country's abundant factors intensively. While trade benefits each country overall, lowering trade barriers will harm some groups, such as industrialists who had enjoyed protection. Therefore, moves toward freer trade are bound to trigger opposition.

On average, the export-to-GDP ratio rises with per capita income, but there are wide variations. Trade is less important for large countries, for example, because they have broader domestic markets. Trade also depends heavily on resource endowments and on government trade strategies. Many developing countries rely heavily on primary exports to earn foreign exchange for importing consumer goods, as well as capital goods and raw materials for domestic industry. Primary exports can promote development by improving factor utilization, attracting investment, and creating linkage effects to support diversification and the development of new, dynamic sources of comparative advantage.

Primary exporters often are thought to suffer from sluggish growth of world demand, declining terms of trade, unstable export earnings, and weak linkage effects. Evidence indicates that world demand for primary products has indeed grown slowly, overall. Yet some commodities face brisk demand, and most primary markets are sufficient to serve as leading sectors for development in low-income countries with rich resource endowments. Studies of long-term data do *not* sustain the claim that primary exports face steadily declining terms of trade, even when fuel products are excluded. Turning to export instability, it is true that world markets for primary products tend to be volatile; this uncertainty can boost savings rates, but it also reduces investment productivity.

There also is validity, in some cases, to the charge that primary exports are produced in enclaves that lack effective links to the rest of the economy. The most serious problem facing primary exporters, however, comes from export booms, or Dutch disease, which can cripple development if not carefully managed. Too often, a rapid influx of foreign exchange earnings leads to currency over-valuation, accelerating inflation, wasteful spending, and imprudent borrowing and leaves the country worse off than if the boom had never occurred.

MAIN LEARNING OBJECTIVES

After studying this chapter, you ought to understand and be able to explain

1. The fundamental concept of comparative advantage as the basis for gains from trade, as well as its major implications.

2. The main export characteristics of developing countries, including the extent to which many of these countries depend on primary exports.

3. How primary exports can serve as an engine of growth by improving resource utilization, expanding factor endowments, and generating various linkage effects.

4. The concepts and facts behind the ongoing debate about barriers to primary-export-led growth due to sluggish demand growth, declining terms of trade, earnings instability, and weak linkage effects.

5. The causes and cures of Dutch disease, which has turned many a commodity boom into a development disaster.

ECONOMIC TOOLS AND TECHNIQUES

From what you have learned in this chapter, you should be able to

1. Demonstrate how the theory of comparative advantage works using a two-country, two-good example and also using a graph of the production frontier.

2. Differentiate among the net barter terms of trade, the income terms of trade, and the single factoral terms of trade and calculate each measure from appropriate data.

3. Define the real exchange rate and explain its role in the propagation of and cure for Dutch disease.

KEY TERMS AND CONCEPTS

comparative advantage
depreciation, appreciation
Dutch disease
export enclave
export share of GDP
exportables, importables
Engel's law
linkage effects, including fiscal linkage
net barter terms of trade, income terms of trade, single factoral terms of trade

permanent-income hypothesis
Prebisch-Singer hypothesis
primary exports
real exchange rate, nominal exchange rate
rent seeking
signaling effect
tradables and nontradables
vent for surplus
world terms of trade, world price

SELF-TEST

Completion

1. Even if one of two countries is more efficient at producing every good, trade between the two countries can still be mutually beneficial. This is the main lesson of the theory of _____ _____.

2. Farm products, timber, metal ores, petroleum, and natural gas are all examples of _____ products that are important export commodities of developing countries.

3. The net barter terms of trade for a country are computed as the ratio of the average price of its _____ to the average price of its _____.

4. Opening a country to trade benefits _____ of imported goods.

5. Government revenues derived from primary exports are referred to as a _____ *linkage*.

6. For industrial countries, the income elasticity of demand for foods is below 0.5. This is consistent with _____ law.

7. A foreign-owned mining complex that purchases locally made construction materials and sells inputs to small metal works is said to have a production _____ effect.

8. The _____-_____ hypothesis implies that more unstable export earnings should be associated with higher savings rates, other things being equal.

9. Industries such as mining and petroleum that remain remote from other centers of production and produce few domestic linkage effects are called *export* _____.

10. The real exchange rate is an index number showing changes in the ratio of home currency per dollar, adjusted for _____.

11. A real _____ of the Mexican peso occurs when the real exchange rate rises.

12. A key cause of Dutch disease is that a commodity boom causes the country's real exchange rate to _____.

True-False

If false, you should be able to explain why.

_____ 1. The theory of comparative advantage explains static trade patterns but not the dynamics of growth or structural change over time.

_____ 2. For nonoil primary products, empirical tests covering the period 1900 to 1988 strongly confirm the Prebisch-Singer hypothesis of declining terms of trade.

_____ 3. The case study of Ghana illustrates successful development through relying on primary products as an engine of growth.

_____ 4. In most developing countries, one or two primary products account for over 90 percent of the country's exports.

_____ 5. Over the period 1965 to 1992, the quantity of nonfuel primary products imported by industrial countries declined.

_____ 6. The real value of a country's earnings from primary exports can be rising even if the country's net barter terms of trade are falling.

_____ 7. Empirical evidence indicates that higher export instability is associated with higher investment rates but not higher growth rates.

_____ 8. A farm lobby in Ethiopia that campaigns for additional investment in farm extension service is engaged in a rent-seeking activity.

_____ 9. Restricting the supply of a primary product improves earnings for the exporters only if world demand is inelastic.

_____ 10. A buffer stock operates by intervening in a commodity market to buy when the price is falling and sell when the price is rising.

_____ 11. Nigeria's agricultural sector prospered from the oil boom in the 1970s and early 1980s.

_____ 12. When a country maintains a fixed nominal exchange rate, the real exchange rate will be appreciating whenever the domestic inflation rate exceeds world inflation.

Multiple Choice

1. Which country sustained relatively rapid growth over the past 30 years through a primary-export-led strategy of development?
   a. Ghana
   b. Malaysia
   c. Nigeria
   d. India

2. In Mexico, a unit of furniture requires nine labor-days and a unit of corn requires three labor-days. In the United States, a unit of furniture requires four labor-days, and a unit of corn requires two labor-days.
   a. The United States should export corn and import furniture.
   b. The United States should export furniture and import corn.
   c. The United States should not trade with Mexico, because it can produce both products at lower cost.
   d. Not enough information is given to determine the efficient pattern of trade.

3. On average the ratio of exports to GDP _____ as a country develops, and on average this ratio is _____ for a small country than for a large country.
   a. rises, lower
   b. rises, higher
   c. declines, lower
   d. declines, higher

4. Tea plantations in Kenya generate large consumption linkage effects if
   a. lots of tea is consumed in Kenya.
   b. the tea plantation uses implements produced in Kenya.
   c. tea exporters spend their foreign exchange earnings on imports of consumer goods.
   d. plantation workers are paid more than they would earn elsewhere; this creates an added demand for domestic consumer goods.

5. When growth of one industry, such as textiles, stimulates domestic production of an input, the effect is called
   a. *vent for surplus.*
   b. a *forward linkage.*
   c. a *backward linkage.*
   d. *comparative advantage.*

6. The income terms of trade is determined by the ratio of export
   a. earnings to import prices.
   b. earnings to expenditures on imports.
   c. prices to import prices.
   d. earnings to export quantities.

7. From 1954 to 1991, the income terms of trade for nonoil developing countries, as a group,
   a. rose by almost 6 percent per year.
   b. fluctuated widely but showed no trend.
   c. fell at an average rate of less than 1 percent per year.
   d. fell steadily until 1980 and then rose sharply.

8. All values here are index numbers defined to equal 100 in 1985. In 1993, Korea's nominal exchange rate was 90.8, its domestic price level was 158.5, and world prices stood at 133.1. What happened to Korea's real exchange rate from 1985 to 1993?
   a. It appreciated by 9 percent.
   b. It appreciated by 24 percent.
   c. It depreciated by 43 percent.
   d. It depreciated by 31 percent.

9. The economic basis for political opposition to freer trade in developing countries is that
   a. only industrial countries gain from trade.
   b. workers in industries facing import competition can be hurt by freer trade.
   c. developing countries cannot compete successfully in world markets.
   d. all the above.

10. The process of mobilizing underutilized domestic resources through exports of primary products is called
   a. *terms of trade.*   c. *permanent income hypothesis.*
   b. *buffer stock.*   d. *vent for surplus.*

11. Which of the following conditions is not a major symptom of Dutch disease sparked by an oil export boom?
   a. Rapidly declining per capita income.
   b. Rising unemployment.
   c. Stagnation or decline in nonoil sectors.
   d. Accelerating inflation.

12. Indonesia dealt successfully with its oil boom through a package of policies. Which of the following was not a key part of this package?
   a. Repeated devaluations were used to avoid real appreciation.
   b. Large wage increases were granted to industrial workers and civil servants.
   c. Investment in agriculture had a high priority.
   d. The government balanced its budget each year.

APPLICATIONS

Worked Example: Comparative Advantage and Gains from Trade

Figure 16–1 shows the production possibilities frontier (PPF) for Imara, a country that produces food (F) and clothing (C). In the absence of international trade, point A represents the combination of F and C that maximizes welfare and achieves the highest attainable social indifference curve (*II*). The slope of the PPF at point A (equal to $-1/4$) indicates the relative opportunity cost of the two goods: One more ton of F could be produced at the cost of giving up four bales of C, or one additional bale of C could be produced by forgoing $1/4$ ton of F. In a market economy the slope at A would also equal the ratio of the product prices, since relative prices would reflect relative costs.

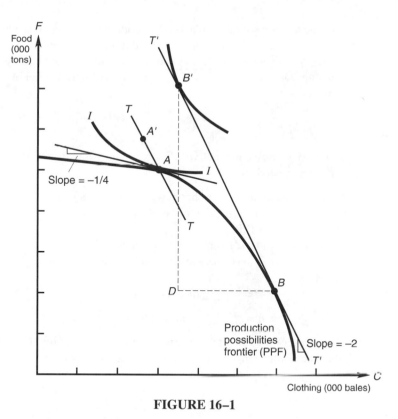

FIGURE 16–1

Suppose that on the world market the price of food is $1,000 per ton and the price of clothing is $2,000 per bale. One can trade $2F$ for $1C$, or vice versa. By producing at A, Imara can attain any point along line TT through trade. Line TT shows the trade opportunities; its slope (-2) embodies the relative price ratio on the world markets, called the *world terms of trade*. Some points on TT (such as point A') clearly lie above indifference curve II, which is the best attainable welfare level in the absence of trade.

But Imara can do even better. For each 1 ton reduction in F output, the economy can produce four extra bales of C. In the world market the four extra bales of C can be sold for $8,000, which buys $8F$. Giving up $1F$ to get back 8 is a good deal. In short, F can be "produced" more efficiently by shifting resources to C and trading. Imara has a *comparative advantage* in producing clothing.

As Imara reallocates resources toward producing more C and less F, the opportunity cost of C increases. At point B, the slope of the PPF equals -2. Up to this point, but no further, specialization and trade continue to be a good deal. With production at B, trade opportunities are given by line $T'T'$. Since $T'T'$ is tangent to the PPF at B, no reallocation of domestic resources would provide more favorable trade opportunities. At B, Imara's domestic price ratio corresponds to relative prices on the world market.

Compared to the best pretrade outcome at A, Imara obtains more C, more F, or more of both through specializing in producing C and trading along line $T'T'$.

The highest possible level of welfare is reached by producing at B and consuming at B' (where there is a tangency between line $T'T'$ and a social indifference curve). The corresponding *trade triangle* involves exporting amount BD of clothing in exchange for amount DB' of imported food or other goods Imara could not produce on its own.

Exercises

1. It is your turn to analyze comparative advantage and gains from trade, along with some related issues.

    a. El Desoto is a small agrarian country with land well suited to grow maize (M) and bananas (B), Figure 16–2 shows El Desoto's production possibilities frontier (PPF).

        (i) Most people in Desoto prefer eating maize. In the absence of trade, social welfare is maximized by producing and consuming at point A, where

$$M = \underline{\hspace{2cm}} \text{ thousand tons,}$$

$$B = \underline{\hspace{2cm}} \text{ thousand tons.}$$

        (ii) The slope of the PPF at point A is equal to _____. (Hint: Calculate the slope of the tangent at A; the slope is an integer here.)

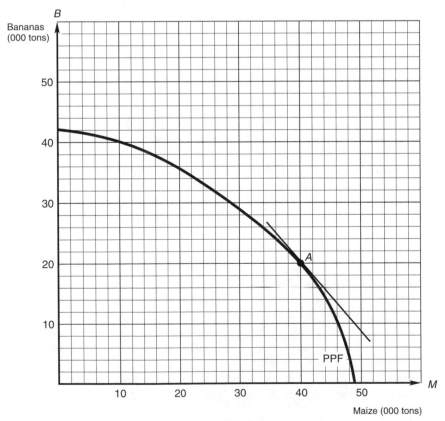

FIGURE 16–2

(iii) The value of the slope at A means that one extra ton of banana output has an opportunity cost equal to _____ of maize. Similarly, the opportunity cost of one extra ton of maize is _____ of bananas.

(iv) At the margin, one ton of maize trades for _____ ton of bananas, so the relative price ratio in the domestic market is

$$P_M / P_B = \text{_____}.$$

b. On the world market maize sells for $2,000 per ton, while bananas sell for $6,000 per ton.

   (i) Hence, on the world market one ton of maize trades for _____ tons of bananas, and one ton of bananas trades for _____ tons of maize.

   (ii) Draw a line through point A showing the trade opportunities open to El Desoto when it produces at point A. Label this line TT.

   (iii) The slope of TT is equal to _____.

   (iv) El Desoto can benefit by reallocating resources (along its PPF) and trading. Specifically, the country can realize a net gain by reducing domestic production of maize by one ton in order to produce an extra _____ ton of bananas.

   (v) This extra banana output can be sold on the world market for $_____, which then can be used to buy _____ tons of maize.

   (vi) In short, by reducing domestic maize output by one ton, El Desoto can obtain _____ tons of maize indirectly through trade. El Desoto has a comparative advantage in producing _____.

c. As resources move to banana production, successive increments of output have increasingly high opportunity costs. At some point X on the PPF, further specialization no longer brings further gains from trade.

   (i) Carefully identify point X in Figure 16–2. Draw a line $T'T'$ showing the trade opportunities open to El Desoto when it produces at point X. (Hint: Lines $T'T'$ and TT reflect the same world terms of trade, but $T'T'$ is tangent to the PPF; point X involves nice round production numbers.)

   (ii) At point X, El Desoto produces

   $$M = \text{_____} \text{ thousand tons,}$$

   $$B = \text{_____} \text{ thousand tons.}$$

   (iii) By producing at X and trading, El Desoto can attain exactly the same maize consumption it had enjoyed at point A, along with an extra

   _____ thousand tons of bananas.

   Or the country can enjoy exactly the same banana consumption as at point A, along with an extra

   _____ thousand tons of maize.

   (iv) Or it can enjoy more of both goods. Draw a point showing the latter outcome and label it X'.

   (v) Draw in what the textbook calls the *trade triangle* for production at X and consumption at X'. Label clearly the corresponding volume of exports and imports.

d. The country as a whole unambiguously gains from trade. Is it possible, though, that some groups in El Desoto are hurt when the country is opened to free trade? Explain.

e. (i) A decline in El Desoto's terms of trade means that the world price of _____ drops relative to the world price of _____.

(ii) How would declining terms of trade alter the position of the optimal production point X' and Desoto's pattern of trade?

While working through the mechanics of this exercise, don't lose sight of the vital lesson: Any country can gain from trade as long as relative prices in the world market differ from what the relative domestic prices would be in the absence of trade.

2. Review the terms-of-trade formulas in the textbook before starting this exercise. Table 16–1 provides data on trade, factor productivity, and exchange rates in Colombia and Malawi for 1980 and 1990. Each figure is an index number defined to equal 100 for 1980. The 1990 values reflect the relative changes between 1980 and 1990. For example, the number 69 in the top row says that Colombia's average export price in 1990 was 69 percent as high as a decade earlier; the average price dropped by 31 percent over this time period. Malawi's average export price also fell but only by 20 percent. Notice in row 5 that GDP growth for the decade was nearly the same in the two countries—40 percent in Colombia versus 36 percent in Malawi. Terms-of-trade measures also are expressed as index numbers. For all of the index measures in this exercise, you have to adjust the units so that the value for 1980 equals 100.

a. What was the value of net barter terms of trade for 1990?

For Colombia: $T_n =$ _____.

For Malawi: T_n = _____.

You should find that the two countries experienced nearly identical declines in net barter terms of trade.

Table 16–1

Trade-Related Indices for Colombia and Malawi, 1980 and 1990
(index numbers, 1980 = 100)

	Colombia		Malawi	
	1980	1990	1980	1990
1. Average price of exports (P_x)	100	69	100	80
2. Volume of exports (Q_x)	100	180	100	119
3. Average price of imports (P_m)	100	113	100	131
4. Labor productivity $(Z_x)^*$	100	163	100	105
5. GDP	100	140	100	136
6. Nominal exchange rate (R_0)	100	1,117	100	321
7. Domestic price level (P_d)	100	913	100	396
8. World price level (P_w)	100	164	100	164

*The variable Z ought to measure total factor productivity, but labor productivity is used here.

Sources: Derived from data in World Bank, *World Tables 1994*, and IMF, *International Financial Statistics Yearbook 1994*.

b. (i) Calculate the *income* terms of trade for 1990.

For Colombia, $T_i =$ _____.

For Malawi, T_i = _____.

(ii) For both countries the income terms of trade index for 1990 is higher than the net barter terms of trade index. Why?

(iii) How is it possible for T_i to exceed 100 for Colombia in 1990, when T_n fell so much during the 1980s?

c. (i) Calculate the single factoral terms of trade index for 1990 (again with 1980 = 100).

For Colombia, $T_s = $ _____.

For Malawi, T_s = _____.

(ii) Although both countries faced similar declines in T_n between 1980 and 1990, the values of T_s were quite different. For Colombia, T_s was virtually unchanged for the decade, but for Malawi, T_s fell. Explain the meaning of these different outcomes for T_s.

d. Overall, how did the two countries fare in terms of their capacity to earn foreign exchange, as purchasing power to buy imports? Explain.

e. A key difference between the two countries was that Colombia's export volume grew much more rapidly. Perhaps this was due to exchange-rate policies.

(i) From the data in lines 6, 7, and 8 of Table 16–1, calculate the real exchange rate in 1990.

For Colombia, $RER = $ _____.

For Malawi, RER = _____.

Again use 1980 = 100 as the base for computing the index number.

(ii) Which country managed its exchange rate in a manner most conducive to stimulating export growth? Explain.

3. This exercise uses a simple supply-and-demand framework to analyze export instability, buffer stock operations, and cartel behavior. Figure 16–3 illustrates conditions in the world market for copper. The supply curve (S) is price inelastic, while the demand curve (D) exhibits unitary price elasticity so that when P goes up 1 percent, the quantity demanded goes down 1 percent. The initial equilibrium price and quantity are P(0) and Q(0); the export revenues earned by copper producers total $R(0) = P(0) \times Q(0)$.

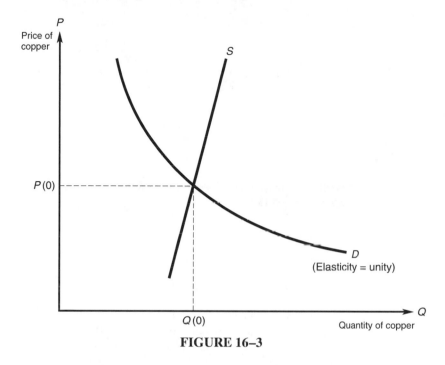

FIGURE 16–3

a. What is the effect on the price of copper (P) and on the export revenues (R) earned by copper producers as a result of
   (i) a 20 percent increase in demand (shift in D)?

   (ii) a 20 percent increase in supply (shift in S)?
       (Hint: Don't forget that the price elasticity of demand is unity here.)

b. Instead of thinking about the effect of a single shift in each curve, consider how the market is affected by a *random series* of shifts, which we can refer to as *instability*.
   (i) How does instability of demand affect copper prices?

    (ii) How does instability of supply affect copper prices?

    (iii) How does instability of demand affect the total revenues earned by copper exporters?

    (iv) How does instability of supply affect the total revenues earned by copper producers? (Again, keep in mind the unitary elasticity of demand.)

    (v) Would any of the answers above be altered if demand was price *inelastic*? Be specific.

c. The major copper-exporting countries band together to form an International Copper Fund to stabilize copper prices at $P(0)$ through buffer stock operations. After investing $5 billion to accumulate an initial reserve stock of copper supplies, the fund goes into operation.

    (i) To stabilize the price, the fund has to _____ copper when market conditions would be pushing the price below $P(0)$. Similarly, the fund has to _____ copper when the market conditions would be pushing the price above $P(0)$.

    (ii) Starting with the conditions shown in Figure 16–3, suppose demand increases by 20 percent. Draw the new demand curve and label it D' (precision is not essential). Show on the graph how much copper the fund must buy or sell to hold the price at $P(0)$.

    (iii) Starting from the same initial conditions, suppose demand declines 20 percent. Draw the new demand curve and label it D''. Show how much copper the fund must buy or sell in this case to hold the price at $P(0)$.

    (iv) Figure 16–4 is just a fresh picture of the same conditions shown in Figure 16–3. Suppose *supply* increases by 20 percent. Draw the new supply curve on Figure 16–4 and label it S'. Show how much copper the fund must buy or sell to hold the price at $P(0)$.

    (v) Starting again from the same initial conditions, suppose that supply drops by 20 percent. Draw the new supply curve and label it S''. Show how much copper the fund must buy or sell to hold the price at $P(0)$.

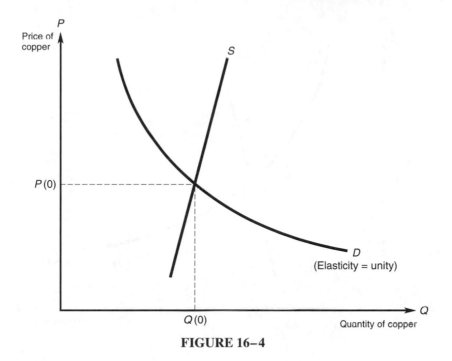

FIGURE 16–4

d. These buffer stock operations succeed in stabilizing the price of copper. But what is the effect on export *revenues* of the copper producers?
 (i) Will fund operations stabilize revenues when the *supply* curve shifts back and forth (as in Figure 16–4)? Explain.

 (ii) Will fund operations stabilize revenues when the *demand* curve shifts back and forth (as in Figure 16–3)? Explain.

e. Figure 16–5 is another fresh drawing of the initial conditions. If the fund continues to operate by the rules established in part c, let's see what happens when there is a *permanent* change in market conditions instead of temporary fluctuations.
 (i) Let *D* increase permanently by 20 percent, while *S* shifts out permanently by 40 percent. Draw the new curves in Figure 16–5 and label them *D'* and *S'*, respectively

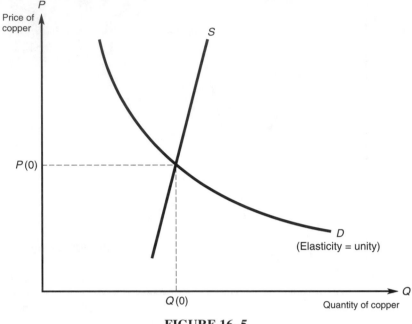

FIGURE 16–5

   (ii) Under these conditions, what will be the fate of the fund if it continues defending $P(0)$?

   (iii) Alternatively, suppose that D increases permanently by 40 percent while S shifts out permanently by 20 percent. Under these new conditions, what will be the fate of the fund if it continues defending $P(0)$?

  f. The initial conditions are redrawn one last time in Figure 16–6. Now the copper exporters decide to form a cartel. They all agree to coordinate production cutbacks such that the supply of copper is fixed at a level that is 25 percent less than $Q(0)$.

   (i) In Figure 16–6, draw a vertical line showing the fixed volume of copper that will be supplied to the market by the cartel. Label it C.

   (ii) Show the price $P(C)$ that the cartel will be able to charge. (Hint: Producers will now charge what the market will bear.)

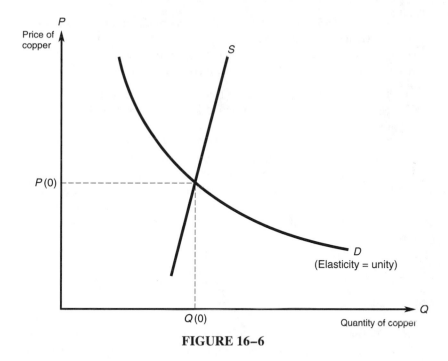

FIGURE 16–6

(iii) Have copper exporters succeeded in increasing their revenues by the action of the cartel? Explain. (Remember, demand elasticity is still unity.)

(iv) In the cartel situation depicted in Figure 16–6, why does each individual exporting country have a strong incentive to cheat on the cartel agreement?

Think about the lessons here. Using supply-and-demand analysis, you have established several important properties of stabilization funds and commodity cartels.

4. This exercise studies the curse of resource riches, also known as *Dutch disease*. Until recently, the economy of Bounty was based on exporting marbles and producing rice for domestic consumption. The government budget was balanced, and there was little inflation, little unemployment, and a very moderate foreign debt.

Then, in 1995, bonanza! An enormous lode of diamonds was discovered in Bounty. Abruptly, export earnings tripled. A large fraction of the new revenue accrued to government in the form of royalties paid by foreign diamond-mining companies. It sounds idyllic, but . . .

a. The rapid increase in supply of foreign exchange caused the home currency (shillings) to appreciate dramatically: from Sh1 = $1 in 1994 to Sh0.4 = $1 in 1995.

   (i) The world price of marbles is $5 per box. At the 1994 exchange rate, marble exporters earned Sh_____ per box. At the 1995 exchange rate, marble exporters received only Sh_____ per box.

   (ii) Assuming the supply curve for marble production has a normal shape, what happened to the volume of marble exports following appreciation of the shilling due to the diamond bonanza?

b. (i) The world price of rice is $200 per ton. At the 1994 exchange rate, the home-currency price of imported rice was Sh_____ per ton. At the exchange rate prevailing after the bonanza, the price in Bounty for imported rice was Sh_____ per ton.

   (ii) Assuming the supply curve for domestic rice production has a normal shape, what happened to domestic rice output when the shilling appreciated due to the diamond bonanza?

   (iii) The rice and marble sectors are very labor intensive, whereas the diamond industry is very capital intensive. How did the diamond bonanza affect employment and real wages in Bounty? Why?

c. The mining royalties paid by diamond companies caused government revenues to swell. The government decided to spend most of this revenue bonanza on domestic services. Since diamond royalties accrued in dollars, the government had to convert the funds to shillings at the central bank.

   (i) When the government converted the huge influx of dollars into shillings and then spent the shillings locally, what happened to the domestic money supply in circulation?

   (ii) With the government spending its foreign exchange bonanza in this manner, what happened to the domestic price level for nontradables?

d. Over the following year, the government of Bounty held the exchange rate fixed at Sh0.4 = $1. Meanwhile, the domestic price level jumped by 40 percent while world market prices rose just 2 percent.

   (i) Did Bounty's real exchange rate appreciate or depreciate between 1995 and 1996? How much? (Give an exact numerical answer, letting 1995 = 100.)

   (ii) Although the official exchange rate remained fixed in 1996, how did the change in the *real* exchange rate affect output in the domestic marble and rice sectors? Explain briefly, with reference to profitability.

e. Recalling the case of Nigeria after the oil boom, explain how Bounty
    might end up with a large government budget deficit and a large
    national debt as a result of its diamond bonanza.

f. The textbook points out that the adverse effects of Dutch disease can be
    avoided if the government responds prudently to the sudden flood of
    revenues.
    (i) What should the government of Bounty do to prevent the diamond
         boom from causing high unemployment and inflation? Explain.

    (ii) What should the government do to convert the diamond windfall
          into a sound foundation for sustained development? Explain.

ANSWERS TO SELF-TEST

Completion

1. comparative advantage
2. primary
3. exports, imports
4. consumers
5. *fiscal*
6. Engel's
7. linkage
8. permanent-income
9. *enclaves*
10. inflation
11. depreciation (or devaluation)
12. appreciate

True-False

1.	T	7.	T
2.	F	8.	F
3.	F	9.	T
4.	F	10.	T
5.	F	11.	F
6.	T	12.	T

Multiple Choice

1.	b	7.	a
2.	b	8.	b
3.	b	9.	b
4.	d	10.	d
5.	c	11.	a
6.	a	12.	b

CHAPTER 17 | Industry

OVERVIEW

The concept of development often is treated as being synonymous with indus-trialization. There is a strong association between rising per capita income and a higher share of manufacturing value-added in GDP up to income levels of $10,000 (1992 PPP$). The relationship, however, is subject to wide variations. Large countries, for example, industrialize more quickly than small countries due to the size of their domestic markets. Other variations stem from resource endowments and development strategies. To serve as an engine of development, manufacturing should generate linkage effects that stimulate production in related sectors; the efficacy of such linkages, however, depends on their economic effi-ciency and not just their technical feasibility through input-output relationships. There also is a strong empirical relationship between industrialization and urbanization. Urbanization creates external economies that stimulate industrial development, but it also entails high infrastructure costs and deleterious congestion effects.

An important aspect of industrial development is the choice of technique. Empirical studies confirm that practical technologies span a wide range of capital-labor ratios. Policies that attempt to stimulate industrialization by holding down the cost of capital relative to labor lead to more capital-intensive techniques that reduce job creation per unit of investment. Scale economies also figure prominently in the patterns of industrialization. For many goods, production becomes more efficient with larger manufacturing facilities, up to a point. Small, low-income countries can produce such goods efficiently only by adopting outward-looking policies that encourage exports. Other goods—especially low-grade consumer goods for the poor—can be produced by local small-scale manufacturers, which often are very labor intensive. Small-scale industry provides a large fraction of the manufacturing jobs in many developing countries. But their productivity usually is quite low, and few such firms have much potential for growth. Develop-ing countries should provide a supporting environment for small-scale industry but avoid costly subsidies that contribute little to development in the long run.

Ultimately, modern manufacturing is a key element of economic development. But equitable and efficient growth for most developing countries requires a balance between industry, agriculture, and services.

MAIN LEARNING OBJECTIVES

After studying this chapter, you ought to understand and be able to explain

1. The empirical patterns of industrialization associated with rising per capita income.

2. The meaning and significance of backward and forward linkages.

3. The strong association between industrialization and urbanization, with its attendant benefits and costs.

4. The wide range of capital-labor ratios that characterize manufacturing and the factors that influence the choice of technology.

5. The importance of economies of scale in manufacturing.

6. The pros and cons of promoting small-scale industry.

ECONOMIC TOOLS AND TECHNIQUES

From what you have learned in this chapter, you should be able to

1. Compute the index of backward and forward linkages from input-output coefficients.

2. Explain the external economies and diseconomies associated with rapid urbanization.

3. Evaluate the appropriate choice of technology using an isoquant diagram.

4. Explain economies of scale in terms of the long-run average cost curve.

KEY TERMS AND CONCEPTS

appropriate technology
backward linkages, direct backward
   linkages, total backward
   linkages
choice of technology or choice of
   technique
costs of urbanization
cottage shops
economies of agglomeration
economies of scale

forward linkages, direct forward
   linkages
industrialization
labor-intensive technology, capital-
   intensive technology
long-run average cost
minimum efficient scale (MES)
small-scale industry
township and village enterprises
   (TVEs)

SELF-TEST

Completion

1. For most developing countries, value added in manufacturing grows

   _____ rapidly than GDP as a whole.

2. Expansion of livestock husbandry leads to new investments for producing

   leather goods. This is a _____ linkage of the livestock industry.

3. Expansion of the cement industry leads to an increase in limestone quarrying. This is a _____ linkage of the cement industry.

4. Manufacturing firms in urban areas benefit from economies of _____ because of the proximity of other firms producing inputs and services.

5. The cost of dispersing industrial developments includes the need to build adequate _____ in numerous small towns.

6. In many developing countries, factor-price distortions have biased technology choice towards more _____-intensive production methods.

7. The minimum efficient scale is defined as the scale of operation beyond which _____-_____ _____ cost ceases to decline.

8. Small-scale industries in many developing countries account for more employment than large-scale industries, because small firms tend to adopt technologies that use more _____ and less _____ per unit of output.

9. Production units with one to four workers are called _____ *shops*.

10. The term _____ *technology* is used in the text to mean the least-cost technology, valued at undistorted factor prices.

11. Linkage measures typically are computed using data from _____-_____ tables.

12. One study found that in brickmaking the most capital-intensive technology has a _____ ratio 13.8 times higher than that of the appropriate technology.

True-False

If false, you should be able to explain why.

_____ 1. The share of GDP attributable to manufacturing rises with per capita income in both large and small developing countries.

_____ 2. If the total backward linkage index equals 2.4 for sector A and 1.2 for sector B, one can conclude that investing in A is more efficient than investing in B.

_____ 3. In almost all cases, the costs of dispersing industrial activity to smaller cities are more than compensated for by the benefits of reduced congestion and infrastructure costs in the large cities.

_____ 4. Empirical studies reveal a very wide scope for factor substitution in many manufacturing activities.

_____ 5. An industry is likely to be dominated by a few oligopolistic producers when the minimum efficient scale (MES) is a large fraction of the national market.

_____ 6. If the minimum efficient scale in gadget production is 10 million units per year and domestic demand in Nerdonia is 4 million units per year, then it is not possible to produce gadgets efficiently in Nerdonia.

_____ 7. Industry-specific studies confirm that large-scale firms are virtually always highly capital intensive.

_____ 8. In many low-income countries, more than 50 percent of all manufacturing jobs are found in enterprises that employ fewer than 20 people.

_____ 9. For most low-income countries, manufacturing grew more slowly than GDP over the period 1965 to 1990.

_____ 10. Primary industries like agriculture and mining are low on the list of in terms of backward-linkage effects.

_____ 11. In even large countries, like China, India, and Brazil, the internal markets for industrial goods are smaller than in Britain.

_____ 12. Many of the cottage shops and small-scale enterprises in low-income countries grow rapidly and modernize quickly once they gain access to inexpensive credit.

Multiple Choice

1. On average for large countries, as per capita income quintuples from $1,000 to $5,000 (using PPP measures), the share of GDP originating in manufacturing rises from
   a. 13 to 22 percent.
   b. 5 to 59 percent.
   c. 2 to 6 percent.
   d. 45 to 67 percent.

2. Which of the following is an early-developing branch of the manufacturing sector with strong backward linkage effects?
   a. Food processing
   b. Textiles
   c. Leather goods
   d. All the above

3. Suppose value-added accounts for 40 percent of the value of toy truck output and payments for imported inputs account for another 15 percent. Then direct backward linkages equal
   a. 85 percent of the value of toy truck output.
   b. 60 percent of the value of toy truck output.
   c. 45 percent of the value of toy truck output.
   d. 40 percent of the value of toy truck output.

4. Which of the following is an external diseconomy of urban industrialization?
   a. Pollution.
   b. Congestion.
   c. Infrastructure costs to support a larger urban population.
   d. All the above.

5. Among the advantages of increased urbanization is that in large cities
   a. crime is relatively easy to control.
   b. proximity to markets reduces distribution costs.
   c. anyone who wants to work can usually find a decent job.
   d. all the above.

6. One is most likely to find technologies that appeal to the "engineering person," but don't minimize cost, in industries that are
   a. highly protected and monopolistic.
   b. highly protected and competitive.
   c. export oriented.
   d. dominated by privately owned firms.

7. China's slogan of "walking on two legs" in the 1970s meant that the country was trying to develop both
   a. rural factories and modern urban industry.
   b. agriculture and manufacturing.
   c. export markets and domestic markets.
   d. the economic sphere and the ideological sphere.

8. The forward linkage from textiles to clothing is an efficient linkage only if
   a. clothing can be produced with labor-intensive technology.
   b. there are no factor-price distortions.
   c. it is backed up by tariffs or quotas to restrict the use of imported textiles.
   d. clothing can be produced at costs below the world price of imported clothing.

9. One empirical study found that for $100 million invested in each of nine industries, a developing country can generate 150,000 more jobs and 70 percent more value added by using the _____ technology rather than the _____ technology.
   a. traditional, modern.
   b. most labor intensive, most capital intensive.
   c. appropriate, most capital intensive.
   d. efficient, traditional.

10. Over the long run, the best way to stem the migration into already over-crowded third world cities is to
    a. ban the entry of new migrants from the countryside.
    b. encourage rural development as well as industrialization.
    c. adopt capital-intensive technologies that create fewer new jobs.
    d. subsidize small-scale industries in towns and smaller urban centers.

11. Scale economies are present when
    a. domestic industry is protected from import competition by tariffs or quotas.
    b. the long-run average cost curve declines over a relevant range of output.
    c. concentrated clusters of firms provide supplies and supporting services to one another.
    d. highly automated production technologies are available.

12. Small-scale firms account for a high share of industrial employment but a low share of industrial value added. These facts imply that small-scale firms
    a. generally are unprofitable.
    b. pay relatively high wages.
    c. employ a relatively large number of workers in low-productivity jobs.
    d. can achieve rapid growth at low cost.

APPLICATIONS

Worked Example: Linkage Effects in Planland

The idea of intersectoral linkages, introduced in Chapter 3 and briefly discussed in this chapter, brings out the evolving nature of the interdependence among the various branches of the economy. Planland is a fictitious developing economy whose input-output table consists of three sectors: (1) agriculture, (2) manufacturing, and (3) services. The interindustry flow matrix of an input-output table is simply an accounting framework, showing the flows output or income between branches of the economy. Looking across a row shows where the sector's output was sold, whereas looking down a column shows where output and input were, by source and by the sector. They both add to total output for the sector. That is why the column total and the row total are identical.

Table 17–1 converts the information on output levels into a matrix consisting of coefficients. Each entry in every column of the flow matrix is divided by the total at the bottom of the column; this gives the amount of each input required per unit of output in the sector, column by column. This information will be used to estimate the direct and indirect amount of output needed, sector by sector, to meet planned targets for final output. Study the data carefully.

The first column shows that each $1 of output in agriculture requires $0.08 worth of agricultural inputs, $0.04 worth of manufactured inputs, and no services. The sum of these three figures (= $0.12) gives the *direct* requirement for domestically produced inputs per $1 of agricultural output. The index of direct backward linkages in this case is

$$L_{b1} = \sum_{i=1}^{3} a_{i1} = 0.08 + 0.04 + 0.00 = 0.12.$$

Table 17–1

Input-Output Coefficient Matrix for Planland

	Agriculture (X_1)	Manufacturing (X_2)	Services (X_3)
1. Agriculture	.08	.20	.375
2. Manufacturing	.04	.40	.25
3. Services	.00	.10	.125
4. Total domestic purchases	.12	.70	.75
5. Imported intermediate goods	.00	.15	.05
6. Payments to labor	.80	.06	.15
7. Payments to capital	.08	.09	.05
Total	1.00	1.00	1.00

This value equals the figure shown in the row 4 for total domestic purchases per unit of agricultural output. For the manufacturing industry, the index of direct backward linkages can be identified in the same manner:

$$L_{b2} = \sum_{i=1}^{3} a_{i2} = 0.20 + 0.40 + 0.10 = 0.70.$$

(The index for the service sector will be dealt with in Exercise 1.)

To calculate the index of *total backward linkages*, one must know the direct plus indirect production requirements, per unit of output for each sector—the r_{ij} matrix. The input-output mathematics required to compute these coefficients cannot be explained here. It suffices to understand that r_{23}, for example, shows the total amount of industry 2 output required per \$1 of final production in industry 3, including the whole chain of interindustry linkages.

For Planland, the appropriate calculations show that \$1 of final demand for agricultural goods requires production of $r_{11} = \$1.11$ of agricultural output (of which \$1.00 is the final output itself and \$0.11 is the required amount of inputs from this sector). The \$1.00 of final demand for agricultural goods also requires $r_{21} = \$0.08$ of manufactured products and $r_{31} = \$0.01$ worth of services. Note that the services requirement is entirely indirect: The agricultural sector itself uses no service inputs, but services are required for production of other *inputs* to agriculture. The sum of these three figures gives the *total* requirement for domestic production per unit of final product in agriculture. Thus, the index of total backward linkages is

$$L_{t1} = \sum_{i=1}^{3} r_{i1} = 1.11 + 0.08 + 0.01 = 1.20.$$

For manufacturing, the corresponding figure is

$$L_{t2} = \sum_{i=1}^{3} r_{i2} = 0.47 + 1.78 + 0.20 = 2.45.$$

Each \$1.00 of manufactured product creates a requirement for \$2.45 worth of domestic output, taking into account the interindustry flows of intermediate goods.

Take note that the previous sentence says "creates a requirement for." Does this mean that $2.45 worth of direct plus indirect domestic output will occur per $1.00 increase in manufacturing-sector production? Maybe not. Domestic suppliers of intermediate goods might be undersold by imports, or they might be unable to increase production capacity to satisfy the increased demand. Also, the input requirements might be met by bidding supplies away from other uses. Or the particular input demands of a specific manufacturing activity may differ from the average coefficients displayed in the input-output table. Then again, inputs previously imported (see line 5 of the coefficients matrix) could be replaced by domestic production. In short, the index of linkages gives only a rough indication of where effective linkages may be lurking.

Exercises

1. Now, it is your turn to calculate linkages from the input-output coefficients, using the Planland data shown in Table 17–1 as your raw material.

   a. (i) The Worked Example showed how to calculate the index of direct backward linkages for the agriculture and manufacturing sectors in Planland. For the service sector, one would apply the formula

   $$L_{b3} = \sum_{?}^{?} a_{??}$$

   Rewrite this equation, replacing the question marks with the proper symbols:

   $$L_{b3} = \sum a.$$

   (ii) Using the appropriate numerical values from Table 17–1, the value of the index of backward linkages for the service sector is

   $$L_{b3} = \underline{\qquad}.$$

   (iii) Compare L_{b3} with the corresponding index value for agriculture and for manufacturing (reported in the Worked Example). It should be clear that the _____ sector has the largest index of direct backward linkages.

   b. To calculate the index of total backward linkages for the service sector, you need to know the following r_{ij} values:

   $$r_{13} = 0.61.$$
   $$r_{23} = 0.54.$$
   $$r_{33} = 1.20.$$

(i) From Table 17–1 you can see that the required input of manufactured goods per unit of services is $a_{23} = 0.25$. What, then, is the meaning of $r_{23} = 0.54$ as reported previously?

(ii) Notice that the value of r_{33} is greater than unity. What does this mean? (Recall that the Worked Example reported values for r_{11} and r_{22} that also exceeded unity.)

(iii) Calculate the value of the index of total backward linkages for the service sector in Planland:

$$L_{t3} = \sum_{i=1}^{3} r_{i3} = \underline{\hspace{2cm}}.$$

(iv) Comparing L_{t3} with the index values for agriculture and manufacturing (reported in the Worked Example), you will find that the _____ sector has the largest index of *total* backward linkages.

(v) Your results should show that the sector with the greatest *direct* backward linkage effect is not the same as the sector with the greatest *total* backward linkage effect. Briefly explain how this can occur.

c. Turn now to forward linkages. It is necessary to refer to the interindustry flow matrix for Planland rather than the coefficient matrix. Table 17–2 provides the required data.

(i) Table 17–2 shows that the total value of output for agriculture is

$$Z_1 = \$\underline{\hspace{2cm}}.$$

Table 17–2

Interindustry Flow Matrix for Planland (dollars)

| | Using sectors | | | Total | Final | Total |
	Agriculture (1)	Manufacturing (2)	Services (3)	intermediate use	use	use
1. Agriculture	20	40	30	90	160	250
2. Manufacturing	10	80	20	110	90	200
3. Services	0	20	10	30	50	80
4. Total domestic purchases	30	140	60	230		
5. Imported intermediate goods	0	30	4			
6. Payments to labor	200	12	12			
7. Payments to capital	20	18	4			
8. Total output	250	200	80			530

(ii) The value of agricultural output used as an input is

To agriculture: $X_{11} = \$$ _____ .

To industry: $X_{12} = \$$ _____ .

To services: $X_{13} = \$$ _____ .

(iii) Altogether, the value of agricultural output purchased as a productive input equaled

$$\sum_{i=1}^{3} X_{1j} = \$ \underline{\hspace{2cm}}.$$

(iv) Therefore, the index of direct forward linkages for agriculture is

$$L_{f1} = (\sum_{i=1}^{3} X_{1j})/Z_1 = \underline{\hspace{2cm}}.$$

(v) Following a similar procedure, you should find that the index of direct forward linkages is $L_{f2} = .55$ for manufacturing and $L_{f3} =$ _____ for services.

(vi) The sector having the largest index of direct forward linkages is _____ .

d. (i) What does $L_{f2} = .55$ mean? More specifically, if production in manufacturing increases by one unit, then the index of direct forward linkages indicates .55 what?

(ii) More generally, what does this index value say about the suitability of manufacturing as a leading sector for Planland's economic development?

Recall the warning from the Worked Example that these indices give only a rough indication of where effective linkages may be lurking. More detailed study would be needed to determine whether the linkages actually would materialize.

2. This exercise investigates the choice of technology in industry. Three alternative technologies for producing knives are available in Republique de Couteau. The data below show the amount of capital (K) and labor (L) required to produce 1,000 knives per year by three alternative methods: the traditional handicraft technology (T1), the labor-intensive intermediate technology (T2), and the automated modern technology (T3).

	Capital required	Labor required
Handicraft technology (T1)	10	80
Intermediate technology (T2)	20	40
Automated technology (T3)	50	20

a. (i) Calculate the capital-labor ratio for each technology:

For T1, $K/L =$ _____.

For T2, $K/L =$ _____.

For T3, $K/L =$ _____.

(ii) The capital-labor ratio for the automated technology is _____ times higher than the ratio for the intermediate technology and _____ times higher than the ratio for the handicraft technology.

(iii) Is this range of capital-labor ratios unrealistic in comparison with the range of technology choice cited in the textbook?

b. In Figure 17–1, plot the point representing the K and L requirements to produce 1,000 knives per year, using each of the three technologies. Label the three points T1, T2, and T3, respectively. Then connect the points to form the corresponding isoquant.

c. Informal-sector firms in Couteau face a market wage that reflects the opportunity cost of labor, but their cost of capital is extremely high due to segmented capital markets. In contrast, modern-sector firms face a subsidized price of capital along with a minimum wage that is higher than the market wage. Specifically, factor prices (in francs) are as follows:

	P_K	P_L
In the modern sector	F100	F200
In the informal sector	F500	F100
At shadow prices reflecting social costs	F175	F100

(i) Given the factor prices faced by firms in each sector, which is the minimum-cost choice of technology?

For firms in the modern sector, T_____.

For firms in the informal sector, T_____.

(Hint: You already know how much K and L are required by each technology choice.)

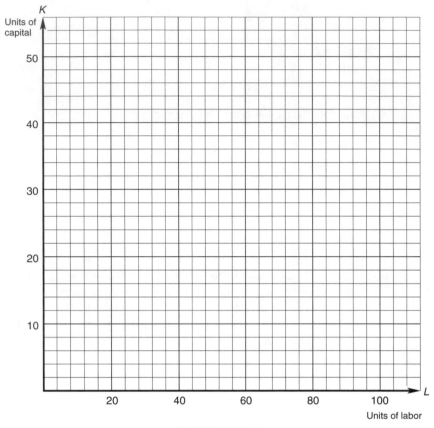

FIGURE 17–1

(ii) Which is the *appropriate* technology for the economy, that is, the one that minimizes costs in terms of shadow prices? T_____.

(iii) Draw a budget line showing the minimum level of costs for modern-sector firms. Label it B_m. (Hint: The line must have a slope equal to $-2 = -P_L/P_K$.)

(iv) Carefully draw a budget line showing the minimum level of costs for informal sector firms. Label it B_i.

(v) Carefully draw a budget line showing the minimum level of costs in terms of shadow prices. Label it B_s.

The graph reveals that T1 is the minimum-cost technology choice for informal-sector firms and that T3 is the minimum-cost choice for modern-sector firms but only because both groups of producers face distorted factor prices. Budget line B_s shows that T2 is much less costly for the economy in terms of appropriate shadow prices.

d. Altogether in Couteau there is a market for 1 million knives per year. Keep in mind that the isoquant in Figure 17–1 is drawn for $Q = 1,000$ knives per year.

(i) How many units of *capital* are required to produce 1 million knives per year with the technology used?

In the modern sector, $K =$ _____ thousand.

In the informal sector, $K =$ _____ thousand.

(ii) How many *workers* are required to produce 1 million knives per year with the technology used?

In the modern sector, $L =$ _____ thousand.

In the informal sector, $L =$ _____ thousand.

(iii) Valuing labor and capital at shadow prices, what is the total factor cost for producing 1 million knives per year?

Using modern-sector technology, F_____ million.

Using informal-sector technology, F_____ million.

Using appropriate technology, F_____ million.

(iv) Compared to production in the informal sector, producing 1 million knives per year in the modern sector requires _____ times as much capital, creates only _____ percent as many jobs, and has an opportunity cost (at shadow prices) that is _____ percent higher.

e. (i) Given the actual factor prices prevailing in each sector, what is the factor cost per 1 million knives?

In the modern sector, $F =$ _____.

In the informal sector, $F =$ _____.

(ii) Given the distorted factor prices that prevail, the _____ sector can easily underprice the _____ sector in market competition. So producers in the _____ sector will be driven out of business.

(iii) Is this an efficient development trend? Explain.

Before going on, think about the loss of efficiency—and the loss of jobs—caused by distorted factor prices in this one small sector of the economy.

3. This exercise examines the relationship between scale economies and the size of the market. Figure 17–2 shows the long-run average cost (including a normal return on capital) for brick production in Amigo. The figure clearly exhibits economies of scale, since long-run average cost declines with the capacity of the production unit.

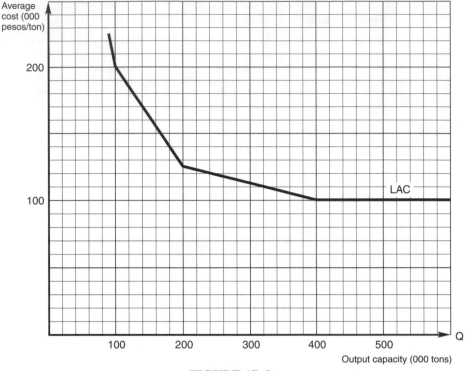

FIGURE 17–2

a. Brick production entails a number of processes, including mixing clays, molding the bricks, firing the bricks in a kiln, and drying the bricks, in addition to handling, storage, and business operations.
   (i) Identify two plausible reasons for the presence of scale economies in the brick industry.

   (ii) What output capacity is the minimum efficient scale (MES) of operation for producing bricks in Amigo?

   MES = _____ thousand tons per year.

   (iii) The graph shows that a production facility with a capacity of 1/2 MES has an average cost that is _____ percent higher than at the MES.
   (iv) A production facility with a capacity of 1/4 MES has an average cost per ton of bricks that is _____ percent higher than at the MES.

b. At the market price of P100,000 (P = pesos) per ton, the quantity demanded in Amigo is 2 million tons of bricks per year.
  (i) The MES in the brick industry equals _____ percent of the annual market volume in Amigo.
  (ii) What does this number imply about the possibility of developing an efficient, competitive brick industry in Amigo?

  (iii) Suppose that brick producers in Amigo can export bricks to El Toro, a neighboring country that lacks high-quality clays. Including exports, the market for Amigoan bricks would equal 8 million tons per year. How would the presence of this export market alter the prospects for developing an efficient, competitive brick industry in Amigo?

c. The main capital goods that are needed to produce bricks in Amigo are clay presses. A study shows that one clay press is needed per 10 thousand bricks and that domestic demand in Amigo is growing by 200 thousand bricks per year.
  (i) To meet the annual growth of domestic demand for bricks, the brick producers have to buy _____ new clay presses each year.
  (ii) Brickmakers also require 50 clay presses per year for replacement purposes. Altogether, then, there is a demand for _____ clay presses per year.
  (iii) Figure 17–3 shows the long-run average cost curve for producing clay presses. The MES in the clay-press industry is reached with a production level of _____ presses per year.
  (iv) How does the domestic demand for clay presses compare with the MES for producing these presses? What does this imply about the cost of producing clay presses locally for the domestic market? Give specific numerical answers.

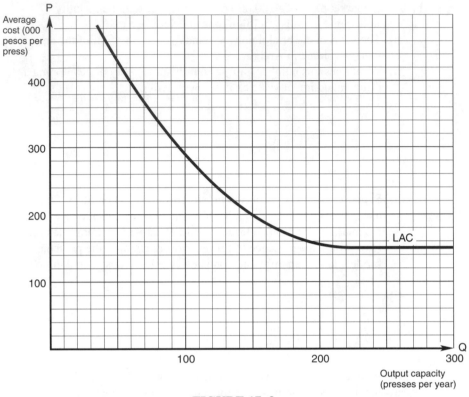

FIGURE 17–3

d. The government is considering banning imports of these presses to take advantage of the backward linkage effects from brickmaking.
   (i) If the government decides to ban imports of clay presses to promote domestic production, would the domestic clay-press industry be competitive or monopolistic? Explain.

   (ii) How would the *brickmakers* be affected by this government decision?

ANSWERS TO SELF-TEST

Completion

1. more
2. forward
3. (direct) backward
4. agglomeration
5. infrastructure
6. capital
7. long-run average
8. labor, capital
9. *cottage*
10. *appropriate*
11. input-output
12. capital-labor

True-False

1.	T	7.	F
2.	F	8.	T
3.	F	9.	F
4.	T	10.	T
5.	T	11.	T
6.	F	12.	F

Multiple Choice

1.	a	7.	a
2.	d	8.	d
3.	c	9.	c
4.	d	10.	b
5.	b	11.	b
6.	a	12.	c

CHAPTER 18 | Trade and Development

OVERVIEW

While factor endowments shape the pace and influence the pattern of the industrialization process, they are not immutable; policies matter, too. Two different trade strategies have been pursued for this purpose: inward-looking import substitution and export-led outward-looking industrialization. The core premise of import substitution is that infant industries need protection to survive, and the premise of outward-looking industrialization is that domestic producers must become internationally competitive.

Import substitution was nearly universal in the 1960s and was still widespread until quite recently. This strategy entails identifying large domestic markets served by imports, assessing the technical feasibility of domestic production, and then erecting protective barriers to shield domestic producers from import competition. After an initial burst of growth, this strategy generally bogs down because domestic markets are limited in size and infant industries remain too uncompetitive to penetrate export markets. In contrast, the export-led strategy pursued by East Asia's "tigers" has been outstandingly successful. These countries intervened in domestic markets to varying degrees, but their interventions shared four key characteristics: a disciplined focus on policies to promote rapid economic development, prudent management of macroeconomic stabilization policies and exchange-rate policy, flexible factor markets, and insulation of export activities from large price distortions.

Governments have four basic policy instruments at their disposal to influence the industrialization process: tariffs on imports, quantitative restrictions on trade, various forms of subsidy, and exchange-rate policy. Protective tariffs involve significant efficiency losses, particularly when effective rates of protection are quite high. Import quotas have similar effects, with the added disadvantage of bestowing monopoly power and scarcity rents on favored firms. Subsidies and other market preferences can achieve similar ends at less cost to consumers. These instruments can be applied to very specific products or firms. Exchange-rate policy, however, affects all tradables producers in a more evenhanded fashion. An overvalued exchange rate renders exports less profitable and imports less expensive, while an undervalued exchange rate has the opposite effect.

Where these instruments have been geared to protect import-substitution industries, they typically impose heavy costs on consumers, discourage exports, induce excessively capital-intensive investments, discourage backward linkages, promote rent-seeking activity in lieu of competitive adjustments, and ultimately lead to arrested growth. Where the instruments have been used to encourage outward-looking industrialization, the results generally have been rapid growth in income and productivity—though the direction of cause and effect remains uncertain.

For domestic entrepreneurs to commit capital to new industries, there may well be a need for some form of protection. Such protection should be selectively applied to infant industries that show clear promise of growing up and becoming competitive. Once this is achieved, no further protection is justified. On balance, well-targeted subsidies are preferred to more distortionary instruments such as trade restrictions.

The spread of outward-looking trade strategies, together with multilateral agreements to reduce barriers to international trade, sparked rapid growth of manufactured exports from developing countries after 1965. This trend benefits all trading countries. Yet within each country there are losers as well as gainers. The benefits of trade tend to be widely spread, while the costs are narrowly borne by particular sectors. As a result, shifts in comparative advantage have fed political pressures in many industrial economies to impose new nontariff barriers to trade. Such reactions are quite costly to the developed country, but even more so for the developing countries that lose access to large export markets. One response to the threat of protectionism has been greater trade among developing countries and moves to establish regional trade arrangements, such as customs unions and free-trade areas. With the establishment of the World Trade Organization (WTO), multilateralism seems to have overtaken the movement toward regional blocs.

MAIN LEARNING OBJECTIVES

After studying this chapter, you ought to understand and be able to explain

1. The premises, objectives, and policy instruments defining import substitution as a strategy for industrialization.

2. The main features of an outward-looking export-led strategy of industrialization.

3. The characteristic outcomes generated from pursuit of the two alternative trade strategies.

4. The economic effects of tariffs and import quotas, including the distinction between nominal and effective protection.

5. How various forms of subsidies are applied to support a country's chosen industrialization strategy.

6. How exchange-rate policy can be managed to influence the pattern of industrialization.

7. How protectionist policies encourage rent-seeking practices in lieu of efforts to improve efficiency.

8. How Asia's newly industrializing countries balanced market interventions with competitive pressures, thereby reconciling import substitution and export promotion strategies.

9. How multilateral agreements have been adopted to move the world economy toward freer international trade (multilateralism).

10. The causes and consequences of the new protectionism in the industrial market economies, such as voluntary export restrictions (VERs) and nontariff barriers (NTBs).

11. The potential advantages and disadvantages of various kinds of regional trade arrangements (regionalism).

12. In general terms, what has worked and what has not, with respect to trade and associated policies for industrialization, and why.

ECONOMIC TOOLS AND TECHNIQUES

From what you have learned in this chapter, you should be able to

1. Use supply-and-demand analysis to evaluate the economic effects—including the deadweight loss of welfare—of protective tariffs and import quotas.

2. Calculate and interpret the effective rate of protection (ERP) for an industry, given data on prices, costs, input coefficients, and tariff rates.

3. Show, using supply-and-demand curves, how subsidies can be used to achieve the same effect as a tariff but with less deadweight loss.

4. Apply and interpret the formula for the effective rate of subsidy (ERS), taking into account tariffs, quota rents, and subsidies affecting incentives for a particular industry.

5. Explain the economic effects of an overvalued or undervalued exchange rate, using a graph of the supply and demand for foreign exchange.

6. Apply the formulas defining the real effective exchange rate (REER) for exportables and importables.

7. Demonstrate the short-run and long-run effects of import-substitution policies, using a graph of the production frontier.

8. Use the distinction between static and dynamic gains from economic integration, including the trade creation and trade diversion effects of regional trade arrangements.

KEY TERMS AND CONCEPTS

Asian tigers, newly industrializing
   countries
border price
effective rate of protection (ERP)
effective rate of subsidy (ERS)
free-trade area, customs union,
   common market
General Agreement on Tariffs and
   Trade (GATT), Uruguay Round
import quotas, quantitative restrictions,
   import licensing
import substitution (inward-looking
   strategy)
most-favored nation (MFN) principle
North American Free Trade Area
   (NAFTA)
nominal rate of protection, protective
   effect, deadweight loss (from a
   protective tariff)

outward-looking trade policies
overvalued exchange rate, undervalued
   exchange rate, fixed exchange
   rate, crawling peg
protection, infant industry, learning
   by doing
quota rent, premium
real effective exchange rate (REER)
   for importables, for exportables
real exchange rate (RER)
rent seeking
static and dynamic gains (from
   preferential trading arrangements)
trade creation, trade diversion
value added at domestic prices and at
   world prices
World Trade Organization (WTO),
   multilateralism

SELF-TEST

Completion

1. An _____ industry is one that requires protection or subsidies to get started, but is expected eventually to become competitive.

2. The margin between the tariff-inclusive price of a product and the tariff-inclusive price of its inputs is called _____ _____ *at domestic prices.*

3. If the effective rate of protection (ERP) is 127 percent for manufacturing and 46 percent for agriculture, the incentive structure will attract investment into _____ and away from _____.

4. A country's exchange rate becomes _____ if there is high domestic inflation without a corresponding devaluation of the home currency.

5. Quality and packaging standards, labeling requirements, and health and safety regulations all may serve as _____ _____ to trade.

6. A trade arrangement that eliminates tariffs between member countries while permitting each member to maintain its own set of tariffs on imports from nonmember countries is called a _____-_____ area.

7. A customs union produces trade-_____ effects when tariffs induce consumers to import goods from a partner country rather than from another country that produces at lower cost.

8. The REER is a gauge of incentives that combines the effects of the real _____ _____ together with the degree of nominal protection.

9. India's exchange rate was overvalued when the rupee price of foreign currency is held artificially too _____.

10. The acronym WTO stands for the _____ _____ Organization, which was established in 1995.

11. The _____ protection created by a tariff is measured by the resulting increase in the domestic price of competing imports.

12. More often than not, the _____-_____ strategy has bred inefficient, high-cost producers rather than successful, competitive industries.

13. The General Agreement on _____ _____ _____ (GATT) was an international agreement to negotiate and monitor multilateral trade negotiations.

14. The term *quota* _____ refers to the windfall profits earned by those who receive import-license allocations under a quota system.

15. A major difference between using protective tariffs and using import quotas is that _____ generate larger deadweight losses by creating monopoly conditions for domestic producers.

True-False

If false, you should be able to explain why.

_____ 1. The development of capital-goods industries generally has the first stage of import-substitution industrialization.

_____ 2. In the 1960s, import substitution was the dominant strategy for economic development.

_____ 3. It is possible for the effective rate of protection on a country's bicycle industry to be 150 percent even if the nominal tariff rate is only 25 percent.

_____ 4. There is no valid economic argument for protection.

_____ 5. Data for 1965 to 1992 show that the highest economic growth rates are found in countries where the ratio of imports to GDP fell sharply.

_____ 6. An overvalued exchange rate increases the domestic-currency cost of imported goods.

_____ 7. Effective protection measures the extent to which the tariff structure allows the value added for domestic producers to exceed the value added for competitive producers in the world markets.

_____ 8. The key to Korea's successful outward-looking development strategy was to let the free market allocate resources.

_____ 9. A real appreciation of the domestic currency reduces the profitability of producing both exports and import substitutes.

_____ 10. Many manufacturers who thrive under import-substitution policies are hurt by a transition to an outward-looking trade strategy.

_____ 11. For an equivalent protection effect, a subsidy creates a larger deadweight loss than an import tariff.

_____ 12. A customs union differs from a free-trade area in that member countries adopt a common set of tariffs on imports from nonmember countries.

_____ 13. In terms of static effects, a country benefits from joining a customs union if trade diversion outweighs trade creation.

_____ 14. Increased competition among producers from different member countries can be an important source of dynamic gains from a customs union.

Multiple Choice

1. Other things being equal, the effective rate of protection on leather shoes will be higher
    a. the higher is the nominal tariff on shoes.
    b. the lower is the nominal tariff on leather.
    c. the smaller is the value added at world market prices.
    d. all the above.

2. Typically, import substitution distorts the structure of effective protection to bias domestic investment in favor of the production of
    a. capital goods.
    b. manufactured consumer goods.
    c. agricultural export goods.
    d. basic food crops.

3. In Figure 18–1, a tariff rate of t is equivalent in most respects to a quota restricting the quantity of imports to
    a. AB.
    b. BC.
    c. BE.
    d. DF.

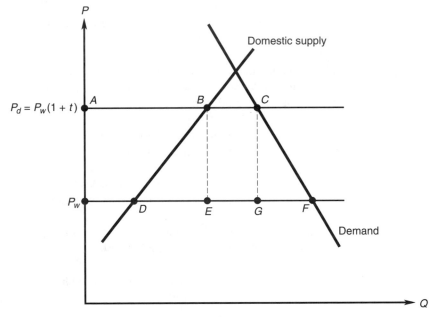

FIGURE 18–1

4. The tariff shown in Figure 18–1 generates government revenues totaling
    a. rectangle $ABEP_w$.
    b. triangle BDE.
    c. rectangle $BCEG$.
    d. zero.

5. The textbook's case study of Kenya illustrates a country where import substitution
    a. quickly led to stagnation.
    b. became an impediment to more rapid growth by the early 1980s.
    c. was never used to promote industrialization.
    d. emphasized agriculture and capital goods industries.

6. In many developing countries the effective rate of protection is especially high for
   a. manufactured consumer goods.
   b. machinery production.
   c. mining.
   d. agriculture.

7. In the long run, import substitution typically leads to which adverse effect?
   a. Encouraging capital-intensive investments.
   b. Creating high-cost noncompetitive industries.
   c. Retarding export growth.
   d. All the above.

8. To promote efficient domestic industrialization, protectionist policies for import substitution should
   a. use import quotas rather than tariffs.
   b. be temporary.
   c. focus on manufactured consumer goods.
   d. maximize the effective rate of protection.

9. Which of the following market interventions is most appropriate for promoting outward-looking industrialization?
   a. Temporary subsidies to exporters.
   b. High protective tariffs for favored industries.
   c. Quantitative restrictions on competing imports.
   d. An overvalued exchange rate.

10. The deadweight loss to the U.S. economy from protecting textile and clothing factories from foreign competition is estimated to be
    a. $14 for every $1 of benefits to the workers whose jobs are saved.
    b. $160 for every $1 of benefits to the workers whose jobs are saved.
    c. $0.25 for every $1 of benefits to the workers whose jobs are saved.
    d. negligible.

11. The hallmark of exchange-rate policy for an outward-looking policy regime is
    a. a stable real exchange rate.
    b. an undervalued exchange rate.
    c. an overvalued exchange rate.
    d. a stable nominal exchange rate.

12. What distinguishes a common market from a customs union?
    a. In a common market, restrictions on the movement of labor and capital among member states are greatly reduced.
    b. In a customs union, tariffs still are levied on imports from other member states.
    c. A customs union does not include common tariffs on imports from nonmember countries; a common market does.
    d. There is no difference; they are two names for the same thing.

13. New methods of protectionism such as quality standards in the industrial countries aim primarily to protect
    a. infant industries that might be hurt by import competition.
    b. declining industries for which comparative advantage has shifted to the developing countries.
    c. industries that have a comparative advantage, but are hurt by unfair competition from cheap labor in developing countries.
    d. industries where the cost per job saved is very low.

14. Which of the following policies increases the effective rate of subsidy (ERS) for producers of cardboard cartons?
    a. Increasing in the nominal tariff on carton imports.
    b. Providing carton producers access to credit at favorable interest rates.
    c. Reducing the nominal tariff on imports of the rough paper for making cardboard.
    d. All the above.

15. Korea's successful export performance was characterized by
    a. intense competition in domestic manufacturing among growing numbers of producers.
    b. government allocation of subsidized credit to firms producing for export.
    c. a large amount of foreign investment in Korea's manufacturing sector.
    d. all the above.

APPLICATIONS

Worked Example: Effects of a Protective Tariff

The Republic of Ecouter imports radios. Figure 18–2 shows that the supply of radios to Ecouter from the world market is perfectly elastic at a price of $P_w =$ $18 = $F6,000 (where F stands for francs, the local currency). At this price, the domestic demand curve (D) shows that 1,000 radios per year are purchased. The market equilibrium is at point E. The line S is the *potential* domestic supply curve; high-cost domestic producers cannot compete against imports as long as the price is under F7,000.

To promote domestic production of radios, the government decides to levy a 50 percent tariff, which increases the domestic market price of imported radios to $P_D = P_W(1 + t) = 6,000 \times (1.5) = $F9,000. This is the *protective effect* of the tariff. The new market equilibrium is at point E'. As you can see from the supply curve S, domestic producers now can compete against imports up to $Q = 500$ units of output. (But it remains unprofitable for them to produce more than 500 radios because the marginal cost of further output exceeds F9,000.) In addition to stimulating domestic production, the high market price reduces the equilibrium quantity demanded to 800 radios. The gap between domestic consumption and production, 300 radios, is filled by imports. With the tariff in place, consumers spend F7.2 million on radios (F9,000 × 800). Of this total expenditure, F1.8 million (area f in the figure) is to pay the world price of the imported radios—quite a drop from the F6.0 million spent on imported radios (area $e + f + g$) before the tariff was imposed. In addition, the consumer expenditure includes F900,000 (area c) that goes to the government as tariff revenue on the imported radios, and F4.5 million (area $a + b + e$) paid to domestic producers.

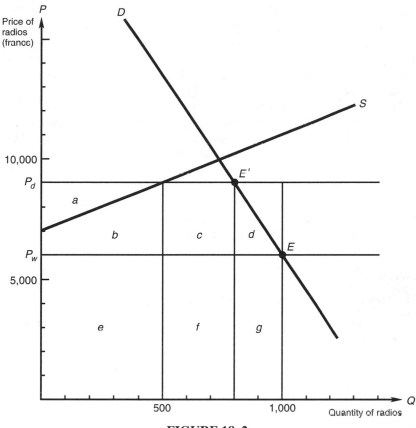

FIGURE 18–2

The height of the demand curve at each point indicates consumers' willingness to pay for the marginal unit of the product. Hence, the area under the demand curve up to any point is a measure of the total value accruing to consumers. Subtracting from this the amount consumers pay for radios gives the *consumer surplus*. Prior to the tariff, at point E, the consumer surplus equaled the entire area enclosed by the demand curve and line P_w. Once the tariff is in place, at point E', consumers pay more and get less. They suffer a loss of consumer surplus equal to area $a + b + c + d$. The protective tariff stimulates domestic production at the expense of consumer welfare; less is available and at higher cost.

Part of the loss to consumer welfare, of course, is offset by the government's gain in tariff revenues (area c). Another part (area a) represents a net gain to domestic producers from receipts in excess of marginal costs. This is the *producers' surplus*. The remainder of the loss in consumer surplus (area $b + d$) is a *dead-weight loss* in terms of social welfare. Notice that area b is part of the revenue earned by domestic producers, but it is not part of the producers' surplus because it represents the *resource cost* of diverting resources to radio production rather than other productive uses.

The welfare and efficiency costs of protection might be worth bearing if the radio industry ultimately became efficient enough to overcome its cost disadvantage and if the interim loss of welfare were more than offset by the subsequent net benefits (all calculated in present-value terms). In the figure, this happy outcome would appear as a downward shift in *S* large enough to allow domestic producers to compete against imports *without* protection. The irony is that domestic producers find it easier to lobby for continued protection than to improve efficiency and compete head-on with imports. As a result, the jobs created in radio production end up reducing overall welfare in Ecouter. That is not a winning formula for sustainable gains in living standards.

The outcome would be even worse if the government used quotas to limit radio imports to 300 units. Once the quota is filled, domestic producers would have monopoly power in the small domestic market, allowing them to boost their profits at the further expense of consumer welfare. In contrast, the government could provide subsidies to lower production costs (and the supply curve) to the point where the domestic industry achieves the same market penetration—500 radios—without causing the price of radios to rise. This would burden the government budget, but the deadweight loss would be much smaller and the cost of protection would be easier to monitor.

Exercises

1. Now it is your turn to analyze the effects of a protective tariff.

   a. Figure 18–3 shows the domestic supply (*S*) and demand (*D*) curves for tires in Kayak.
      (i) Domestic production will be undertaken only if the market price of tires is at least Ksh_____. (Ksh stands for the Kayak shilling, the local currency.)

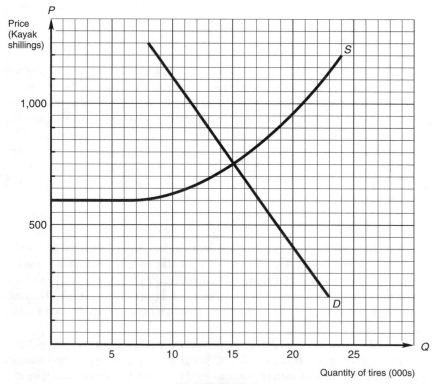

FIGURE 18–3

    (ii) Imported tires sell for Ksh400. Draw the line representing supply from the world market, and label it P_w.

    (iii) Under these conditions the quantity demanded is _____ thousand tires. The market price is Ksh_____ per tire. Consumer spending on tires totals Ksh_____ million.

    (iv) Imports account for _____ percent of the market.

    (v) The exchange rate is Ksh10 = \$1. Hence, the foreign exchange cost of imported tires is \$_____.

b. To foster domestic tire production, the government introduces a 100 percent tariff on imports.

    (i) With this tariff, the domestic price of imported tires rises to Ksh_____.

    (ii) Draw a line in Figure 18–3 showing this new price of imports; label it P_w'.

    (iii) Label as point E the new market equilibrium, showing the price and quantity of tires bought and sold after imposition of the tariff. (Hint: Think carefully about the new equilibrium, this problem is a bit different from the Worked Example.)

    (iv) At the new market equilibrium the quantity demanded is _____ thousand tires; label this Q_E. The new equilibrium price is Ksh_____; label this P_E.

    (v) Total spending on tires now equals Ksh_____ million, and imported tires account for _____ percent of the market.

    (vi) Government tariff revenues total Ksh_____.

    (vii) The foreign exchange cost of tire imports is \$_____.

    (viii) The tariff's protective effect stimulates new domestic production of _____ thousand tires.

c. Carefully add labels a, b, c, and so forth, as needed, in Figure 18–3 to identify:

    (i) The loss of consumer surplus due to imposition of the tariff.

    (ii) The producer's surplus resulting from the tariff.

    (iii) The deadweight loss associated with the tariff.

d. Still maintaining the 100 percent import tariff, how would domestic tire production, the volume of tire imports, and the equilibrium price change if

    (i) Domestic production becomes less efficient, and this causes costs to rise 50 percent?

(ii) Demand increases by 50 percent?

In both cases you should find that import competition protects *consumers* from excessive domestic price increases, even with the 100 percent tariff. This stands in sharp contrast to the situation under import quotas, examined below.

e. What long-run change in the supply curve in Figure 18–3 would characterize *successful* import substitution in Kayak's tire industry?

f. Rather than levying a tariff, suppose the government of Kayak simply bans tire imports by setting a zero quota, which is enforced by denying import licenses for procuring foreign-made tires.
  (i) Under these conditions what point in Figure 18–3 represents the equilibrium price and quantity in the domestic tire market?

  (ii) Compare the market outcome with a ban on tire imports against the outcome with a 100 percent tariff. In particular, compare these two alternative forms of protection in terms of their effect on domestic production and consumption of tires.

g. With tire imports banned, how would the domestic price and quantity adjust if
  (i) Domestic producers became less efficient, and this caused supply costs to rise by 50 percent?

  (ii) Demand increased by 50 percent?

(iii) The minimum efficient scale for tire production exceeded the size of the domestic market, and this led to the emergence of a monopoly producer?

Your answers should reveal why tariffs are more efficient than import quotas as an instrument for protection. Even with a high tariff, imports can serve as a buffer to cushion changes in demand, without pushing up prices. The use of tariffs limits the extent to which high costs and inefficiencies can be foisted onto consumers. It also limits the potential for abuse of domestic market power by monopolistic producers. And not incidentally, tariffs generate revenue for the government.

2. This exercise works through several calculations of the effective rate of protection (ERP).

   a. Automobiles can be imported into the Republic of Motokah at a cost of $P_w = \$10,000 = 100,000$ rupees (the local currency is the rupee, at Rs10 = \$1).

      (i) Component kits for assembling automobiles in Motokah can be imported at a cost of $C_w = \$9,000$ per car. In local currency, the component kits cost _____ rupees per car.

      (ii) What is the value added at *world* prices of the car assembly operations in Motokah?

      $$V_w = P_w - C_w = \$\rule{2cm}{0.4pt}.$$

      Expressed in local currency units, the value added at world prices is

      $$V_w = \text{Rs}\rule{2cm}{0.4pt}.$$

   b. The government of Motokah levies a tariff of $t_o = 25$ percent on imported cars. Component kits for domestic assembly can be imported duty free, so $t_i = 0$ percent. (The text uses t_o for the tariff on imported output and t_i for the tariff on imported inputs.)

      (i) With this tariff structure, the domestic price of an imported car is

      $$P_d = \text{Rs}\rule{2cm}{0.4pt}.$$

      (ii) The domestic price of imported component kits is

      $$C_d = \text{Rs}\rule{2cm}{0.4pt}.$$

      (iii) Domestic automobile assemblers can compete against import competition as long as the cost of the domestic resources used to convert component kits into finished products (that is, the value added at domestic prices) is no higher than

      $$V_d = P_d - C_d = \text{Rs}\rule{2cm}{0.4pt}.$$

    (iv) Compare V_d with V_w, both in rupee units. Domestic assembly can compete with imports as long as the resource cost of domestic assembly (V_d) exceeds value added at world prices (V_w) by no more than _____ percent.

    (v) The *effective* rate of protection for domestic automobile assembly operations is ERP = _____ percent, even though the nominal rate of protection is only 25 percent.

  c. Suppose all conditions remain the same except that the government switches to a *uniform* 25 percent tariff on all imports. This means that $t_o = t_i = 25$ percent.

    (i) With a uniform 25 percent tariff on all imports, the effective rate of protection on domestic car assembly is ERP = _____.

    (ii) In this case the domestic industry can compete against imported automobiles as long as the resource cost of domestic assembly exceeds V_w by no more than _____ percent.

    Notice that a uniform import tariff covering inputs as well as outputs causes the effective and nominal rates of protection to converge.

3. This exercise examines how foreign exchange controls can be used as a tool to protect domestic industry. In the republic of Cabana, the supply of foreign exchange (dollars) is generated entirely by coffee exports. The demand for foreign exchange comes from importing machinery and blue jeans. In Figure 18–4, curves S and D show the supply and demand for dollars as functions of the exchange rate R, which is measured in pesos per dollar.

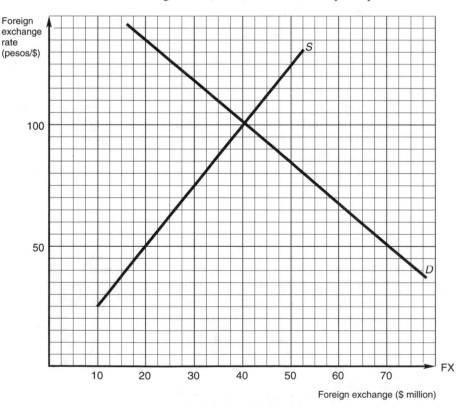

FIGURE 18–4

a. (i) The market equilibrium exchange rate is

$$R = \underline{\hspace{2cm}} \text{ pesos per dollar.}$$

  (ii) At this exchange rate (and with no tariffs or quotas to muddy the exercise), coffee that sells for $1 per pound in the world market is worth _____ pesos per pound to Cabanian exporters.

  (iii) For a machine priced at $5,000 on the world market, the equivalent price in Cabana is _____ pesos.

  (iv) For a pair of blue jeans selling at $20 on the world market, the equivalent price in Cabana is _____ pesos.

b. The government passes a law requiring coffee exporters to turn over all their foreign exchange earnings to the central Bank of Cabana at an exchange rate of $R' = 50$ pesos per dollar. The central bank then sells available dollars to *licensed* importers at the rate R'. At the controlled exchange rate of $R' = 50$ pesos per dollar:

  (i) Coffee selling for $1 per pound in the world markets is worth _____ pesos per pound to Cabanian exporters.

  (ii) A machine selling for $5,000 on the world market costs _____ pesos to a buyer in Cabana.

  (iii) A pair of blue jeans selling for $20 on the world market costs _____ pesos to a buyer in Cabana.

c. (i) Compared to the equilibrium exchange rate, Cabana's peso in part b has become _____-valued.

  (ii) At the controlled exchange rate R', exporting coffee becomes _____ profitable, while imports become _____ expensive.

  (iii) Figure 18–4 shows that at $R' = 50$ pesos per dollar, the quantity of foreign exchange demanded equals $_____ million; the quantity of foreign exchange supplied equals $_____ million.

  (iv) Hence, there is $_____ million of excess demand for foreign exchange.

d. To cope with this disequilibrium in the market for foreign exchange, the government begins to license access to dollars sold by the Bank of Cabana. Officials decide that no licenses will be granted for importing blue jeans, in order to promote import substitution in the clothing industry. But licenses are readily available to obtain foreign exchange for importing machines.

  (i) The new system of foreign exchange licensing is equivalent to a quota of _____ on imports of blue jeans.

  (ii) Comparing the peso prices of coffee before and after imposition of exchange controls, one finds that the exchange-rate policy imposes an implicit tax of _____ percent on coffee exporters.

  (iii) Comparing the peso prices of imported machinery before and after imposition of exchange controls, one finds that the exchange-rate policy creates an implicit subsidy of _____ percent on purchases of imported machines.

(iv) How does the protectionist exchange-rate policy affect incentives for producing coffee, clothing, and machines in Cabana?

(v) How does the exchange-rate policy affect incentives for using capital-intensive versus labor-intensive techniques to produce trousers? What does this imply about job growth?

e. Return to the initial situation in which the market determines the exchange rate, without direct government interventions. Let's see how protectionist policies affect the exchange rate anyway.

(i) The government of Cabana decides to protect the domestic clothing industry by setting a high tariff rate on imports of blue jeans. This makes imported jeans so expensive that the demand curve for foreign exchange shifts to the left by 25 percent. Carefully draw the new demand curve in Figure 18–4. Label it D'.

(ii) What is the effect of the import tariff on the equilibrium exchange rate? Why?

(iii) How does this change in the exchange rate affect the peso earnings from coffee exports and the peso price of imported machinery? Be as specific as possible.

(iv) Compared to the free-trade situation, how does the protectionist tariff for *trousers* affect incentives for *exporting coffee*? Explain.

4. This exercise examines effective rates of subsidy for various industries in Zimba. In the past the country's sole export product was copper (C). Now, the government is promoting exports of beef (B) as well. The government also is promoting local production of aspirin (A) as an import-substitution industry. Each product happens to be packaged in quantities that sell *in the world market* for $10, or Kw400 at the official exchange rate of 40 kwacha per dollar.

Like the effective rate of protection (ERP) measure, the effective rate of subsidy (ERS) is a gauge of government support per unit of *value added* in each industry. This is reflected in the formula

$$\text{ERS} = [(t_o + s_o + q_o) - \Sigma a_i(t_i - s_i + q_i) + s_t + s_b]/(1 - \Sigma a_i).$$

The denominator is the value added (domestic factor cost) per unit of output. Recall that a_i is the cost of intermediate input i per unit of output.

The ERS formula supplements the ERP measure of *tariff* protection by also incorporating direct subsidies on inputs (s_i) and outputs (s_o), any quota premium due to import controls (q_o), and implicit subsidies in the form of special tax breaks (s_t) or privileged access to cheap bank credit (s_b). All these terms usually are defined per kwacha of output, expressed in decimal form.

a. For *aspirin* production, the intermediate inputs consist of $6 (Kw240) of imported chemicals and Kw80 of local packaging, per unit of output. For *beef* production, the only intermediate input is Kw160 of local feed grain, per unit of output. *Copper* production requires $3 (Kw120) of imported shovels and Kw 60 of locally generated energy, per unit of output.

   (i) With free trade, domestic aspirin producers can compete against imports if their total cost per unit of output is no higher than Kw400. Given the cost of intermediate inputs, as given above, this means that factor costs—which compose value added—can be no higher than $VA_a = 400 - 240 - 80 = $ Kw80 per unit of output. What is the maximum level of factor costs that can be incurred per unit of output in each of the other two industries?

$$VA_b = \text{Kw} \underline{\hspace{2cm}}.$$

$$VA_c = \text{Kw} \underline{\hspace{2cm}}.$$

   (ii) For the aspirin industry, the denominator of the ERS formula is

$$1 - \Sigma a_i = 1 - (240/400 + 80/400) = .20.$$

This means that value added payments account for 20 percent of the product price, while intermediate inputs account for 80 percent. What is the denominator of the ERS formula?

For the beef industry: \underline{\hspace{1.5cm}} .

For the copper industry: \underline{\hspace{1.5cm}}.

b. It so happens that domestic factor costs are too high for beef exports and domestic aspirin production to be profitable with free trade. But Zimba's trade policies include a 50 percent tariff on aspirin imports and a direct subsidy of 25 percent to beef exporters. To raise revenue, the government also imposes a 33.3 percent tariff on shovel imports. Therefore,

$$t_o = 0.50 \text{ for aspirin.}$$

$$s_o = 0.25 \text{ for beef.}$$

$$t_i = 0.333 \text{ on shovels used for copper.}$$

No quota premiums or subsidies in the form of special tax status or low-cost bank credits are present (so $q_o = q_i = s_t = s_b = 0$). Let's consider the effects of Zimba's trade policies on the profitability of each industry.

(i)   With the 50 percent tariff, imported *aspirin* is priced at $400 + 0.50(400)$ = Kw600 per unit. So local producers can charge as much as Kw600 to compete against imports. Netting out intermediate input costs, domestic factor costs can run as high as $VA_a = 600 - 320 = $ Kw280 per unit of aspirin, versus just Kw80 under free trade. The 50 percent tariff permits value added to swell by $280/80 - 1 = 2.50 = 250$ percent. Plug the appropriate numbers into the ERS formula to confirm this result.

(ii)   For each unit of *beef* exported, producers earn $10. After changing the dollars into local currency and collecting their 25 percent subsidy, they end up with revenues of Kw_____ per unit of exports.

(iii)   After netting out the cost of intermediate inputs, beef producers can now export profitably with domestic factor costs as high as $VA_b = $ Kw_____ per unit of beef, versus just Kw_____ under free trade.

(iv)   The 25 percent subsidy permits value added to swell by _____ percent. Plug appropriate numbers into the ERS formula to confirm this result.

(v)   After netting out the cost of intermediate inputs, including the tariff on imported shovels, copper producers can export profitably with domestic factor costs as high as $VA_c = $ Kw_____ per unit of copper, versus Kw_____ under free trade.

(vi) Qualitatively, what does the 33.3 percent tariff on imported shovels do to profitability of copper exports? Plug appropriate numbers into the ERS formula to compute the ERS for the copper industry, and briefly explain the result.

(vii) Briefly, how do Zimba's trade policies alter the allocation of resources between the three industries?

c. Suppose the government institutes a trade policy reform that eliminates the great differences in nominal protection. In place of the original tariffs and subsidy, all exports now receive a flat 10 percent subsidy, while all imports (including aspirin and shovels) are charged a 10 percent tariff.

(i) The effective rates of subsidy are now

$$ERS_a = \underline{\hspace{1cm}}\%,$$

$$ERS_b = \underline{\hspace{1cm}}\%,$$

$$ERS_c = \underline{\hspace{1cm}}\%.$$

(ii) Does the new trade policy make the economy more efficient or less efficient now than it was under the former trade policy? Why?

(iii) The industry with the highest profit margin per unit of output is now _____ production, and _____ production is now unprofitable.

Two closing observations: First, while nominal rates of protection are equalized by the reform, effective rates of subsidy still differ. Why? Because the value-added share of unit cost differs across industries. Second, a simple 10 percent devaluation of the kwacha would have the same effect as the uniform tariffs and subsidies.

5. The real effective exchange rate (REER) is a comprehensive indicator of the influence of trade and exchange-rate policies on incentives for resource allocation. Study the text discussion of REER carefully, including the notation, before tackling this exercise.

    The Republic of Pampas exports wheat and produces clothing as an import-substitution industry. Table 18–1 presents data for both goods on world prices, tax and tariff rates, domestic production costs, and the exchange rate in pesos per dollar for 1995. Notice that wheat exports are subject to a 10 percent tax while clothing imports bear a 25 percent tariff to protect domestic producers. To keep things simple, the quota premiums and all forms of subsidy equal zero initially.

Table 18–1

Pampa's Wheat and Clothing Industries

	1995	1996	1996a
Wheat			
1. World price ($ per bushel)	4	4.40	4.40
2. Exchange rate (P per $)*	20	_____	_____
3. Exporter receives (P per bushel)	80	_____	_____
4. Export tax rate (%)	10	_____	_____
5. Net revenue per bushel, after tax (P)	72	_____	_____
6. Domestic production cost per bushel (P)	64	80	80
7. Exporter's profits per bushel (P)	12	_____	_____
Clothing			
8. World price ($ per unit)	50	55	55
9. Exchange rate (P per $)	20	_____	_____
10. Border price (P per unit)	1,000	_____	_____
11. Tariff rate (%)	25	_____	_____
12. Domestic price (P per unit)†	1,250	_____	_____
13. Domestic production cost per unit (P)	1,100	1,375	1,375
14. Domestic producer's profits per unit (P)	150	_____	_____

*P = pesos.
†Domestic price = (border price)(1 + tariff), where the tariff is expressed as a decimal.

a. In 1996, world prices for all tradable goods rose by 10 percent, while prices and production costs in Pampas rose 25 percent. The official exchange rate, the tax rates, and the tariff rates were still at 1995 levels.
   (i) On the basis of this information, fill in the column headed 1996 in Table 18–1. (To assist you, some numbers are provided.)
   (ii) To facilitate calculation of the REER, Table 18–2 restates the basic data for the wheat industry as index numbers, defined so that 1995 = 100. As shown in the book, the REER for exportables is given by the formula

$$REER_e = R_o N_e P_w / P_d,$$

where N_e is a measure (in decimal format) of nominal protection:

$$N_e = (1 + t_e + S_e)^t / (1 + t_e + S_e)^o.$$

There are no changes in trade policy here, so N_e stays fixed at 1.00.
Fill in the 1996 column in Table 18–2.

Table 18–2

Index Numbers for Wheat Exports

	1995	1996	1996a	1996b
1. R_o	100	_____	_____	100
2. N_e	1.00	_____	_____	_____
3. P_w	100	_____	_____	110
4. P_d	100	_____	_____	125
5. REER$_e$	100	_____	_____	100

(iii) Briefly explain how the change in REER$_e$ has affected the
profitability of producing wheat for export in 1996.

b (i) Using Table 18–2 as your model for tabulating the required
information, calculate the 1996 REER$_m$ for clothing imports.

$$REER_m = _____.$$

(ii) How does the change in REER$_m$ between 1995 and 1996 affect the
profitability of producing clothing as an import substitute?

c. Let's rerun history. This time the government of Pampas decides to
devalue the peso by 15 percent, to 23 pesos per dollar, to offset
(approximately) the excess of domestic inflation over world inflation.
All other conditions for 1996 remain as above.
(i) Fill in the columns labeled 1996a in Tables 18–1 and 18–2, as
appropriate to reflect the new official exchange rate.
(ii) Using Table 18–2 as a model, calculate the 1996 value of the real
effective exchange rate for clothing imports after the devaluation.

$$REER_m = _____.$$

(iii) Looking at your calculations, how does the 1996 devaluation affect the profitability of producing exportables (wheat) and importables (clothing) in Pampas?

d. Wind the clock back once again. This time the government chooses to maintain the fixed exchange rate and to support domestic producers using tax and tariff policies, instead. Stated more formally, the government aim is to hold $REER_e = 100$ and $REER_m = 100$ in 1996 by altering N_e and N_m, while holding R_o fixed at 20 pesos per dollar.

(i) Compute the value for N_e required to maintain $REER_e = 100$ in 1996. Write the answer in the column labeled 1996b in Table 18–2. (Hint: In this case $R_o = 100$; given P_w and P_d for 1996, find N_e such that $REER_e = 100$.)

(ii) From the formula

$$N_e = (1 - t_e)_{1996}/(1 - t_e)_{1995},$$

use the value for N_e that you just calculated to find the necessary export tax rate t_e for 1996:

$$t_e = \underline{\hspace{2cm}}.$$

(Hint: The answer is negative; this indicates that an export *subsidy* is needed. Note that the textbook formula for N_e adds a term s_e for export subsidies; it is easier here just to treat subsidies as negative taxes.)

e. (i) Following a parallel procedure, calculate the value of N_m needed to maintain $REER_m = 100$ in 1996, if the peso is not devalued.

$$N_m = \underline{\hspace{2cm}}.$$

(ii) In the absence of any quota premium, the formula for the nominal protection index for importables is

$$N_m = (1 + t_m)_{1996}/(1 + t_m)_{1995}.$$

Find the tariff on clothing imports, t_m needed to achieve REER$_e$ = 100 in 1996.

$$t_m = \underline{\hspace{2cm}}.$$

In general, domestic producers of exportables and importables suffer when domestic inflation outpaces world inflation. The government can cure the adverse effects by devaluing the home currency or by increasing protection for tradables producers. Of the two options, devaluation is far simpler to administer—especially in countries where domestic inflation exceeds world inflation year after year. Also, ever increasing protection invites all the distortions commonly associated with import-substitution regimes. The best policy, of course, is to avoid high inflation in the first place.

6. This exercise examines the dynamics of import substitution using a general equilibrium framework like the one in the textbook. Figure 18–5 shows the production possibilities frontier (PPF) for Anglia back in 1970. The world price was $1,000 per ton for both coconuts (C) and steel (S). Hence, line TT, showing the world terms of trade, has a slope equal to –1.0. With free trade, Anglia produces at point A and trades along TT to the optimal consumption point A'.

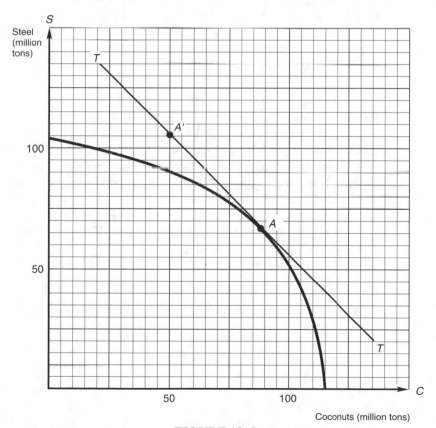

FIGURE 18–5

a. At point *A* the slope of the PPF equals _____; if resources were reallocated to produce one extra ton of steel, the opportunity cost would be a reduction in coconut output by _____.

b. To promote the domestic steel industry, the government levies a 100 percent tariff on steel imports, which doubles the *domestic* price of steel. The domestic price of coconuts remains initially unchanged.
    (i)   At domestic prices, 1 ton of steel is now worth _____ tons of coconuts.
    (ii) The protective tariff gives entrepreneurs an incentive to reallocate resources to produce more steel and fewer coconuts. To be precise, it is profitable to shift resources in this manner as long as each ton of lost coconut output is replaced by at least _____ of additional steel production.
    (iii) So entrepreneurs continue to shift resources to the northwest from point *A* as long as the slope of the PPF is greater than _____ (in absolute value).
    (iv) In Figure 18–5, carefully determine the outcome of this tariff-induced reallocation process. Label the new production choice as point *B*.

c. (i)   Carefully construct a line showing the various *trade* possibilities open to Anglia when the economy *produces* at point *B*. Label this line *T'T'*. (Hint: World prices have not changed, so the slope of the line showing the world terms of trade has not changed either.)
    (ii) When producers operate at point *B* in response to the tariff, Anglia trades along line *T'T'* to achieved its preferred consumption outcome. Label as *B'* some plausible point on *T'T'* showing the consumption outcome. (Point *B'* should entail lower consumption of both goods compared to the original free-trade outcome at *A'*.)

d. Figure 18–6 reproduces Anglia's PPF for 1970.
    (i)   Over the ensuing 25 years, Anglia's import-substitution policy is *successful*. Draw in a new production frontier for 1995 showing a successful growth outcome. Label it PPF_{95}.
    (ii) For simplicity, suppose the tariff on steel is still in force in 1995 and relative prices remain unchanged in the world markets. Identify the point along PPF_{95} showing the production outcome in 1995. Label it B_{95}.
    (iii) Draw the line through point B_{95} showing the world terms of trade. Label this $T_{95}T_{95}$. What is the slope of this line?

    (iv) Identify a plausible point on line $T_{95}T_{95}$ representing the preferred consumption outcome, given production at B_{95} and the prevailing terms of trade. Label this point as B'_{95}.

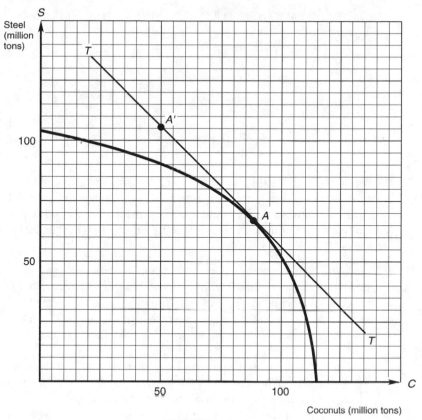

FIGURE 18–6

e. The success of Anglia's import substitution policy means that the country's GDP has grown rapidly and consumption of both steel and coconuts is much higher than in 1970.

   (i) Even so, is point B_{95} the best production point for the country in the year 1995? In particular, would the country be better off by eliminating the tariff on steel imports and moving toward less distorted trade flows in 1995? Explain.

   (ii) What would a case of *unsuccessful* import substitution 25 years later look like on the graph? (Don't draw it; just explain it in words.)

(iii) What accounts for the fact that import-substitution strategies have more often than not turned out to be unsuccessful in the long run?

7. *Harder.* This exercise explores the trade creation and trade diversion effects of a customs union between Tanya and its neighbor Kenzania. The exchange rate between the Kenzanian shilling and the Tanyan shilling is Ksh1 = Tsh1; each currency is worth $0.10. Consider first the static effects for Tanya.

a. Tanya can obtain gaskets, pumps, and tractors from three supply sources: the goods can be produced in Tanya, imported from Kenzania, or imported from other countries. Initially, Tanya levies a 40 percent tariff on all imports. Table 18–3 shows how the acquisition cost of each product varies according to the source of supply. Take a moment to study the setup of this table.
   (i) Fill in the blanks in the left-hand side of Table 18–3, to find the domestic price in Tanya for each good, for each supply source. The column for gaskets is worked out in full as an example. This calculation reflects conditions prior to the creation of a customs union between Tanya and Kenzania.
   (ii) With a 40 percent tariff on all imports into Tanya, the cheapest source of supply:

   For gaskets is _____,

   For pumps is _____,

   For tractors is _____.

b. *After* entering the customs union Tanya sets to zero the tariff on imports from Kenzania. Imports from other countries still face a 40 percent tariff.
   (i) Based on the new tariff structure, fill in the blanks in the right-hand side of Table 18–3.
   (ii) How does Tanya's entry into the customs union alter its pattern of production and trade?

   For gaskets:

Table 18–3

Acquisition Costs for Tanya

Source of supply	Prior to customs union			After customs union		
	Gaskets	Pumps	Tractors	Gaskets	Pumps	Tractors
A. Imports from Kenzania						
1. Price of imports (Ksh)	Ksh 18	Ksh 6,000	Ksh 100,000	Ksh 18	Ksh 6,000	Ksh 100,000
2. Price of imports (Tsh)	Tsh 18	——	Tsh 100,000	——	——	——
3. Tariff charged (Tsh)	Tsh 7.2	Tsh 2,400	——	——	0	——
4. Domestic price (= 2 + 3)(Tsh)	Tsh 25.2	——	——	——	——	——
B. Imports from other countries						
1. Price of imports ($)	$2	$500	$8,000	$2	$500	$8,000
2. Price of imports (Tsh)	Tsh 20	——	Tsh 80,000	Tsh 20	——	Tsh 32,000
3. Tariff Charged (Tsh)	Tsh 8	Tsh 2,000	——	——	——	——
4. Domestic price (= 2 + 3) (Tsh)	Tsh 28	——	——	——	——	——
C. Production in Tanya						
1. Domestic production price (Tsh)	Tsh 24	Tsh 8,000	Tsh 95,000	Tsh 24	Tsh 8,000	Tsh 95,000

For pumps:

For tractors:

   c. (i) In what sense does Tanya benefit from trade creation as a result of the customs union?

      (ii) In what sense does Tanya lose from trade diversion as a result of the customs union?

ANSWERS TO SELF-TEST

Completion

1. infant
2. *value added*
3. manufacturing, agriculture
4. overvalued
5. nontariff barriers
6. free-trade
7. diversion
8. exchange rate
9. low
10. World Trade
11. nominal
12. import-substitution
13. Tariffs and Trade
14. *premium* (or *rent*)
15. quotas

True-False

1.	F	8.	F
2.	T	9.	T
3.	T	10.	T
4.	F	11.	F
5.	F	12.	T
6.	F	13.	F
7.	T	14.	T

Multiple Choice

1.	d	9.	a
2.	b	10.	a
3.	b	11.	a
4.	c	12.	a
5.	b	13.	b
6.	a	14.	d
7.	d	15.	b
8.	b		

CHAPTER 19

Managing an Open Economy

OVERVIEW

Short-run stabilization problems often dominate the policy agenda in developing countries that face serious macroeconomic imbalances resulting from external or internal shocks or from the cumulative effects of prior mismanagement. Stabilization problems were widespread during the 1970s and 1980s due, in part, to wide swings in oil prices, real interest rates, major exchange rates, and the availability of foreign financing.

The basic model for analyzing stabilization policies, known as the *Australian model*, starts by recognizing that most developing countries are small, open economies. They are small in the sense of being price takers in the world markets for tradable goods (including both importables and exportables). And they are open in that the domestic economy is heavily affected by international trade and finance. Still, a significant share of economic activity involves nontradables, which include most services. The domestic price of tradables is determined by the world price and the nominal exchange rate, while the price of nontradables is a function of domestic supply and demand conditions. The relative price of tradable to nontradable goods provides a measure (P) of the real exchange rate.

External balance is defined as equality between the supply and demand for tradables. This boils down to having a zero balance of trade or a balance of trade that matches the net inflow of foreign financing, where such financing is available and sustainable to augment the supply of tradables. External *imbalance* can take the form of an unsustainable trade deficit or, less critically, an excessive trade surplus. In like fashion, *internal balance* is defined as equality between the supply and demand for tradables. Internal *imbalance* can take the form of excess demand, which produces inflation, or excess supply, which entails idle factors of production, including high unemployment.

The two key variables determining the outcome are aggregate expenditure (or absorption) and the real exchange rate P. A rise in absorption increases the demand for both tradables and nontradables. A rise in the real exchange rate, by altering relative prices, induces consumers to shift spending toward nontradables (which become relatively cheaper), while it induces producers to shift resources toward more tradables (which become relatively more profitable). Although these markets possess self-correcting tendencies, the adjustment process can be slow to work due to structural rigidities or adverse policy responses.

The model reveals the combination of changes in absorption (A) and real exchange rate (P) that are needed to restore macroeconomic balance, starting from any situation of external and internal imbalances. In the phase diagram, the external balance line delineates combinations of A and P where the tradables market has a surplus, a deficit, or a zero balance. Similarly, the internal balance line shows the combinations of A and P for which the market for nontradables has surplus capacity (unemployment), excess demand (inflation), or balance.

Two main instruments are available to the government to help move the system toward overall balance. First, monetary and fiscal policies directly affect absorption; second, official exchange-rate policy affects the real exchange rate.

The Australian model can be used to analyze the nature of a country's macroeconomic imbalances and the mix of policies needed to achieve stabilization. In general, the two policy instruments must be used in a coordinated fashion to reach the equilibrium. The essence of stabilization policy is to identify the disequilibrium condition and then to determine the policy adjustments needed. For countries suffering large external deficits and high domestic inflation, the indicated response is austerity, through tight fiscal and monetary policies to reduce absorption, combined with exchange-rate depreciation. This is the standard IMF prescription. One important detail is that aid inflows make the adjustment process less onerous by reducing the necessary dose of devaluation and austerity. The model also provides a basis for analyzing Dutch disease, the nature of the debt repayment problem, and the macroeconomic effects of economic shocks such as drought.

MAIN LEARNING OBJECTIVES

After studying this chapter, you ought to understand and be able to explain

1. The distinction between tradable and nontradable goods and services.

2. How the prices of tradables and nontradables are determined and how the ratio of these prices provides a measure of the real exchange rate.

3. The definition of external and internal balance and the nature of external and internal imbalances.

4. How changes in gross national expenditure (or absorption) and changes in the real exchange rate affect the demand for tradables and nontradables.

5. How fiscal and monetary policies can be used to influence absorption and how official exchange-rate policy affects the real exchange rate.

6. Why the self-correcting tendencies in the market for tradables and nontradables often fail to cure imbalances quickly.

7. How to determine the changes in absorption and real exchange rate needed to correct any situation of external and internal imbalance.

8. How to determine the policy changes needed to facilitate stabilization.

9. Why two policy instruments generally are needed to achieve simultaneous internal and external balance.

10. How foreign aid, foreign capital inflows, or debt relief helps to alleviate the burden of adjustment.

ECONOMIC TOOLS AND TECHNIQUES

From what you have learned in this chapter, you should be able to

1. Demonstrate the macroeconomic equilibrium in the Australian model using a graph of the production frontier.

2. Define the determinants of the real exchange rate in this model.

3. Define absorption and external balance in terms of national accounts variables.

4. Show how the markets for tradables and nontradables adjust to external shocks and changes in absorption, using supply and demand graphs defined with the real exchange rate (*P*) as the price variable.

5. Analyze the various zones of external and internal imbalances in the phase diagram defined in terms of absorption and the real exchange rate.

6. Identify the appropriate monetary, fiscal, and exchange-rate policies to move the economy toward equilibrium, starting from any condition of macroeconomic imbalance.

7. Apply the phase-diagram model to analyze Dutch disease, a debt-repayment crisis, drought, and the standard IMF stabilization package.

KEY TERMS AND CONCEPTS

appreciation, depreciation (of the official exchange rate)
austerity
Australian model
balance of trade
Dutch disease
exchange-rate anchor (stabilization)
expenditure, absorption
fiscal policy, monetary policy
fixed, floating, or crawling peg official exchange-rate regime

internal and external balance, imbalance
International Monetary Fund (IMF)
phase diagram, zones of imbalance
real exchange rate (as the relative price of tradables to nontradables)
small, open economy
stabilization program
tradable and nontradable goods and services
tradables market, nontradables market

SELF-TEST

Completion

1. A country where trade and capital flows significantly affect the domestic economy is called an _____ *economy*.

2. Equilibrium in the Australian model occurs where a community indifference curve is tangent to (that is, just touches) the _____

_____.

3. In the Australian model, importables and exportables are combined as
   _____ goods.

4. In this model the real exchange rate is measured as the price of
   _____ relative to _____.

5. A rise in aggregate expenditure, also called _____, increases
   demand for both tradables and nontradables.

6. To maintain internal balance, an exogenous rise in aggregate expenditure
   must be accompanied by _____ of the real exchange rate.

7. The _____ balance curve in the phase diagram shows
   combinations of absorption and the real exchange rate for which the
   tradables market is in equilibrium.

8. In the phase diagram for the Australian model, any point to the
   _____ of the *EB* line entails an unsustainable balance-of-trade
   deficit.

9. _____ programs often are supported with funds from the IMF.

10. IMF stands for _____ _____ _____.

11. A rise in the real exchange rate causes the demand for _____
    goods to fall and the demand for _____ goods to rise.

12. A _____-_____ exchange-rate regime involves
    frequent adjustments in the official exchange rate in order to maintain a
    stable real exchange rate.

True-False

If false, you should be able to explain why.

_____ 1. Some governments, especially in Asia, managed their economies
           well enough to adjust smoothly to the external shocks in world
           markets during the 1970s and 1980s.

_____ 2. In a small, open economy the domestic price of tradable goods is
           given by $P_t = P_t^*/e$, where e is the official exchange rate and P_t^* is
           the world market price.

_____ 3. One big problem with macroeconomic imbalances is that there are no automatic tendencies for the markets to self-correct.

_____ 4. A rise in the real exchange rate (that is, a real devaluation) induces a shift toward producing more nontradable goods.

_____ 5. Even though it is expressed differently, the real exchange rate P_t/P_n in the Australian model is identical to the real exchange rate defined as $R_o(P_w/P_d)$, as in Chapter 18.

_____ 6. External balance can occur with a balance-of-trade deficit as long as a country is the recipient of a long-term inflow of foreign capital.

_____ 7. To maintain external balance, a rise in absorption has to be accompanied by a rise in the real exchange rate (devaluation).

_____ 8. In the phase diagram for the Australian model, any point to the right of the *IB* curve entails inflationary pressure in the market for nontradables.

_____ 9. The internal balance curve (*IB*) in the phase diagram shows equilibrium in the nontradables market as a function of absorption and the official exchange rate.

_____ 10. Taiwan built up large foreign exchange reserves by maintaining an undervalued real exchange rate.

_____ 11. Usually a government can restore both internal and external balance using just one of its two main policy instruments.

_____ 12. Smaller government deficits, credit restraint, and official devaluation form the core of most stabilization packages.

Multiple Choice

1. Many developing countries suffered macroeconomic imbalances during the 1970s and 1980s because of changes in
   a. the world price of oil.
   b. real interest rates in the world financial markets.
   c. major exchange rates.
   d. all the above.

2. In the market for tradables, a decline in absorption causes the demand curve to shift to the _____ and the real exchange rate (*P*) to _____.
   a. left, rise   c. right, rise
   b. left, fall   d. right, fall

3. Which of the following is true?
   a. All small economies are open.
   b. All open economies are small.
   c. All small economies are price takers in world markets.
   d. All developing-country economies are small and open.

4. Which of the following will cause the real exchange rate to depreciate, other things being equal?
   a. A rise in the official exchange rate.
   b. A fall in the world price of tradables.
   c. A rise in the domestic price of nontradables.
   d. All the above.

5. Long-run equilibrium in the Australian model occurs at the point where
   a. the relative price of tradables to nontradables equals the slope of the production possibility frontier at the highest attainable community indifference curve.
   b. the quantities of tradable and nontradable goods demanded exactly match the quantities supplied.
   c. national income and welfare are at the highest possible sustainable levels.
   d. all the above.

6. When a country confronts high domestic inflation with no external imbalance, as did Brazil, the indicated policy response is to
   a. reduce absorption and allow the exchange rate to appreciate.
   b. reduce absorption and allow the exchange rate to depreciate.
   c. increase absorption and allow the exchange rate to appreciate.
   d. increase absorption and allow the exchange rate to depreciate.

7. Dutch disease is caused by
   a. a sudden decline in access to foreign capital inflows.
   b. the onset of a recession in the industrial countries.
   c. a sharp rise in the price or volume of exports of a natural resource such a natural gas.
   d. cutbacks in domestic government spending.

8. In the phase diagram for the Australian model, a point exactly to the left of where *EB* and *IB* intersect represents a situation of external
   a. deficit and excess domestic unemployment.
   b. deficit and domestic inflation.
   c. surplus and excess domestic unemployment.
   d. surplus and domestic inflation.

9. The case study of Chile illustrates a case in which the adjustment program
   a. was so well managed that the economy stabilized in a few months.
   b. adopted an exchange-rate anchor when inflation remained high despite tight fiscal and monetary policies.
   c. produced a real exchange-rate appreciation that stimulated rapid export growth.
   d. failed because no effort was made to reduce the fiscal deficit.

10. For an economy with an external _____ and internal balance, a devaluation is needed to restore external balance, but taken alone this would push the domestic economy into _____.
    a. deficit, inflation
    b. deficit, high unemployment
    c. surplus, inflation
    d. surplus, high unemployment

11. For an economy facing a large external deficit and domestic inflation, an inflow of foreign aid will
    a. worsen the internal imbalance.
    b. reduce the magnitude of the required austerity and devaluation.
    c. reduce the magnitude of the required devaluation, but not the degree of austerity.
    d. reduce the magnitude of the required austerity, but not the amount of devaluation.

12. In the context of the phase diagram, a major drought will cause a
    a. leftward shift in the *IB* line, with no change in the *EB* line.
    b. rightward shift in the *EB* line, with no change in the *IB* line.
    c. rightward shift in both the *IB* and *EB* lines.
    d. leftward shift in both the *IB* and *EB* lines.

APPLICATIONS

Worked Example: A Sad Tale of Macroeconomic Populism

To grasp the analysis of macroeconomic imbalances, a good starting point is to look at how the imbalances may originate. The simplest tool to use for this purpose is the graph of supply and demand in the markets for tradables (*T*) and nontradables (*N*), as shown in Figure 19–1.

Notice that the vertical axis measures the price of tradables *relative* to the price of nontradables, $P = P_T/P_N$. In the Australian model, *P* defines the real exchange rate, which is the key determinant of the allocation of consumption and production between *T* and *N*. In panel A, the real exchange rate is a natural measure of the price of tradables. But *P* is an *inverse* measure of the price of nontradables. A higher *P* indicates a fall in the relative price of nontradables; a lower *P* indicates a rise in the relative price of *N*. Since the price measure in panel B is inverted, so are the supply and demand curves. It may look odd for the curves in panel B to be drawn with the "wrong" slopes, but they reflect the ordinary market behavior: a fall in the relative price of nontradables—meaning a rise in *P*, as defined—causes a decline in the quantity supplied and a rise in the quantity demanded. As usual.

The starting point in each panel is point 1. Both markets are at equilibrium. In the market for tradables, the quantity demanded (T_1) is consistent with the quantity supplied, which is determined by exports (X_T) plus net inflows of foreign financing (*F*). In the market for nontradables, the equilibrium quantity (N_1) is consistent with the economy's noninflationary production capacity. (Line X_N shows that nontradables output still could rise but not without pushing up prices and shifting resources out of tradables.) The situation is one of external and internal balance.

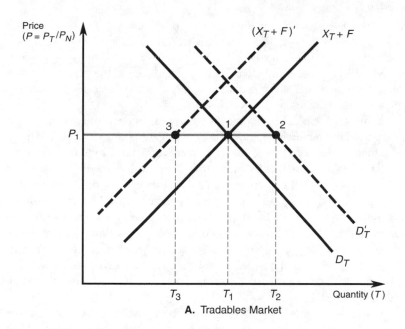

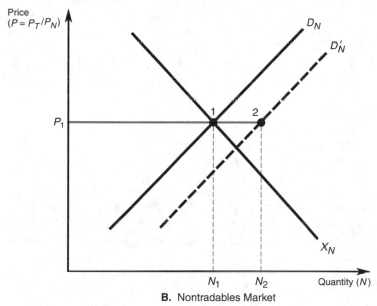

FIGURE 19–1

What can go wrong? One common source of trouble is imprudent macro-economic management—macroeconomic populism. The government spends more than it can afford on nifty programs like subsidies, roads, bailouts for mismanaged parastatal (state-owned) companies, and military equipment; the deficit is financed by inflationary credit from the central bank. These loose fiscal and monetary policies cause absorption to rise, and this leads to rightward shifts in the demand curves in *both* markets, to D'_T and D'_N. The outcome in panel A is a balance-of-trade deficit (distance $T_1 T_2$) that is not supported by sustainable foreign financing; in panel B, the excess demand for nontradables (distance $N_1 N_2$) provokes inflation. In this particular case, the cure is simply to reverse absorption and shift the demand curves back to their initial positions by tightening fiscal and monetary policies.

Keep in mind that tightening means cutting the budget for subsidies, roads, bailouts, and military equipment. Stabilization is not popular. That is why governments often try to avoid the adjustments and paper over the imbalances. For example, the external imbalance can be covered by drawing down foreign exchange reserves, building up unsustainable foreign debt, defaulting on debt-service payments, or imposing foreign exchange controls. Domestic inflationary pressures can be suppressed with price controls or accommodated with indexing arrangements. These expedients only delay the day of reckoning; meanwhile they create distortions and imbalances that make the adjustment more costly when it comes. Eventually, the economy has to restore a balance between supply and demand in each market, without suppressing the competitive market forces that drive long-run growth.

External shocks may serve as the trigger for adjustments. A cutoff of foreign financing or an adverse movement in the terms of trade, for example, would shift the supply curve in panel A leftward, to $(X_T + F)'$. (The external shocks may also affect P and D_N, but we limit attention to the main impact.) This accentuates the external imbalance (distance $T_3 T_2$). To deal with the crisis, the government asks the IMF for support in the form of financing to increase F; but support is available only on the condition that steps are taken to redress the underlying imbalances.

Must the government take action? The market's self-correcting mechanisms may not work quickly or smoothly, and they can be thwarted by government policies. For example, excess demand for nontradables increases P_N, this lowers the real exchange rate, and this stimulates supply and demand responses that move the N market toward equilibrium, perhaps slowly. But a drop in P *worsens* the external imbalance, as you can see in panel A. If the external imbalance is covered by having the central bank sell foreign exchange reserves, this will reduce the money supply and dampen absorption, and this helps to restore balance in both markets. But the monetary contraction is easily offset by the government's profligate spending.

The whole analysis is neatly displayed in the phase diagram in Figure 19–2. By increasing absorption, loose macroeconomic policy pushes the economy from point 1 to point 2, in the deficit-plus-inflation zone. A cutoff of foreign aid shifts EB to the left, to EB', worsening the external imbalance. With the economy at point 2, a drop in the real exchange rate due to rising domestic prices moves the economy closer to line IB, but then we are farther than ever from external balance. The solution is to reduce absorption. Foreign financing can alleviate the crisis by shifting EB' back toward its initial position.

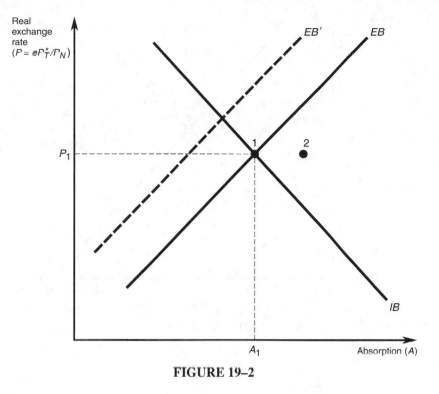

FIGURE 19–2

Exercises

1. Before tackling applications of the Australian model, it is a good idea to practice the mechanics. *All the questions in this exercise refer to the immediate impacts and exclude subsequent adjustments that may occur due to self-correcting tendencies of the market.*

    a. Figure 19–3 reproduces the supply and demand curves for tradables (T) and nontradables (N). As pointed out in the Worked Example, notice that in panel B the vertical axis is an inverse measure of the price of nontradables, so the demand curve for N slopes up and the supply curve for N slopes down.

        (i) Starting at point 1 in panel A, how does each of the events listed below affect the market for *tradables*? Each answer should cover the following points: Does either curve shift? If so, which way? If not, how does the impact show up in the graph? And what is the nature of the resulting imbalance?

            Event 1. A decline in absorption due to tight fiscal and monetary policies.

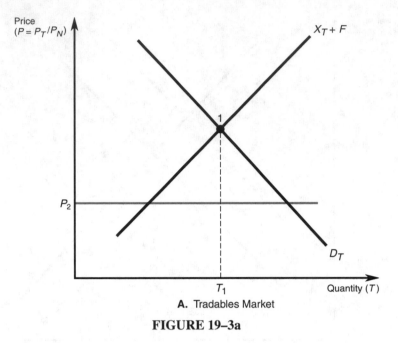

A. Tradables Market

FIGURE 19–3a

Event 2.   An increase in foreign aid receipts.

Event 3.   A killer frost that decimates the harvest of the main
           export crop.

Event 4.   A devaluation of the official exchange rate.

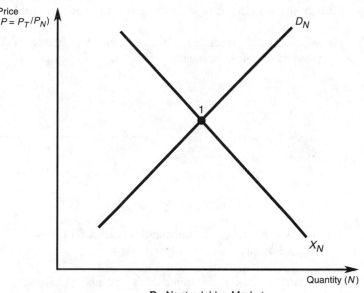

B. Nontradables Market

FIGURE 19–3b

(ii) Starting at point 1 in panel B, how does each event affect the market for *nontradables*? Answer in the same manner as previously.

Event 1. A decline in absorption due to tight fiscal and monetary policies.

Event 2. An increase in foreign aid receipts.

Event 3. A killer frost that decimates the harvest of the main export crop.

Event 4. A devaluation of the official exchange rate.

b. Such events can also occur when the economy is not at equilibrium to start out.

   (i) When the real exchange rate is P_2 in panel A of Figure 19–3, what is the nature of the imbalance in the market for *tradables*?

   (ii) In panel B, what is the nature of the imbalance in the market for *nontradables*?

   (iii) Briefly explain how the imbalance in the market for *tradables* is affected by each of the following events:

   Event 1. A rise in absorption due to loosening of fiscal and monetary policies.

   Event 2. A cutoff of access to foreign loans.

   Event 3. A bountiful harvest of the main export crop.

   Event 4. An appreciation of the *official* exchange rate. (Remember that $P_T = e \times P_T^*$.)

(iv) How is the imbalance in the market for *nontradables* affected by each event?

Event 1. A rise in absorption due to loosening of fiscal and monetary policies.

Event 2. A cutoff of access to foreign loans.

Event 3. A bountiful harvest of the main export crop.

Event 4. An appreciation of the *official* exchange rate.

c. Figure 19–4 reproduces the basic phase diagram for the model.
  (i) Explain why the *EB* line slopes upward. Use the following opener as the start for your answer: "The *EB* line has a positive slope because external balance can be preserved only if a rise in absorption . . ."

  (ii) Explain why the *IB* line slopes downward. Start your answer with the following opener: "The *IB* line has a negative slope because internal balance can be preserved only if a rise in absorption . . ."

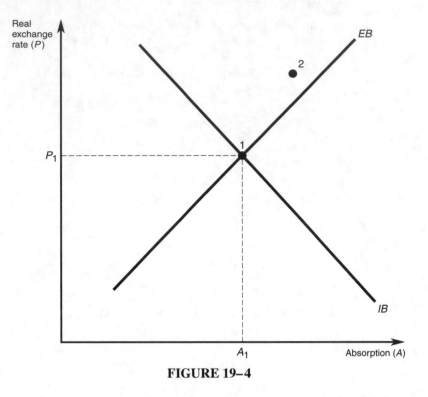

FIGURE 19–4

d. The economy begins at point 1, with internal and external balance.
   (i) Other things held constant, how does each event listed below affect
       the economy's *external* balance? Will the *EB* curve shift? If so,
       which way? If not, how does the impact on the external balance show
       up in the graph? What is the nature of the resulting imbalance?

   Event 1. A decline in absorption due to tight fiscal and monetary
             policies.

   Event 2. An increase in foreign aid receipts.

   Event 3. A decline in the world price of the main export good.

Event 4. A devaluation of the official exchange rate.

(ii) How does each of the following events affect the economy's *internal* balance?

Event 1. A decline in absorption due to tight fiscal and monetary policies.

Event 2. An increase in foreign aid receipts.

Event 3. A decline in the world price of the main export good.

Event 4. A devaluation of the official exchange rate.

e. Similar events can occur when the economy has not initially achieved external and internal balance.

(i) At point 2 in Figure 19–4, what is the nature of the external imbalance?

(ii) At point 2, what is the nature of the internal imbalance?

(iii) Briefly explain how the external imbalance is affected by each of the following events:

Event 1. A rise in absorption due to tight fiscal and monetary policies.

Event 2. A cutoff of access to foreign loans.

Event 3. A rise in the world price of the main export good.

Event 4. An appreciation of the official exchange rate.

(iv) Briefly explain how the internal imbalance is affected by each event:

Event 1. A rise in absorption due to tight fiscal and monetary policies.

Event 2. A cutoff of access to foreign loans.

Event 3. A rise in the world price of the main export good.

Event 4. An appreciation of the official exchange rate.

2. The Worked Example illustrated one way for a small, open economy to get into and out of trouble in terms of macroeconomic imbalances. It is your turn to consider a different situation. The scene is the tiny Kingdom of Antiquity, which produces one tradable good, elegant pottery for export, and one nontradable, banquet services. Everything else is imported using the proceeds from exports plus foreign loans from a wealthy moneylender in nearby Carthage. The story starts with the economy operating at point 1 in Figure 19–5.

a. Overnight, pottery from Antiquity becomes a favorite in fashionable homes from Cathay to Gaul. Earnings from pottery exports double.
  (i) How will the export boom affect the external-balance line? Why?

  (ii) Draw the new external-balance line as a dashed line in Figure 19–5. Label it *EB*2.

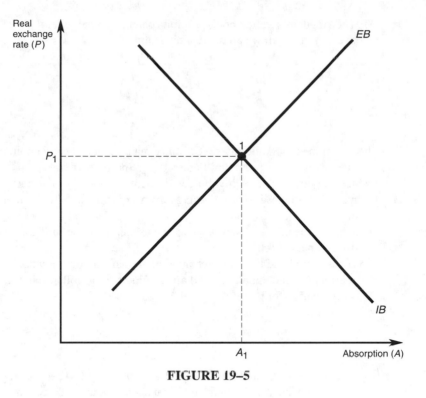

FIGURE 19–5

(iii) If absorption (A) and the real exchange rate (P) were to remain
unchanged at point 1, describe the nature of the macroeconomic
imbalance that arises following the export boom.

(iv) What combination of changes in A and P is needed to restore overall
macroeconomic balance? Label the new equilibrium point 2.

(v) Since the fashion boom does not expand the kingdom's production
frontier, how can an increase in absorption—which boosts the
demand for nontradables—be accommodated without causing
inflation?

402 / CHAPTER 19

    (vi) The kingdom's sacred book prohibits changes in the *official* exchange rate. How can the real exchange fall to P_2?

b. The government of Antiquity successfully manages its macroeconomic policies and achieves point 2 in Figure 19–5. Shortly thereafter, fashionable homeowners grow bored with Antiquarian pots and start buying Greek statues instead. Earnings from exporting pots fall to half the original level.

    (i) Draw in the new external-balance line as a dashed line in Figure 19–5; label it *EB3*.

    (ii) If absorption and the real exchange rate remain at point 2, what macroeconomic imbalance will arise following the collapse in the world market for pottery?

    (iii) Could external balance be restored by a change in the real exchange rate alone, with absorption fixed? What about overall macroeconomic balance? Explain.

    (iv) Could external balance be restored by changing absorption alone, with the real exchange rate fixed? What about overall balance? Explain.

c. The King of Antiquity refuses to take the necessary steps to adjust to the loss of export earnings. As a result, Antiquity's credit rating is downgraded; the moneylender in Carthage boosts the interest rate on all the kingdom's external debt.

(i) How does this new external shock affect the position of the curves in Figure 19–5, the macroeconomic imbalances, and the magnitude of the required policy adjustments? (Answer in words; the graph is messy enough.)

(ii) The Samaritan League learns of the Antiquity's plight. They offer a package of low-interest financial support large enough to cover the increase in market interest rates, plus compensatory financing to offset part of the decline in export earnings. How does this foreign financing affect the position of the *EB* curve, the macroeconomic imbalance facing Antiquity, and the magnitude of the required policy adjustments?

3. Now try applying the model to more realistic settings.

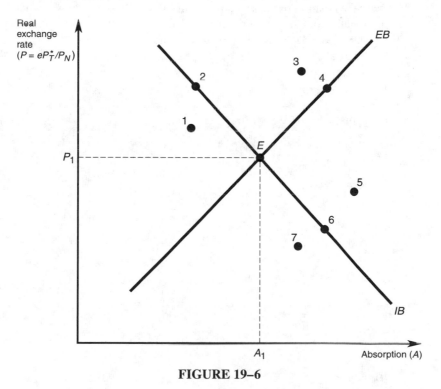

FIGURE 19–6

a. Seven points are marked in Figure 19–6. Each point corresponds to one of the following economic conditions. Match the descriptions of conditions to the appropriate point numbers from the graph.

(i) Through effective exchange-rate management, Brazil in the early 1990s had a stable balance-of-trade situation despite chronically high inflation: point _____.

(ii) In the early stages of its adjustment efforts, Chile experienced an unsustainable inflow of foreign savings with high domestic unemployment and falling real incomes: point _____.

(iii) Several African countries, such as Kenya, had moderate inflation and reasonable output growth along with serious foreign exchange constraints due to excess demand for tradables: point _____.

(iv) Prior to implementing a very successful adjustment program in 1993, Peru encountered high inflation and a debilitating balance-of-payments crisis: point _____.

(v) In the 1980s, Taiwan's economic management led to stable prices with full employment together with a balance-of-payments surplus that resulted in a large buildup of foreign exchange reserves: point _____.

(vi) In 1975 Korea nearly tripled its foreign exchange reserves, but the inflation rate reached 25 percent: point _____.

(vii) During the 1980s, several African countries, like Tanzania, faced severe balance-of-payments constraints despite economic growth so sluggish that per capita income declined: point _____.

b. Study the position of the seven points in Figure 19–6. As drawn, what combination of changes in the real exchange rate (P) and absorption (A) would be needed to achieve simultaneous internal and external balance in

(i) Brazil?

(ii) Chile?

(iii) Kenya?

(iv) Peru?

(v) Taiwan?

(vi) Korea?

(vii) Tanzania?

   c. The country at point 7 starts out with excessive slack in its economy, yet the model indicates that a contraction in absorption is needed to bring absorption to the level consistent with macroeconomic balance. Why is a contraction needed when the economy is weak at the outset?

ANSWERS TO SELF-TEST

Completion

1. *open*
2. production frontier
3. tradable
4. tradables, nontradables
5. *absorption*
6. appreciation (which means a decline in P)
7. external
8. right
9. Stabilization
10. International Monetary Fund
11. tradable, nontradable
12. crawling-peg

True-False

1.	T	7.	T
2.	F	8.	T
3.	F	9.	F
4.	F	10.	T
5.	F	11.	F
6.	T	12.	T

Multiple Choice

1.	d	7.	c
2.	b	8.	c
3.	c	9.	b
4.	a	10.	a
5.	d	11.	b
6.	a	12.	d